OFFICE SKILLS

Thelma J Foster

Fellow of the Royal Society of Arts, Dip RSA

Chief Examiner to the Royal Society of Arts for
General Reception

Formerly Senior Lecturer, Business Studies Department,
Worcester Technical College

Second Edition

Stanley Thornes (Publishers) Ltd

First published in 1981 by Stanley Thornes (Publishers) Ltd.
Old Station Drive, Leckhampton
CHELTENHAM GL53 0DN

Reprinted 1982 twice
Reprinted 1983
2nd edition 1984
Reprinted 1985
Reprinted 1986

British Library Cataloguing in Publication Data

Foster, Thelma J
    Office skills.   2nd ed.
    1. Office practice
    I. Title
    651.3′7   HF5547.5

ISBN 0 85950 222 8

Printed and bound in Great Britain at the Bath Press, Avon

Contents

Acknowledgements

I am grateful to Mr R A D Foster (my husband) for his advice on charts and graphs; to Dr RL Nowill for his advice on computers; and to Mr T Edwards, Mr D Manley and the staff of Stanley Thornes (Publishers).

The author and publishers are grateful to the following who have provided material and given permission to reproduce:

Barclays Bank plc (p. 391); British Rail (p. 184); British Telecom (p. 81); Coutts & Co (p. 391); Her Majesty's Stationery Office (p. 254); Lloyds Bank plc (p. 391); London Transport (Abridgement of London Underground Map, Registered User Number 84/268) (p. 188); Midland Bank plc (p. 391); The Post Office (p. 236); Williams & Glyn's Bank plc (p. 391).

Preface to 2nd Edition

A second edition of *Office Skills* has become necessary for several reasons. The first one is that since 1981 (when the first edition was published) many changes have taken place in Post Office, telephone, banking and building society services. Updating is essential — there is now no point in teaching students about telegrams!

Secondly, changing technology has affected offices in many ways, and while there are still thousands of small firms all over the world operating very competently with a typewriter, a telephone, a filing cabinet, a box of stamps and a postage book, it is the duty of teachers and lecturers to make their pupils and students aware of developments in office automation, not least because it is one of the important factors contributing to the fewer number of vacancies for school and college leavers. Therefore, I have incorporated brief outlines of the way automation will affect office procedures, where applicable, in the hope that it will be possible for young people to be taken into firms to see the latest developments for themselves.

Finally, after research into examination syllabuses and the needs of YTS and other courses, I have enlarged the scope of *Office Skills* to include sections on charts and graphs, the use of underground maps and railway timetables, travel itineraries and keeping diaries — all topics that appear regularly in examination papers.

I hope that these changes will make *Office Skills* even more useful for hard-pressed teachers of Office Practice, and, what is just as important, more interesting for those pupils and students being introduced to the commercial world through its pages.

THELMA J FOSTER
Studley, 1984

Preface to 1st Edition

I have written this book in the hope that young people will enjoy reading it. My experience of teaching the subject over the past 20 years has shown me that pupils in schools and students in colleges will not read their textbooks unless absolutely obliged to do so and I have tried to make this one interesting, attractive, funny (in places), and, perhaps most important, simple — especially when dealing with points which I know very well young people find confusing,

Ideally, Office Practice should be correlated with Commerce, Economics and Accounts — not to mention typewriting, but I know this is a counsel of perfection and difficult to achieve. What I hope this book will do is to enable teachers in schools and colleges to make Office Practice as practical as possible; even where equipment is inadequate, it is possible to organise supplies of forms so that the lessons can be interesting and imaginative. Typewriting lessons could be used for this purpose, once some degree of proficiency has been reached.

Technology is bringing changes in offices, as elsewhere, but the fundamental principles of storing and finding information, dealing with visitors to firms and answering the telephone, will remain for many years to come and study of Office Practice can only be of use to the office workers of the future.

Office Skills will be especially useful for pupils in schools studying the CSE syllabuses on Office Practice, and also for students in Colleges of Further Education working towards the Secretarial Studies Certificate. BEC/General students should also find much of this book relevant.

My most heartfelt thanks are due to my husband for his patience and help, to my colleagues for their interest and encouragement and, especially, to all those students who have worked painstakingly through the exercises and shown me the error of my ways. I should also like to acknowledge Mr Tony Edwards, who made helpful comments and suggestions on the first draft, and the staff of Stanley Thornes (Publishers) who turned the final draft into a book.

Finally, I am grateful to the Bank of Education, the Post Office and ROSPA for permission to use some of their material.

THELMA FOSTER
Worcester, 1981

List of Topics For Your Folder

*The cartoon 'What's Wrong?' is reproduced by kind permission of The Royal Society for the Prevention of Accidents.

List of Exercises

SECTION A **THE OFFICE WORLD**

CHAPTER 1

The Departments of a Company

Introduction

Most companies are divided up into departments, with a manager to take responsibility for each one. The managers report to the managing director, who in turn works in close cooperation with the board of directors and the chairman.

The organisation chart below shows the responsibilities of each manager, including the manager in charge of office services.

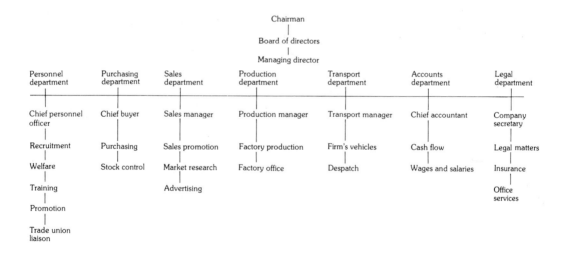

A typical organisation chart. The exact structure of any firm will of course depend on the particular type of business being conducted

A separate chart (see p. 5) shows what office services consist of, with each department controlled by a supervisor under the authority of the company secretary. The supervisors have the responsibility of ensuring that the work of their staff is carried out efficiently, accurately and promptly.

The Purpose of the Office

An 'office' is a place where any clerical work is done, and the word 'clerk' means any office worker – typist, computer programmer, receptionist, for example. Offices exist in firms mainly to receive, record and find information. In a small one-man business, separate office services will not be necessary. The manager can receive and give information himself. In larger businesses the managing director cannot deal personally with all inward and outward communications (see pp. 124 – 36); nor can he supervise everything that takes place. The office services are there to carry out these functions on his behalf.

The Key People

THE CHAIRMAN OF A COMPANY

The chairman is the most important member of the board of directors (and is usually elected by them). He represents his company both outside the firm to the public (shareholders, for example) and in the firm – he may make presentations to employees with long-service records or who have given exceptional service. He takes the 'chair' (i.e. presides – see p. 137) at board meetings and presents the annual report on the company's progress to shareholders. The chairman depends upon his fellow directors for information and advice – no single individual could be expected to know every detail of what is going on in a large firm.

BOARD OF DIRECTORS

Each director may be responsible for a particular section of the business – production, sales or buying, for example – but they are also responsible to the managing director and have to accept the board of directors' decisions.

MANAGING DIRECTOR

The managing director's chief responsibility is to see that the decisions made by the board of directors are carried out. He works in close cooperation with the chairman; in order to achieve this he also spends a great deal of time with the managers (known as 'executives') of the various departments. It is through the managing director that important matters are passed to the board of directors for discussion and decision.

THE COMPANY SECRETARY

The company secretary is mainly responsible for making sure that his company does not break the law (taking care of legal matters). He also acts as a link between the company and the shareholders and sends them information about their shares, and the company's financial position (i.e. how much profit or loss it has made in the previous 12 months). The company secretary is responsible for keeping an account of proceedings at all meetings (minutes: see pp. 138 — 9) and that the company keeps proper records of its financial transactions (buying, selling, borrowing, paying wages). The company secretary works closely with the chief accountant. As well as legal matters, the company secretary handles insurance matters. In many firms he is responsible for the office services. In all firms he is the link between the board of directors and the office staff.

The organisation of office services in a typical large firm may look like this

The People and Departments in a Large Firm

We now look at the departments in a large firm and see 'who does what'.

THE PERSONNEL DEPARTMENT

The word 'personnel' means 'the persons employed in any service', and the main duties of the staff working in a personnel department are connected with people. Such duties may include:

- Advertising vacancies for jobs.
- Training employees; promoting them.
- Transferring employees from department to department.
- Keeping staff records.
- Looking after the welfare of staff.
- Organising negotiations with trade unions.
- Dealing with resignations and dismissals.
- Helping to run social events and 'public-relations' exercises such as open days for visitors.

The first step towards obtaining a job in a large firm is usually taken by completing an application form for the personnel department. This may be a general form (suitable for any vacancy in the firm) or a specialised one – perhaps (say) suitable for office staff only. A completed application form will tell the firm whether an applicant is suitable enough to be interviewed. If so, he or she is put on what is called a 'short list'.

EMPLOYMENT APPLICATION FORM (Office Staff)

Surname (in CAPITAL letters, please) . . . .

Forename(s) . . . . Mr/Mrs/Miss

Address . . . .

. . . .

Date of birth . . . . Nationality . . . .

Education

	Name	From	To
Last school attended	. . . .	. . . .	. . . .
Further education	. . . .	. . . .	. . . .

Examinations passed

Subject	Board	Grade
. . . .	. . . .	. . . .
. . . .	. . . .	. . . .
. . . .	. . . .	. . . .
. . . .	. . . .	. . . .
. . . .	. . . .	. . . .
. . . .	. . . .	. . . .

Previous office experience

Name of firm	Position held	From	To
. . . .	. . . .	. . . .	. . . .
. . . .	. . . .	. . . .	. . . .
. . . .	. . . .	. . . .	. . . .

Any other work experience

. . . .	. . . .	. . . .	. . . .
. . . .	. . . .	. . . .	. . . .

Hobbies and other interests

. . . .

. . . .

Please tick any of the positions below in which you are interested and for which you consider you would be suitable. Number them in order of interest and suitability.

☐ Audio-typist   ☐ Receptionist

☐ Book-keeper   ☐ Secretary

☐ Copy-typist   ☐ Shorthand-typist

☐ Filing clerk   ☐ Switchboard operator

Signed . . . . Date . . . .

An application form for employment

This list will give the names of the half-dozen or so really first-class applicants for a particular post.

After interview, and appointment, details on an application form are transferred to a staff record sheet. In the one shown this will go on to the left-hand side; the right-hand side is for information relating to the employee's career with the firm and this will be kept up-to-date continuously. Some employees stay with one firm all their lives, and obviously one staff record would not be large enough to contain all the relevant information, so after a number of years there could be a series of such sheets.

Personnel records contain a great deal of information which is confidential and must be filed in lockable cabinets, which should never be left open when the office is unattended. Staff working in a personnel department have to be trustworthy and discreet – never passing on information about staff to anyone outside or inside the firm.

STAFF RECORD SHEET

Name . . . . First name(s) . . . .
. . . .

Address . . . .
. . . .

Tel No . . . .   Nationality . . . .
Next of kin . . . .   Address . . . .
Tel No . . . .
Date of birth . . . .   M/F   Married/single
Children . . . .
. . . .

Education: To/From   To/From
Secondary . . . .   Further . . . .

Qualifications:

Subjects	Examining boards	Dates
. . . .	. . . .	. . . .
. . . .	. . . .	. . . .
. . . .	. . . .	. . . .
. . . .	. . . .	. . . .
. . . .	. . . .	. . . .
. . . .	. . . .	. . . .

Previous employment

Firms	Positions held	Dates
. . . .	. . . .	. . . .
. . . .	. . . .	. . . .

National Insurance No . . . .
Referees given: . . . .
. . . .

Department . . . .
Position   . . . .
Salary (starting) . . . . Date . . . .
Salary increases . . . . Date . . . .
. . . . Date . . . .
. . . . Date . . . .
. . . . Date . . . .

Date of appointment . . . . Age on appointment . . . .
Transfers or promotions: . . . .   Date . . . .
. . . .   Date . . . .
. . . .   Date . . . .
. . . .   Date . . . .

Training record:
In the firm: To: From . . . .
Day release   To: From . . . .
Block release   To: From . . . .

Additional qualifications gained: Date
. . . .
. . . .

Periods of illness
From: To: Nos of days absent . . . .   Reason . . . .
From: To: Nos of days absent . . . .   Reason . . . .

Absences for reasons other than illness:

Date	Cause
. . . . .	. . . .
. . . . .	. . . .
. . . . .	. . . .

Pension scheme   Joined . . . .   Due to retire . . . .
Retired . . . .
Date of leaving . . . .
Reason (other than retirement) . . . .

A staff record sheet

PURCHASING DEPARTMENT

The purchasing department is the responsibility of the purchasing officer (sometimes called the 'chief buyer'). The chief buyer carries out three important duties:

- He must make sure that value for money has been received.
- He must make sure that accurate records of money spent are kept by his department.
- He must authorise all payments made on behalf of his department.

The purchasing department arranges for the buying of raw materials to be used by the production department, as well as office equipment, stationery and possibly the food and other requirements of the canteen. Frequent visitors to the purchasing department are salesmen from other firms, hoping to be given orders for the goods they are trying to sell. Invoices from suppliers are sent to the purchasing department for checking, after which they are sent to the accounts department for payment. Other forms used are orders and enquiries. Another important responsibility of the purchasing department is stock control.

Stocktaking

The 'stock' in a firm consists of supplies of everything likely to be needed. Because it costs money, it is very important to make sure that too much stock is not piling up on the shelves. Money can earn interest – idle stock on shelves which is not likely to be required for months earns nothing. The supervisor in charge of stock control has to arrange security for the goods in store so that they cannot easily be stolen, and he also has to prevent stock being wasted. Stock record cards (see p. 253) enable him to see at a glance how much of any article is in stock, and who is 'requisitioning' it from him. Stock requisitions (see pp. 253 – 55) are forms completed by employees requiring goods from the stores.

SALES DEPARTMENT

The work of the sales department is very important because without sales a firm would go out of business. A large sales department may be divided into two – one for supervising sales overseas (export market) and one for supervising sales in this country (home market). The organisation of the sales department is carried out by the sales manager who may attend directors' meetings at which sales policy is decided. The sales manager also supervises his assistant managers and sales representatives. An advertising section often forms part of the sales department, and its main job is to arrange sales 'promotion' – to bring the products of the firm to the attention of the public by free offers, advertising in magazines, newspapers, on television and arranging exhibitions and special campaigns. Other ways of advertising are by 'direct mail' – sending circulars through the post to people living in a selected area or having a particular interest. Market research (interviewing passers-by in the street or calling at their homes in certain neighbourhoods and asking them to fill in questionnaires) enables the advertising section to find out what the public wants to buy.

Clerical workers in the sales department spend part of their time sending out catalogues and price-lists to customers, and typing invoices.

Customers' complaints may also be dealt with by the sales department, and in some firms, this department provides a repair service to customers for goods they have purchased from the firm.

PRODUCTION DEPARTMENT

The production manager is responsible for the factory which manufactures the goods sold by the firm. A works manager is usually in direct control of the factory, and the factory office is the link between the factory and all the other departments in the firm. When an order is received by the sales department, it is sent to the factory office, and the factory office must ensure that orders are correctly delivered without delay.

The production manager may also be responsible for the maintenance in a firm – repairing roads, buildings and machinery in the factory. This work is carried out by supervisors with technicians and workmen under their control.

TRANSPORT DEPARTMENT

The manager in charge of transport has the responsibility of arranging for the goods manufactured by the firm to be delivered to the customers. This may be done by the firm's own vehicles – vans or lorries – or by British Rail or transport firms. The transport manager has to decide upon the safest, quickest and cheapest methods. If the firm's own vehicles are used, he also has to make sure that they are always in a good state of repair and that there are always some available when required. Company cars, mini-buses and coaches may also be the responsibility of the transport manager.

The transport manager and the works manager have to work closely together.

ACCOUNTS DEPARTMENT

The chief accountant is the head of the accounts department, which is one of the most important in the firm. It is the job of the accounts department to see that all the bills sent to the firm by its suppliers are paid promptly and, similarly, that all bills are sent out punctually to the customers of the firm, and that they are also paid promptly.

At the end of the 'financial year' (this is often the income tax year: see pp. 381 — 2) the records kept by the accounts department are checked by an independent outside accountant (this is known as an 'audit').

A copy of the audited accounts is sent to the shareholders. These audited accounts enable the accounts department to produce a 'balance sheet' which shows how much profit or loss the firm has made during the preceding financial year.

Payment of wages and salaries is often a part of the accounts department's responsibilities, and it may be dealt with by a separate section. Employees in the wages section are busy working out the amounts due to workers each week, or each month, and what amounts have to be deducted for income tax, national insurance and other deductions (see pp. 379 — 83). The busiest time in the wages section is towards the end of each week — most firms pay out wages on Thursdays or Fridays. Since much of the work in this section is concerned with figures, much of it today is completed by machines — for example, calculating machines and computers (see pp. 165 — 9).

FOR YOUR FOLDER

1. THE DEPARTMENTS OF A COMPANY

Write these notes in your folder, filling in the missing words and phrases.

1) An organisation chart shows the responsibilities of each _____ in a firm.

2) An 'office' is a place where any _____ work is done.

3) The word 'clerk' means any _____ worker — typist, computer programmer, receptionist.

4) Offices exist in firms mainly to receive, record and _____ information.

5) The chairman _____ his company both inside and outside the firm.

6) The chairman is usually _____ by the board of directors and is the most important member of this board.

7) The managing director's chief responsibility is to see that decisions made by the _____ are carried out.

8) The company secretary is mainly responsible for legal and _____ matters.

9) In many firms he is also responsible for _____ services. In all firms he is the link between the board of directors and the _____.

10) The main duties of the staff working in the personnel department are connected with _____.

11) Staff working in a personnel department have to be _____ and _____.

12) The purchasing department arranges for the _____ of raw materials to be used by the production department, as well as many other requirements of the firm.

13) Documents sent out by the purchasing department are _____ and _____.

14) Another important responsibility of the purchasing department is stock _____.

15) Forms used in connection with this are _____ record cards and _____.

16) The sales manager organises the sales department and also supervises _____ and _____.

17) An _____ section often forms part of the sales department.

18) Clerical workers in the sales department spend part of their time sending out catalogues and price-lists to customers and typing _____.

19) The production manager is responsible for the _____ which manufactures the goods sold by the firm.

20) A works manager is usually in direct control of the factory and the _____ office is the link between the factory and all other _____ in the firm.

21) The transport manager has the responsibility of arranging for the goods manufactured in the firm to be delivered to the _____.

22) The transport manager has to decide upon the safest, quickest and _____ methods of transport.

23) The head of the accounts department is the _____.

24) It is the job of the accounts department to see that all the bills sent to the firm by its suppliers are paid promptly and that all bills are sent out of the firm punctually to the _____ of the firm.

25) Each year, the records kept by the accounts department are checked by an independent accountant – this is known as an _____.

26) Also part of the accounts department's responsibilities may be the payment of _____ dealt with by a separate section of the department.

Exercise 1

QUESTIONS ON THE DEPARTMENTS OF A COMPANY

1) Describe the work of the personnel department.

2) What is the purpose of an office?

3) What is the importance to a firm of the chairman, board of directors and managing director?

4) Explain the importance of stock control in a firm.

5) What are 'sales promotion' and 'market research'?

6) The transport department and the production department have very important links. What are they?

7) Explain what a 'balance sheet' is and its importance to the shareholders in a firm.

Office Services

The tendency in many large firms is towards centralisation of office services. There are many advantages of centralisation:

- *Reduction of noise.* All noisy equipment such as typewriters can be located away from staff who need quiet in order to concentrate.
- *Economy.* When work is centralised it is carried out by clerical staff who are specially trained in that type of work more efficiently and quickly.
- *Better equipment.* It is worth spending more money on better equipment because it is being shared by many.
- *Efficiency.* The work is done under experienced supervision.
- *Spreading the work.* The work load can be spread evenly, perhaps reducing the need for overtime.

The disadvantages of centralisation are:
- Work can become monotonous.
- No training is given in any other type of work – promotion prospects may be lessened.
- There is a loss of personal contact with staff engaged on other work, as most communication is done through the supervisor.

TYPING POOL

This is an example of centralisation, where all the typing, audio-typing and shorthand-typing carried out in a firm is done in one department under a trained supervisor. The typing pool provides an excellent training for the school or college-leaver, as working directly under experienced supervision is of great benefit to beginners. The work in a typing pool consists of typing circular letters, form letters, schedules, ink stencils, envelopes or letters. Word processors are beginning to take the place of copy-typists in some large firms, but audio-typists and shorthand-typists are still in great demand.

MAIL ROOM

In many firms, all the mail is collected and dealt with by a centralised mail room, who also distribute incoming mail after it arrives in the mornings. Many school-leavers are first appointed to work in the mail room, which gives them an opportunity to get to know their way around a large firm and to find out who works where.

COMPUTER SECTION

The computer section has to be housed in special air-conditioned rooms, as the equipment is affected by changes in temperature. Computers are used in large firms to work out the payroll, sales account records, stock control and production planning. Clerical workers in the computer section include 'programmers' – people trained to work out a set of instructions for a computer to perform a complete operation (see pp. 165 – 7).

REPROGRAPHY DEPARTMENT

The reprography department is where all the duplicating and photo-copying needed in the firm is centralised. The workers in a reprography department may produce a wide variety of jobs — staff handbooks, price-lists, instruction sheets, office stationery, internal telephone directories, copies of minutes and agenda.

They work closely with the typing pool in many large firms. The equipment used in reprography includes: photocopiers, ink duplicators, spirit duplicators and offset-litho duplicators (see Chapter 12). Clerical workers in the reprography department have an opportunity to become familiar with all these machines.

FILING DEPARTMENT

In many firms, one department is responsible for the sorting and filing of all the papers in the firm which are required to be stored for future reference. Centralised filing saves space, ensures a uniform method of filing and makes better use of both filing staff and equipment. Papers may be out when required, and the filing department may be some distance from many of the offices, thereby causing a waste of time when clerical workers go to borrow files.

Don't let this happen!

RECEPTIONIST

The receptionist is almost the first person callers see when they come to a firm and therefore her job is most important. She must be pleasant, polite, tactful and well-groomed; in addition she should learn all she can about her firm and what it does so that she can answer callers' questions. To learn about reception work, a school or college leaver should look for a job as an assistant receptionist (see Chapter 4).

FACTORY OFFICE

Clerical workers in the factory office have to work closely with the factory workers (the people actually engaged in making the firm's products). The factory office keeps records of all manufacturing and production operations – the factory office is the link between the factory and all the other departments in a firm.

A modern office

FOR YOUR FOLDER

2. OFFICE SERVICES

Write these notes in your folder, filling in the missing words and phrases.

1) The department where all the typing, audio-typing and shorthand-typing carried out in a firm is done under one trained supervisor is the _____.

2) The department which deals with all outgoing letters and parcels, as well as the incoming ones, is the _____.

3) Clerical workers in the computer section trained to work out a set of instructions to a computer are _____.

4) The department where all the duplicating and photocopying is carried out is the _____ department.

5) Centralised filing saves _____ ensures a uniform method of _____ and makes better use of both filing staff and _____.

6) The receptionist's job is important because she is almost the _____ _____ callers see when they come to a firm.

7) The factory office is the _____ between the factory and all the other departments in a firm.

8) Centralisation of office services has many advantages; economy, reduction of noise, better equipment, efficiency and _____.

9) Disadvantages of centralisation are: monotony, fewer promotion prospects and _____.

CHAPTER 2

Today's Office

Health and Safety

Most offices today, even those in old, inconvenient buildings, are warm in winter, well-lit and have up-to-date equipment and furniture. If office staff are uncomfortable, they will soon look for another job.

It was not always so. Until 1946 there were no regulations at all for the protection of office workers and many firms failed to provide even the most elementary standards of lighting, heating or adequate space for their office staff. The description in Dickens' *Christmas Carol* of the office where Scrooge was the employer could almost have been true of many offices in the twentieth century! Factory workers and mine-workers had been protected by law since 1802 – it took over a century and a half for anything to be done for office workers.

The Industrial Injuries Act of 1946 provided a scheme of insurance against accidents at work for *all* employees, including office workers, and this was at least a beginning. Seventeen years later, in 1963, the Offices, Shops and Railway Premises Act was passed. This Act laid down conditions for lighting, heating, washing and toilet facilities, as well as minimum space (400 cubic feet) for each office worker. Regulations about first aid and safety were also laid down in this Act – firms employing over 150 people had to arrange for one person to be trained in first aid. The Offices, Shops and Railway Premises Act did not, however, apply to schools and colleges – and these have office workers, too.

First-aid box needed!

Workers in many small offices continued to endure miserable conditions – larger firms had more money and provided better facilities. Eventually, the shortage of office workers forced employers to improve working conditions – even a generous salary does not compensate for shivering through the winter or stifling in the summer.

The formation of trade unions for office workers has also influenced working conditions and helped to improve them.

The most recent and important development in office workers' conditions is an Act passed in 1974 called the Health and Safety at Work Act, which includes all the regulations in the Offices, Shops and Railway Premises Act of 1963 but which is much more comprehensive and also applies to schools and colleges. HASAWA (for short) lays responsibility on employees as well as employers, especially for safety and security.

Accidents can be caused in offices (as in homes) very easily by carelessness or thoughtlessness, and it is now the duty of everyone, from the executives to the youngest employees, to help to prevent accidents in offices. HASAWA makes it plain that although employees now have rights, they have duties, too.

The following is a list of suggestions for office workers to help to make their places of work safer for all:

- Gangways between desks should not be blocked with boxes, files or wastebins.
- Fire exits must be kept clear, too.
- Fire doors must be kept closed (not propped open).
- Filing cabinet drawers must be closed after use, it is easy to trip over an open bottom drawer.
- Smouldering cigarette ends are one of the main causes of fire, and smokers should observe non-smoking rules.
- Electrical appliances must be unplugged and switched off at the end of each day.
- Adaptors and trailing wires are dangerous and should be avoided. Any faulty electrical equipment must be repaired by an expert electrician.
- Tops of high cupboards should not be stacked with files and boxes.
- Torn or frayed floorcovering should be reported to a supervisor and then barricaded off until it has been repaired.
- First-aid boxes must be clearly displayed and contents replenished frequently.
- Unguarded electric fires must never be used.
- All employees should be familiar with the use of fire extinguishers and know the firm's fire drill – fire drills are usually carried out regularly in most firms. If they are not, they should be.
- Any cupboards containing valuables (see p. 345) should be locked at the end of the day, and filing cabinets with confidential documents also. Office doors should be locked and windows firmly

secured — this will not prevent a burglar gaining entrance if he really is determined to, but it will make it more difficult for him.

Employers, office staff, trade unions — all have to work together to improve the safety of their places of work.

FOR YOUR FOLDER

3.   SAFETY FIRST!

How much do you remember about safety? Look at the picture below and list 'what's wrong'. Remember to avoid these hazards if you go to work in an office!

What's wrong with this office?

Location of Offices

The location of offices is very important to different types of office worker for many reasons.

● Their special type of work may require peace and quiet.
● They may need to be accessible to frequent outside callers or to staff from other departments.
● Privacy may be necessary — some interviews with other members of staff should not be overheard.
● Good lighting is essential for all office workers.
● Ventilation is vital too — in summer and winter.

The siting of firms comes before the location of the offices inside them and here it is important to take into account:

● Nearness to public transport (trains, buses).
● Nearness to shops, banks and post office, cafés and restaurants.
● Allocation and provision of adequate parking space.

Once the building has been completed, it is then necessary to decide where the various offices shall be located inside.

Obviously the reception area and receptionist's desk must be near the main entrance, so that visitors can easily find them (see Chapter 4). Also, the personnel department should not be too far away from the main entrance, as they will have many callers from outside — people coming for interviews for instance. The buying department, too, will have representatives calling from other firms, so should not be far from the main entrance.

It makes good sense to site on the ground floor any department using heavy machinery — the reprographic department, for example.

Services which are centralised in many firms — mail room, filing, typing pool, messenger, reprographic, wages and accounts — should be central and convenient to other departments, not on the top floor which necessitates all staff wasting time and energy unnecessarily. (And lifts do not always work!)

There must be toilet and cloakroom facilities on every floor, and fresh drinking water should be available, as well as hot water for washing. The canteen and surgery ought to be close to offices to avoid staff having to walk long distances in cold or wet weather.

The Layout of an Office

PLANNING OFFICES

Siting of office buildings and location of offices inside the building is important to those who work in them; just as important is the right type of furniture and equipment, but, before this is chosen, another decision has to be made — the layout of each office.

CELLULAR OFFICES

The traditional type of office is rectangular, similar to a medium-sized room with doors and windows, and is known as a 'cellular' office.

The advantages of cellular offices

- They are lockable, providing security for anything confidential or valuable.
- They are private.
- There is peace and quiet for work which requires concentration.
- Special conditions can be provided for equipment which needs controlled temperature and humidity (e.g. a computer).

The disadvantages of cellular offices

- They require more space in a building, because of partitioning, doors and windows.
- They are more expensive to maintain – redecoration, heating, lighting.
- More supervision is required as each office operates behind its own walls.

OPEN-PLAN OFFICES

An open-plan office is where a large space is furnished as one integrated whole, with or without the use of screens (sometimes provided by plants in pots or plant stands). It generally accommodates several grades of staff from typists and clerical workers to managers and directors.

A scheme of a typical open-plan office

The advantages of open-plan offices

- They are easy to supervise, as all the staff are on view.
- Communication between sections and departments can be carried out without delay, since everyone is on view.
- Flow of work is speeded up since it is from desk to desk rather than from office to office.
- They enable centralisation of office services to be organised easily.
- Managers and senior staff are in constant contact with the work of all staff.
- They are cheaper to maintain – there is more economical use of space, heating, and lighting, and cleaning is straightforward.
- Layout in certain areas can be changed quickly if required.

The disadvantages of open-plan offices

- They are noisier, because of the lack of partitions.
- Workers are distracted, because of people passing to and fro.
- Security is reduced because there are no lockable doors.
- Privacy is difficult to obtain.
- Infections (coughs, colds, 'flu) spread more quickly.
- Some office machines are noisy (typewriters, duplicators) and unsuitable for an open-plan area.
- Senior staff prefer their own offices which they regard as status symbols (marks of seniority).
- It is difficult to arrange lighting and ventilation for all tastes.
- The atmosphere is impersonal – many people like their own office walls on which to hang pictures, photographs etc.

CENTRALISATION

This is an arrangement in firms where services used by all departments are under the control of one or two supervisors – e.g. the typing pool, the mail room, the filing and reprography departments and the wages and accounts departments.

The advantages of centralisation

- The work load can be spread more evenly among specially trained staff.
- All noisy machinery can be contained in one area and away from other staff.
- Expensive equipment is not installed in many offices in several departments.
- A more efficient service can be provided by the specialist staff.

The disadvantages of centralisation

- Centralised services may be a long way from some offices and time is wasted while staff walk to and fro.
- The staff engaged on work in a centralised office may find it monotonous.
- Contact may be lost with staff in other departments.

Office Furniture

Well-designed office furniture, suitable for the work of the user, helps health and efficiency. The heights of desks and chairs should be appropriate to avoid slumping and discomfort.

Steel furniture is less of a fire risk than plastic, which causes suffocating smoke within seconds after the outbreak of a fire.

For typists, and keyboard operators, shaped modules provide a working and a typing area. A swivel chair enables both areas to be used easily. The height of seat and back should be adjustable. Footrests should be available for all typists and clerical workers.

An Anglepoise desk lamp gives lighting which can be adjusted to suit individual needs and is used by many typists in addition to the overhead lighting.

A shaped module and swivel chair

Specialised furniture is required for workers in the drawing office and artists in the advertising department.

The reception area has special furniture for people waiting so that they may relax comfortably (see Chapter 4).

Diaries

Diaries are an essential part of daily planning. They give the day's programme at a glance, and, in addition, they enable a secretary to space out her employer's engagements and to allow time between callers, visits, meetings, luncheon and dinner engagements for him to carry out his own job.

THE THREE DIARIES

Two of the three diaries are kept in the office — one on the manager's desk and another identical one on the secretary's desk. Frequent checks must be made during the day to make sure all engagements have been entered in each diary — this is easy to do and is a very important part of the daily routine.

The third diary is the one kept by the manager in his pocket, and in which he jots down engagements made over luncheon or dinner. Tact and diplomacy are called for on the part of the secretary, who must make a regular, brief enquiry about the pocket diary, perhaps at the end of the morning's dictation, and transfer any engagements to the two desk diaries kept in the office.

Diaries are also extremely useful as 'reminders' — about making telephone calls for instance — and provide a valuable record for reference if any queries should arise at a later date. The manager should decide when the diaries may be scrapped (a minimum period should be 5 years).

Entries in diaries must be clearly written (or printed if handwriting is not clear) to avoid any possibility of misunderstandings. Provisional arrangements should be entered in pencil, which can be easily altered (if necessary) at a later date. Name, initials, address (home or company) and telephone number are all essential information to be entered when making appointments. Vague notes such as 'Miss Jones 10 am' may mean nothing a week later. A quick check in the diaries should be one of the first duties a secretary carries out each morning.

Friday 20 March 198___

0930	Mrs Mary Wyman, Office Equipment Ltd, Kingston-upon-Thames (Buyer).
1100	Mr K Knight, Assistant Manager, Williams and Glyn's Bank Ltd, Chancery, London.
1300	Lunch at the Hilton International, with 3 directors from J Law & Sons, Glasgow.
1430	Meeting with Accountants, Thompson and Gregory, Whitaker Lane, Aldwych.
1630	Mr K Evans, Sales Manager, Everton Engineering Co, Bristol.
1930 for 2000	Dinner at the Plaza Restaurant, Piccadilly Circus, with 2 directors from Rank Xerox, London. Wife to accompany me.

A typical page in an executive's diary

Friday 20 March 198___

0930	Mrs Mary Wyman, Office Equipment Ltd. Henley Road, Kingston upon Thames (Buyer) Tel 295 491 Ex 15
1100	Mr K Knight, Assistant Manager, Williams + Glyn's Bank Ltd, Chancery Lane, London Tel 665 430 Ex 73
1300	Mr Barber to lunch at the Hilton International, with 3 directors from J Law + Sons Ltd, Mackenzie Street, Glasgow Tel 537 888
1430	Mr Barber to attend meeting with his accountants, Thompson + Gregory, Whitaker Lane, Aldwych Tel 987 554
1630	Mr K Evans, Sales Manager, Everton Engineering Co Ltd. Ship Street, Redlands, Bristol Tel 993 871 Ex 42
1930 for 2000	Dinner at the Plaza Restaurant, Picadilly Circus, with two directors from Rank Xerox, Hammersmith, London. Mrs Barber included.

A typical page in a secretary's diary

Friday 20 March 198___

0930	File needed for Office Equipment Ltd.
1100	File needed for Williams + Glyn's Bank Ltd. Franking machine meter due for re-setting. Cheque (£100) for PO to be signed.
1300	Book table - Hilton International for 4 (Tel 263 540 Ex 367). Book accommodation (HI) one night - 3 single rooms + baths (Tel Ex 221)
1430	Files needed - give to Mr Barber before he leaves for Hilton Int.
1630	File needed. Appointment to be confirmed in writing. I may have to take notes.
1930 for 2000	Notify Mrs Barber. Offer to babysit. Tell her dress is informal. (Tel 771856)

A secretary's own reminders

Above are the reminders a secretary might make on the engagements covered by the pages in the two diaries for Friday, 20 March.

She will have to remember what is needed in the way of files for the meetings, as well as to book the table for lunch at the Hilton International and the accommodation for the three guests.

THE RECEPTIONIST'S DIARY

This is more usually known as an 'appointments book' (see p. 66) and, in a large firm, information about appointments is given to the receptionist by the secretaries, ideally, not later than the day before.

FOR YOUR FOLDER

4. TODAY'S OFFICE

Write these notes in your folder, filling in the missing words and phrases.

1) The Industrial Injuries Act of _____ provided a scheme of insurance against accidents at work for all employees, including office workers.

2) In 1963, the Offices, Shops and Railway Premises Act was passed, which laid down conditions for lighting, heating, washing and toilet facilities as well as minimum space for _____.

3) The Offices, Shops and Railway Premises Act did not, however, apply to _____.

4) The formation of trade unions for office workers has also influenced their conditions and _____.

5) The most recent and important development in office workers' conditions was passed in 1974 and is called the _____.

6) The location of offices is very important to office workers for many reasons:
   peace and quiet
   privacy
   good lighting
   ventilation
   _____.

7) Reception area and personnel department should be near the main entrance as also should the _____ department.

8) Any department using _____ machinery (such as the reprography department) should be on the ground floor.

9) Centralised services, such as mail room, filing, typing pool, messenger, reprographic, wages and accounts should be central and _____ to other departments, not on the top floor which necessitates staff wasting time and energy.

10) The traditional type of office is rectangular, similar to a medium-sized room and is known as a _____ office.

11) Where a large space is furnished as one integrated whole, with several grades of staff (typists, clerks and managers), this is an _____ office.

12) A very large area with a minimum of 50/100 occupants is a _____ office.

13) Open-plan offices are not always popular, because they are noisier, there is more distraction for workers, security is reduced and _____ spread quickly.

14) Centralisation in firms is an arrangement where _____.

15) Two examples of centralisation are _____ and _____.

16) The advantages of centralisation are the spreading of a more even workload and _____.

17) The disadvantage of centralisation is _____.

18) Well-designed office furniture helps _____ and _____.

19) Typists' chairs should have seats and backs which are _____.

20) Specialised furniture is required in drawing offices and for artists in advertising departments. The _____ area also has special furniture for people _____.

21) Items of equipment on a secretary's desk might include an Anglepoise lamp, telephone, stapler, perforator and _____.

22) Diaries are important because they record the appointments and meetings of the manager for the day. Provisional arrangements should be entered in diaries in _____.

23) There should be a diary on the desk of a secretary which is an exact match of the one on her employer's desk. Frequent checks must be made during the day to make sure that all engagements have been _____.

24) The 'third' diary is the _____ diary and tact and diplomacy are necessary to make sure that appointments made during lunch or dinner are _____ to the two main desk diaries.

25) Information about appointments is passed by secretaries in large firms to the _____ so that they are able to enter them in the appointments book.

Exercise 2

PLANNING AN OFFICE LAYOUT

Make a plan to scale (¼ inch to 1 foot).

Mark doorways and windows.

Decide on furniture and equipment.

Cut out templates of all furniture and equipment to scale.

Arrange templates on plan.

Mark in names of workers, telephones etc.

Submit for approval.

Exercise 3

QUESTIONS ON TODAY'S OFFICE

1) Compare the Offices, Shops and Railway Premises Act of 1963 with the Health and Safety at Work Act of 1974.

2) Explain six ways in which office workers can help to make their places of work safer.

3) What five factors have to be taken into account when deciding on the site of an office?

4) Why do many senior members of staff prefer their own offices? Explain two reasons why open-plan offices are not popular with office workers.

5) Make a plan to scale of an office, with furniture, equipment and staff, remembering that 40 square feet is the allowance of space (minimum) laid down by law for office workers.

CHAPTER 3

Finding a Job and Starting Work

Types of Job in the Office

OFFICE JUNIORS

Some firms will employ school-leavers as office juniors. An office junior will learn to do many different sorts of job and will often be asked to help out a department if it is short of staff – perhaps because of sickness or holidays or when someone has recently left the firm. The junior may even be asked to make the tea or coffee — see Appendix 2, pp. 439–40.

AUDIO-TYPISTS

Someone new to the office may be introduced to 'audio' typing. An audio-typist listens to a cassette through headphones and types what she hears. She has to be very good at spelling and punctuation because she has nothing to guide her.

An audio-typist

COPY-TYPISTS

Copy-typists type from handwritten or corrected typescript. Their typing speeds range from 35 words a minute (a junior copy-typist) to about 60 words a minute (an experienced copy-typist). A junior typist may also be sent on a day-release course to the local college to learn shorthand and improve her typing speed.

SHORTHAND-TYPISTS

A shorthand-typist has to have a good typing speed (50 words a minute) and also be able to write shorthand at about 100 words a minute. In addition her English must be very good, because she is typing from shorthand not longhand.

A shorthand-typist

A filing clerk

FILING CLERKS

Some office workers specialise in filing, an important job which requires great care and efficiency (see Chapter 13).

VDU OPERATORS

A visual display unit (VDU) is a screen resembling a television screen, on which the 'input' (see p. 166) from a computer, teleprinter or word processor is displayed.

Keyboard or VDU operators should be accurate typists. Speed is less important than accuracy when operating a computer keyboard, as mistakes are not so easy to correct. Keyboard operators may be computer programmers or computer terminal operators (see p. 166).

A VDU operator

RECEPTIONISTS

Many school-leavers are attracted by the idea of becoming reception-ists. A receptionist in a firm is the first person a caller may speak to and her speech, manner and appearance are very important. Usually, a firm's receptionist will be around 20 years of age, but in a very large firm she will need an assistant and a school-leaver could be considered for this job. Some receptionists also look after switchboards and are able to type. There is more about receptionists later on in the book (Chapter 4).

A receptionist

A switchboard operator

TELEPHONISTS

Another important key post in a firm is that of the telephonist or switchboard operator. Many of these are trained by British Telecom before going to work in a firm as they must be efficient, polite, tactful, calm and helpful. There is much more about telephonists in Chapter 5.

In some firms the jobs of receptionist and switchboard operator are combined and done by one person.

SECRETARIES

A secretary is a very good shorthand-typist or audio-typist (or someone who can do both audio and shorthand-typing) who has worked in a firm, or several firms, and gained experience of what the firm does and of her employer's duties in the firm. She is thus able to take over much of the day-to-day running of the office, screening callers on the telephone and personal callers, organising the diary, making travel arrangements, taking minutes at meetings and finding information for her employer, so saving him time and enabling him to work without interruption in his own specialised field. Many good shorthand-typists or audio-typists become excellent secretaries when they have gained sufficient experience to use their initiative in this way.

A secretary dealing with callers

FOR YOUR FOLDER

5. TYPES OF JOB

Write these notes in your folder, filling in the missing words and phrases.

1) An audio-typist has to be very good at spelling and punctuation because she listens through _____ and then types what she has heard.

2) A book-keeper in a firm works with accounts. Although in a large firm much of this work is done on accounting machines or computers, a book-keeper would have to be very good at _____.

3) Copy-typists type from handwritten or corrected typescript. Their typing speeds range from 35 words a minute (a junior copy-typist) to about 60 words a minute (an experienced copy-typist). More important than speed, however, is _____.

4) A filing clerk spends most of her time putting away letters and other documents so that they can be _____ quickly. She must be an especially careful worker, as looking for missing papers is a waste of valuable time.

5) A receptionist's speech, manner and appearance are very important, as she is likely to be the first person to whom a caller will go when he visits a firm. In a small firm, she may look after a switchboard as well as looking after all the _____ to a firm.

6) A shorthand-typist has to have a good typing speed and also to be able to write shorthand at about 100 words a minute. In addition, her English must be very good, because she is typing from _____ and not words.

7) A secretary has to have good typing speeds and be able to write shorthand at over 100 words a minute. She must also have very good English. In addition to these qualifications, she needs several years' _____ in a firm so that she is able to help her employer with a great deal of his office work.

8) A switchboard operator may be trained by British Telecom before she goes to work for a firm, as she has the very important job of dealing with all the incoming and outgoing _____ calls, and she must be efficient, polite, tactful, calm and helpful.

Exercise 4

QUESTIONS ON TYPES OF JOB

1) Explain the difference between a shorthand-typist and a secretary.

2) Why do audio-typists and shorthand-typists have to be especially good at English?

3) In some cases, who trains switchboard operators?

4) A switchboard operator must be very efficient. What else should she be?

5) In a small firm, one member of the office staff might look after a switchboard as well as doing another job. What other job would this be?

Vacancies

The employment exchange run by the Government's Manpower Services Commission is known as a 'Jobcentre'. There is one in most towns and cities. There is also a Careers Advisory Centre for school and college-leavers. Employers may notify Jobcentres of vacancies they wish to fill.

There are also employment agencies run by private firms. They keep a register of people who are looking for jobs, and put them in touch with firms who have vacancies. There is *no charge* to the people looking for jobs – it is the firms with the vacancies who pay, when the job is taken.

Advertisements in local papers are another source of information about vacancies.

**RECEPTIONIST/
TYPIST**

Hours 3 p.m.-7 p.m., Monday-Friday evenings; one Saturday morning in four 9 a.m. 1 p.m.
Salary at age 21 plus £2,625 pro rata, per annum. Box 891

Sometimes there is a box number in place of a firm's name, so that the applicant does not know *where* the job is when she applies. The reason for box numbers is to prevent people calling at firms instead of writing in the first place.

Another way of finding out about vacancies is to write to firms and enquire if there are likely to be any in the near future. If you are especially interested in working in a building society, a bank, an estate agent or a travel agent, for instance, the addresses are in the *Classified Trade Directory* (Yellow Pages) and a letter can be sent to them, with brief details of education etc. Calling personally is not a good idea as firms are too busy to cope with you and you will be politely asked to write in, anyway.

Letter of Application

Ideally, this should be typed, but often this is not possible and some employers prefer a handwritten application. The letter should, therefore, be written as neatly and clearly as possible, with spelling checked and double-checked! It is a great saving of time and of considerable help to a prospective employer if a letter of application is short, with most of the details set out plainly on a separate sheet. This separate sheet should be headed 'curriculum vitae' (this means 'life history'). Curricula vitae can be duplicated (if possible) or typed with five carbon copies, so that they are ready for sending with letters applying for jobs. These letters (known as 'covering letters' since all the information is on a separate sheet) must be written or typed for each firm applied to. Making carbon copies of curricula vitae, or duplicating them, saves time when several jobs are being applied for, and also avoids the possibility of omitting an important piece of information, but the 'covering letter' must *not* be a carbon copy. This would not give a good impression to the firm reading it.

Application Forms

Many firms send these to applicants for jobs, even though full details have been supplied to them on a curriculum vitae. An application form must be completed and returned to the firm as quickly as possible, with a brief 'covering letter' simply stating that the completed application form is enclosed.

Exercise 5

APPLICATION FORM

Copy out the application form on p.6 and fill it in with your own personal details.

For which of the jobs listed is typing not required?

For which jobs is good English important?

Exercise 6

SITUATIONS VACANT

From the advertisements on the following page:

1) Place the jobs in order of suitability for application by yourself.

2) Give reasons for your first, second and third choice.

3) What would you ask about during an interview for your first choice?

4) What would you ask about during an interview for your third choice?

5) Why in advertisement No 1 do you think a handwritten reply is asked for?

6) What is meant by 'competitive salary' in No 2?

7) What is a 'relief telephonist' in No 3?

8) What is meant by 'Person Friday' in No 4?

9) What does 'salary negotiable' mean in No 5?

10) What might 'wider responsibilities' mean in No 5?

11) What does 'capable of working on own initiative' mean in No 6?

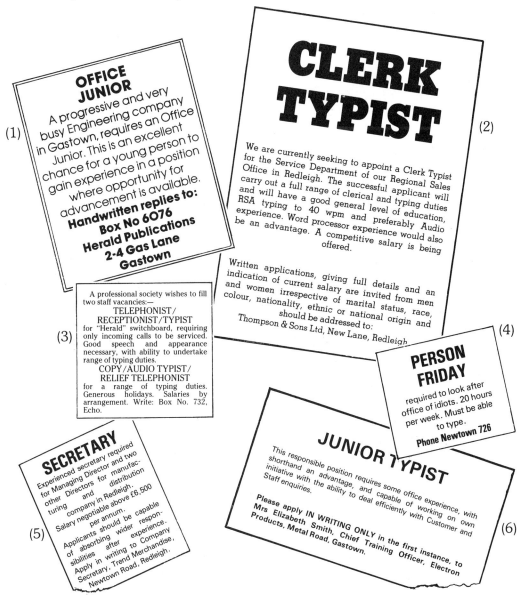

(1)

OFFICE JUNIOR

A progressive and very busy Engineering company in Gastown, requires an Office Junior. This is an excellent chance for a young person to gain experience in a position where opportunity for advancement is available.

Handwritten replies to:
Box No 6076
Herald Publications
2-4 Gas Lane
Gastown

(2)

CLERK TYPIST

We are currently seeking to appoint a Clerk Typist for the Service Department of our Regional Sales Office in Redleigh. The successful applicant will carry out a full range of clerical and typing duties and will have a good general level of education, RSA typing to 40 wpm and preferably Audio experience. Word processor experience would also be an advantage. A competitive salary is being offered.

Written applications, giving full details and an indication of current salary are invited from men and women irrespective of marital status, race, colour, nationality, ethnic or national origin and should be addressed to:
Thompson & Sons Ltd, New Lane, Redleigh

(3)

A professional society wishes to fill two staff vacancies:—
TELEPHONIST/
RECEPTIONIST/TYPIST
for "Herald" switchboard, requiring only incoming calls to be serviced. Good speech and appearance necessary, with ability to undertake range of typing duties.
COPY/AUDIO TYPIST/
RELIEF TELEPHONIST
for a range of typing duties. Generous holidays. Salaries by arrangement. Write: Box No. 732, Echo.

(4)

PERSON FRIDAY

required to look after office of idiots. 20 hours per week. Must be able to type.
Phone Newtown 726

(5)

SECRETARY

Experienced secretary required for Managing Director and two other Directors for manufacturing and distribution company in Redleigh. Salary negotiable above £6,500 per annum.
Applicants should be capable of absorbing wider responsibilities after experience. Apply in writing to Company Secretary, Trend Merchandise, Newtown Road, Redleigh.

(6)

JUNIOR TYPIST

This responsible position requires some office experience, with shorthand an advantage, and capable of working on own initiative with the ability to deal efficiently with Customer and Staff enquiries.

Please apply IN WRITING ONLY in the first instance, to Mrs Elizabeth Smith, Chief Training Officer, Electron Products, Metal Road, Gastown.

1. Godliness, Cleanliness and Punctuality are the necessities of a good business.

2. This firm has now reduced the hours of work, and the clerical staff will now only have to be present between the hours of 7.00 a.m. and 6.00 p.m. on week days. The Sabbath is for worship, but should any man-of-war or other vessel require victualling, the clerical staff will work on the Sabbath.

3. Daily Prayers will be held each morning in the main office. The clerical staff will be present.

4. Clothing must be of a sober nature. The clerical staff will not disport themselves in raiment of bright colours, nor will they wear hose unless of good repair.

5. Overshoes and top-coats may not be worn in the office, but neck-scarves and headwear may be worn in inclement weather.

6. A stove is provided for the clerical staff. Coal and wood must be kept in the locker. It is recommended that each member of the clerical staff bring four pounds of coal, each day, during the cold weather.

7. No member of the clerical staff may leave the room without permission from Mr. Ryder. The calls of nature are permitted, and the clerical staff may use the garden below the second gate. This area must be kept in good order.

8. No talking is allowed during business hours.

9. The craving for tobacco, wines or spirits is a human weakness and, as such, is forbidden to all members of the clerical staff.

10. Now that the hours of business have been drastically reduced the partaking of food is allowed between 11.30 a.m. and noon, but work will not, on any account, cease.

11. Members of the clerical staff will provide their own pens. A new sharpener is available, on application to Mr. Ryder.

12. Mr. Ryder will nominate a senior clerk to be responsible for the cleanliness of the main office and the private office, and all boys and juniors will report to him forty minutes before prayers, and will remain after closing hours for similar work. Brushes, brooms, scrubbers and soap are provided by the owners.

13. The new increased weekly wages are as hereunder detailed:

	s.	d.
Junior boys (to 11 years)	1	4
Boys (to 14 years)	2	1
Juniors	4	8
Junior Clerks	8	7
Clerks	10	9
Senior Clerks (after 15 years with the owner)	21	-

The owners hereby recognise the generosity of the new labour laws, but will expect a great rise in output of work to compensate for these near Utopian conditions.

OFFICE STAFF PRACTICES: 1853

Times have changed!

The Right Way to Apply for a Job

> JUNIOR TYPIST required for busy office in local firm centrally situated. Shorthand not necessary but good standard of English essential – 'O' level or CSE equivalent. Apply by letter to: Office Manager, Millard & Perkins Ltd. St Christopher's Trading Estate, Bromswood B95 8BT.

Below you can see how Margaret Atkins applied for this job. She has typed her letter nicely and sent in a very useful curriculum vitae – so naturally she hopes to get an interview.

8 Rose Crescent
Garden View Estate
BROMSWOOD
Essex
G45 8TA

Telephone: 432 990

30 June 198-

The Office Manager
Millard & Perkins Ltd
St Christopher's Trading Estate
BROMSWOOD, Essex
G45 5TB

Dear Sir

Re: Vacancy for Junior Typist

I am interested in your advertisement in today's issue of the "Daily News" for the above vacancy, and enclose details of my education and training, together with a photocopy of my latest school report.

I am 16 years of age and have finished my examinations, so should be able to leave school at any time.

If you would like me to call for an interview, I shall be pleased to do so on any day and at any time to suit your convenience.

Yours faithfully

Margaret Atkins

Margaret Atkins (Miss)

Encls

The letter of application

```
Name:              ATKINS Margaret        Nationality:    British

Address:           8 Rose Crescent        Marital status:  Single
                   Garden View Estate
                   BROMSWOOD
                   Essex
                   G45 5TB

Tel:               432 990

Date of birth:     16 May 1967

EDUCATION:         St Mary's Comprehensive School, Bromswood.   1978-83

QUALIFICATIONS:    (Examination results not yet known)
                   O level

                   English
                   Mathematics
                   History
                   Geography

                   CSE

                   Typewriting
                   Office Practice
                   Commerce
                   Home Economics


EXPERIENCE:        Working on Saturdays for Nevinson's Stationers, High St,
                   Bromswood - typing envelopes, filing, helping in the shop
                   at busy times.  Also dealing with incoming and outgoing
                   post and paying money into the bank.

                   From August 1982 to the present day.

HOBBIES:           Swimming, gymnastics, hockey, cooking.

OTHER INTERESTS:   Raising money for muscular dystrophy (have helped to
                   organise a sponsored walk), disco-dancing.

REFERENCES:        These may be obtained from:

                   Miss N Keene              Mr G Dunn
                   Headmistress              The Manager
                   St Mary's Comprehensive School   Nevinson's Stationers
                   Bromswood                 High Street
                                             Bromswood
                   Tel:  33501
                                             Tel:  32411
```

A curriculum vitae

Interviews

Many applications for jobs do not result in an interview. One of the reasons is that the applicant has not read the advertisement properly and has applied for a job for which she is totally unsuitable. Points to check especially are: age, experience, skills needed. The other main reason for no interview following a letter of application is that the letter was badly spelt and untidily written and set out or did not supply the information requested (unlike the one written by Margaret Atkins!).

BEFORE AN INTERVIEW

If you are successful with your application and receive a letter asking you to attend for an interview, there are several things which will improve your chances of success before you even set out:

1) Find out what you can about the firm – its history, what it makes or what it does, when it was founded, how many people it employs etc. (The local library may have some books or they may be able to help if you ask an assistant. Alternatively you may be able to talk to someone already working at the firm.)

2) Locate the building beforehand, so that you know exactly where it is, and find the main entrance and the reception area. This will save valuable time on the day of the interview.

3) Check bus and/or train times making sure that you will arrive near the firm with time to spare. You can always 'kill time' near the firm taking a walk or having a cup of coffee in a snack bar.

4) Make a list of suitable questions to ask your interviewer – his job is to try and get you to talk to him so that he can find out more about your personality; he already has the basic facts in your letter of application and curriculum vitae. Some topics for you to ask about could be:

- What other duties would be involved besides typing
- What sort of typewriter – electric or manual
- Any possibility of further training or day release
- Pension scheme
- Promotion and pay increases – on merit or automatically
- Welfare and medical service
- Social activities and sports clubs
- Canteen
- Hours of work
- Holidays
- Pay (if not mentioned by interviewer — this is one of the main reasons why you are going to work, after all).
- Fringe benefits (e.g. Luncheon Vouchers)

Before an interview try to think of the questions you may be asked. One question frequently asked is 'Why do you want to come and work here?' A sensible answer to this might be 'I have always been interested in banking (or travel, or whatever the firm's type of business is)'. Another question will almost certainly be about any hobbies or special interests mentioned on your curriculum vitae, so it is important to be honest when mentioning these and not just to try and impress. It's no good, for example, listing 'horse-riding' if the only time you mount a horse is once a year when you're staying with a friend, or 'reading' if you only glance through weekly magazines.

Finally, on the day of the interview:

- Dress carefully – smart but not startling and above all, comfortable.

- If it's a hot day, wear something loose and cool in preference to a very new outfit which is really too heavy for a summer's day.
- If it's very cold, wrap up warmly – arriving looking blue and shivering will not create a good impression.
- Wear comfortable shoes – those 4″ heels are fine for the evening but not for tottering into a strange building with unfamiliar stairs and (possibly) polished floors.
- Pay especial attention to hair, hands, shoes and tights.
- Be prepared for a typing test and take with you a typewriter eraser and a backing sheet; a ruler may be useful.
- Take the letter asking you to come to the interview with you.

DURING THE INTERVIEW

The interviewer's job is to make you feel at ease, so you will be pleasantly surprised to find that you stop feeling nervous quite soon. Sit down when you are asked to do so. Talk naturally and avoid 'you know' – nervous people often use this phrase out of sheer fright. At the end of the interview, the interviewer will usually say 'we will let you know' – it is not often that a decision is given there and then. If you decide that you don't want the job anyway, don't say so – you might change your mind later on, or the job may not even be offered. Thank your interviewer for seeing you and say 'Goodbye' with a smile – the last impression is just as important as the first.

Making you feel welcome

SUCCESS OR FAILURE?

If you receive the long-awaited letter offering you a job, reply at once by letter accepting it, or, tell them you have decided not to accept it, if that is the case. You may receive a letter telling you you have not been successful. If so, do not be too discouraged – every interview and interviewer is different and adds to your experience. Next time you will have a great deal more confidence.

FOR YOUR FOLDER

6. FINDING A JOB

Write these notes in your folder, filling in the missing words and phrases.

1) A 'curriculum vitae' is a _____.

2) It is useful to have several ready to send with letters of application for jobs because _____ and _____.

3) Questions may be asked at an interview about hobbies or interests listed in a curriculum vitae so it is important to be _____.

4) Before attending for an interview, it is a good plan to find out what you can about a firm, visit it beforehand to locate it exactly and _____ so that you will not be late.

5) A list of suitable questions to ask the interviewer could include:
   a _____
   b _____
   c _____
   d _____
   e _____

6) You may be given a typing test as part of an interview for a typist's job. It will create a good impression if you take with you _____.

7) It is also important to have with you your letter _____.

8) At the conclusion of an interview, you should _____ – the last impression is just as important as the first.

9) If an important letter arrives offering you the job you should _____.

10) If after all you have decided you do not want the job, you should _____.

Exercise 7

QUESTIONS ON FINDING A JOB

1) There are several ways of finding out about job vacancies. Explain three of them.

2) What is a 'box number' and why do firms use them?

3) On Margaret's curriculum vitae (p. 38) she gave 'date of birth' and not her age. Why was this?

4) What was the distinction between her 'hobbies' and 'other interests'?

5) Why did she include two names of people to whom application could be made for references?

6) Write a letter to the Office Manager, Millard & Perkins Ltd, accepting the post in the advertisement.

7) Write a letter to the Office Manager, Millard & Perkins Ltd, explaining that you do not wish to accept the post. You do not have to give a reason.

8) Write a letter to the Office Manager, Millard & Perkins Ltd, in reply to his asking you to come for an interview on Monday 1 July 198—, explaining that you are ill and unable to come on that day, but would be pleased to come a week later.

9) Draw a map showing the way to a firm in your town, marking any landmarks such as a river, bridges, cathedral, railway and bus stations.

10) Find out what you can about this same firm on the lines suggested in this chapter, and type (or write) it out in a suitable form to take with you to an interview (A5 paper, so that you could slip it into your pocket or handbag for quick reference during an interview if needed).

Starting Work

CONTRACT OF EMPLOYMENT

If you are offered a job, you will sooner or later get a contract of employment.

This may be in the form of a letter of appointment, or it may be oral, in which case the terms of appointment must be set out in the form of a notice on the wall of the office, so that employees are aware of the conditions of their contract of employment.

The contract of employment must set out the following details and must be supplied by your employer within 13 weeks of your starting the job:
- Rates of pay (and whether paid weekly or monthly)
- Hours of work
- Sick pay
- Pension
- Holidays and holiday pay
- Length of notice to be given by either side
- The right to belong to a trade union of choice
- The right *not* to belong to a trade union
- The person to whom a grievance can be made
- Date of commencement of employment.

The minimum periods of notice which must be given to employees are based on length of service:

After four weeks' service – one week's notice *and then*
one week's notice for each completed year of service up to a maximum of 12 weeks' notice.

THE FIRST DAY

Your first day in an office is very important, and also rather alarming to contemplate. It helps to get ready the evening before. What to wear should be decided, clothes laid out, shoes cleaned, and alarm clock set – it would never do to be late on the first morning!

Many firms have what is known as an induction course for new employees.

An induction course is actually an introduction to the firm, its departments and its organisation and procedures. Many firms have a printed handbook which will be given to you to keep with all this information contained in it.

An induction course will normally occupy most of the first morning, so it will be after lunch before you get down to finding out what you actually have to do in the firm's office where you are to work. By this time you will have found out where the canteen is, where the cloakrooms are and whether you clock in and out when you leave. It is also important to remember where the sick room is, in case you feel ill at any time. Some firms arrange a medical inspection for each new employee, either just before or just after they start work.

WHAT TO TAKE WITH YOU

A National Insurance number is necessary for your first job and this is obtainable from the Department of Health and Social Security. Your National Insurance contributions will be deducted along with your income tax by your employer. If you have not worked before, you will not have a P45 form, which is a record of income tax deducted by your previous employer. You will be given an emergency code until your income tax form (Claim for Allowances) has been completed by you (see Chapter 16).

You will be introduced to the person to whom you will be responsible and who will tell you what your duties will be. An office junior, straight from school, without any training in office routine or typewriting, may be shown how to collect the mail from the other offices and take it to the mail room. She may be given messages to take around the firm (so it is important to remember how to find your way around); she may be shown how to collect filing and pre-sort it (see Chapter 12); she may make tea or coffee for other people in the office – or fetch it from vending machines for them. One day a week may be spent at the local college learning to type and write shorthand – this is a 'day-release course'. The firm itself may run a training section of its own.

CLOTHES AND MAKE-UP

The right clothes give you confidence. This is particularly important for a new job. Also, an outfit must be comfortable when you are going to wear it all day.

All large firms have centrally heated offices and it is not necessary to wear thick clothes indoors, in the winter.

Trousers, well-pressed and part of a matched outfit look smart, but any old jeans and T-shirt will *not* do.

Warm summer days may have chilly mornings, so a cool dress with a matching jacket is useful.

High heels *look* pretty and feminine but can easily cause an accident while going up or down stairs carrying files. Besides, they are tiring to wear all day, especially as some office jobs involve hours of standing or walking. A spare pair of shoes with lower heels kept at the office may be the answer to the footwear problem.

What is wrong? Why did she fall?

Jewellery worn to the office should be simple and inexpensive.

Leave anything really precious at home. Long dangly ear-rings or necklaces may be caught up in typewriters or other equipment which could be dangerous.

Hands and nails are conspicuous when typing, answering the telephone or filing, and should be well-cared for. Dark nail varnish is attractive but it must be unchipped and perfect (all part of the good grooming). A paler varnish is easier to keep in a good state of repair as it needs replacing less often. Filing nails a little shorter than usual is sensible as this avoids tearing them on a typewriter or other office equipment.

Perfume is pleasant — in moderation. A light toilet water and matching talc is ideal.

Personal freshness should be an automatic part of the day's grooming routine, but it is worth remembering that in a centrally heated office during a busy day, a deodorant may need re-applying.

A spare make-up kit containing everything necessary for a quick repair job to face and nails should be kept in your office drawer. This, together with aspirins, tissues, plasters, needle, cotton and scissors, and a spare pair of tights, will enable you to cope with most minor emergencies, as well as that exciting unexpected date!

Good grooming is essential, and a simple, basic plan is a great help, because it means you arrive at the office looking your best *every* morning. Spending the first 15 minutes in the cloakroom putting on make-up is not a good idea – it is no better than arriving late at the office – and will soon get you a reputation for being slack.

Hair should be shining clean and if short or medium length, well-cut so that it looks its best with very little trouble. If it is long, experiment with taking it up, or back, so that it does not obscure your view during the day.

Finally, a word for young men. A jacket, trousers, shirt with collar and tie are the right wear in an office, jeans and T-shirts are *not* suitable, with the alternative of a polo-necked sweater under a jacket if the weather is wintry. Shoes must shine, please!

Not ideal hair-styles for the office!

FOR YOUR FOLDER

7. OFFICE CLOTHES

Either: trace a winter and summer outfit from a magazine

or: (if you can draw) design a summer and winter outfit.

Complete all these drawings with suitable shoes for wearing in an office.

Some Do's and Don'ts

Do Arrive a little early – this helps you to feel calm and relaxed.

Do Try to learn your way around a firm as quickly as possible. Draw a rough plan of the various buildings and write their names on it.

Do Try to remember people's correct names and titles. Use names when you say 'good morning' or 'good afternoon'. It sounds polite and efficient.

Do Make sure you do everything you have been asked to do before you go home. Keep a little notebook so that you can jot down any points you may forget, and cross each job off as it is completed. This will avoid anything being overlooked.

Do Keep your desk, desk drawers and area around you neat and tidy, not like the office squirrel below. You cannot work in a clutter nor can you find anything quickly when you are asked for it.

The office squirrel!

Clocking in

Don't

Be a clock watcher and vanish at the first stroke of the hour you are allowed to leave. Finish off any work which you know may be needed. Some firms operate what is known as flexible working hours and you are able to 'save' extra time and take a half-day off when you have sufficient time in the 'bank' (there is more information about this on p. 48). To operate this system it is necessary to clock in and clock out so that your employer knows exactly when you arrived and when you left.

Don't Gossip. What you hear may not be true and will only hurt someone's feelings if they hear it.

Don't Criticise. If you can't think of anything nice to say, say nothing. This is known as 'being tactful'!

Don't Take your troubles with you to the office. Try to forget them and concentrate on your job. You may find that by the time you go home your problems will not seem nearly as bad as they did in the morning.

Don't Sit and look bored when you have finished all the work you have been given to do. Keep busy by cleaning your typewriter or tidying desk drawers. Later on, when you are more experienced, you will be able to see what else needs doing, without being told. This is known as 'using your initiative'!

Don't Forget to let your employer know, before 9 o'clock if possible, that you will not be coming to the office (if you are ill, for instance). This is known as 'being polite'!

Don't Regard small items of stationery, such as pencils, ball-point pens, envelopes, erasers, rubber bands, paper clips, or typing paper, supplied to you at the office, as being yours to take home.

Don't Be disloyal to your employer. This means that you do not discuss what you may consider to be his faults with anyone, either in the firm or outside it.

Exercise 8

CROSSWORD ON STARTING WORK

Make a copy of the crossword square below and see if you can solve it.

Across
1 You may be wearing the wrong kind of shoes if your feet _____ (4)
3 Some firms require their workers to clock _____ and out (2)
5 Hands and _____ are so much on view they must be well-cared for (5)
6 People who criticise without thought _____ tactless (3)
7 If you have work to do when it is time to go home _____ a little later to get it done (4)
10 Spending the first 15 minutes of each morning in the cloakroom to put on make-up is as bad as arriving _____ (4)
11 As well (4)

Down
2 Taking home small items of stationery is not _____ (6)
3 If you are _____ you must let your employer know (3)
4 Arrive at the office a few minutes _____ if you want to start the day calm (5)
8 It may be your job to make this! (3)
9 Should long hair be styled so that it is off the face in an office? (3)

Flexible Working Hours

This is a system whereby office workers can vary their starting and finishing times to suit their own convenience, so long as they work an agreed minimum number of hours per week. They may prefer to start early (0800 hours) and finish early (1600) to fit in with family commitments (children at school, for example) or start later (1000) and finish later (1800) to avoid rush-hour traffic.

There are usually periods when all workers have to be in the office. One is in the morning (perhaps 1000–1200) and the other in the afternoon (perhaps 1400–1600). These periods are known as 'core time'. The lunch hour may be taken at any time between the two core periods. Different workers may choose different lunch hours so that, for instance, the reception desk always has someone in attendance (see pp. 61 — 2).

Time may be 'banked' by working overtime – hours in addition to the agreed minimum and half-days taken by arrangement with the firm. Banked time is generally limited to a certain number of hours per week.

Clocking in and out is an essential part of flexible working hours in order to keep an accurate record of time actually spent in the office.

Flexible working hours have proved to be popular with office workers, especially women, who are able to fit in working time with looking after school-age children and shopping. They are also popular with office workers who travel long distances as they can fit in travelling time with less busy periods on rail or road.

FOR YOUR FOLDER

8. FLEXIBLE WORKING HOURS

Write these notes in your folder, filling in the missing words and phrases.

1) Flexible working hours is a system whereby office workers can _____ their starting and finishing times to suit their own convenience.

2) They have to work an agreed _____ per week.

3) The period of time when all workers have to be in the office is known as _____ time.

4) By working overtime, it is possible to _____ time which can then be taken in half-days off, by agreement with the firm.

5) An essential part of flexible working hours is _____ in and _____ out, in order to keep an accurate record of hours actually spent at work.

6) Flexible working hours are popular with married women who work in offices because they are able to fit in _____ with working time.

7) Flexible working hours are also popular with people who _____ long distances.

Holiday Rotas

Office workers cannot all take their main summer holidays at the same time (unless their firm closes down) so they have to 'stagger' their holidays. This means they have to spread their holiday period over several months, so that the work of the office is still carried out promptly and efficiently.

A rota is arranged early in the year and office workers are usually given a choice of weeks which they may take for holidays. Longer service in some firms entitles workers to a number of extra days of holiday. Some firms do not allow 'key' workers (those with important jobs such as managers, supervisors, switchboard operators or wages clerks) to be away on holiday for more than two weeks at any one time — their remaining weeks have to be taken separately.

A holiday rota could look like the one below or it could be a visual planning chart (see p. 147).

HOLIDAY ROTA FOR JUNE – JULY 198__

Personnel Department

Name		From	To
STRIDE	Mrs K. (Supervisor)	4 June	18 June
ABBOTT	Anne	11 June	25 June
CARTER	Lucy	18 June	2 July
LINEHAM	Jane	25 June	9 July
MASON	Debbie	2 July	16 July
PRATT	Gloria	9 July	23 July
RUSSELL	Paula	16 July	30 July

Exercise 9

HOLIDAY ROTAS

Answer the following questions about the rota above:

1) Gloria and Debbie want to plan 7 days' holiday together in July. What will be the dates at the beginning and end of their 7 days?

2) Jane's fiancé cannot have his holiday starting on 25 June and Jane wants to change to his dates, which are 11 June to 18 June. Who will Jane have to change holiday dates with?

3) If this change is possible, and is agreed, a new rota will have to be made out. Rewrite it as it will appear when the new arrangements have been made between Jane and the person concerned.

Exercise 10

ASSIGNMENT ON HOLIDAY ROTA

OCTOBER						
SUN	MON	TUE	WED	THUR	FRI	SAT
						1
2	3	4	5	6	7	8
9	10	11	12	13	14	15
16	17	18	19	20	21	22
23	24	25	26	27	28	29
30	31					

From the calendar above for October, work out a rota for 5 days' holiday to be taken for the staff in Exercise 9. Not more than two members of staff may be away at the same time. Holidays need not start on Mondays, or end on Fridays, but Saturdays and Sundays are not usually working days, so are not counted as holidays.

Trade Unions

THE TRADE UNION AND THE INDIVIDUAL

If you go to work for a large firm, where a particular trade union is represented, you may be asked to join that union by the union representative who also works for the firm – his wages are paid by his employer, not by the trade union. He (or she) is elected as a representative by the trade union members. The representative is known as a shop steward, and he is the link between the union and its members at that particular workplace. He will give you details of subscriptions and rights and privileges which you are entitled to. He is also the person to whom you should complain if you feel that your pay and/or conditions of work need to be improved. The shop steward will also keep you informed of union policy as it affects you.

As a union member you will be attached to a local 'branch' of the union. Here you may make your views known about any aspect of your local working conditions to the branch officials. A vote is taken on all issues and decisions discussed at the branch meeting, with the majority view being accepted.

Two ways of voting

Many offices, particularly the small ones employing just a few people, may not have any union representative. In fact, none of the people who work in small offices may ever belong to a trade union. Whether you belong to a trade union is usually a matter of your choice, but there are a few exceptions.

In some companies the union to which most of the employees belong may negotiate an agreement with the employer that he will not engage anyone unless that person is prepared to join the union. This is known commonly as a 'closed shop' agreement. Usually such agreements are made by particular craft unions so that office workers (typists, shorthand-typists, receptionists) may not be affected by such a closed shop agreement. In any case, it is possible to refuse to join a union on religious or conscientious grounds, and if neither of these apply and you do not wish to join a union, you simply find a job elsewhere – whether to join a union or not is a matter for the individual to decide.

DISPUTES

If a dispute or disagreement arises between an employer and members of a union working at that particular place, the union members concerned may be called upon to 'strike' – that is; withdraw their labour from that particular employer. It sometimes happens that only members of a particular union withdraw their labour – other colleagues who may belong to a different union, but work at the same place, may continue to work. If the dispute is regarded as very serious by all the unions represented in a firm, then all the workers are called out on strike, irrespective of which union they may belong to. In all circumstances of strikes, any person who does not belong to a union has the right to go to work at his place of employment, even though some of his colleagues may try to persuade him not to work by means of 'picketing' which simply involves using 'peaceful persuasion' at the entrance to the firm.

In many cases disputes arise, and workers may be called upon to strike by a shop steward, which they are expected to do. Nevertheless, until the union's senior officials approve of strike action, the strike is 'unofficial'. Some strikes take place, are settled and never become officially recognised. Others may start as unofficial strikes and become official later on when senior officials of the union engage in 'negotiation' (discussions between union and management of the firm).

Usually strikes are settled by negotiation between the employer and trade union representatives, but in the occasional cases where a settlement cannot be reached, both sides may agree to refer the facts to the government's Advisory, Conciliation, and Arbitration Service (ACAS).

Officials of ACAS listen, separately, to each side and suggest some common grounds for discussion in order to end the strike.

If ACAS cannot end the dispute, the government may appoint an independent body to negotiate and to make recommendations for a settlement.

There are trade unions for professional people (such as doctors, lawyers, teachers), for particular trades (engineers, construction workers, plumbers, electricians) and for specialised workers in industry, retail and office work (railway workers, shop workers, miners, local government officers, civil servants, public employees and health service workers). Some of these unions are:

Association of Scientific Technical and Managerial Staffs   ASTMS

Association of Professional Executive and Computer Staffs   APEX

National Union of Public Employees   NUPE

There are also unions which cater for those whose work does not fall into a particular group but is of a more general nature:

The Transport and General Workers Union   TGWU

The General and Municipal, Boilermakers and
   Allied Trade Union   GMBATU

These last two unions can look after the interests of clerical workers, secretaries and other office workers. Office workers form only a small proportion of these unions' total membership.

TRADES UNION CONGRESS (TUC)

The Trades Union Congress was founded in 1868 and is a voluntary association of trade unions. Representatives of the trade unions meet annually to consider matters of interest to their members. The Congress is made up of delegates from the unions on the basis of one delegate for every 5000 members. In 1981 – 82 affiliated unions totalled 105, with a total membership of 11 005 984.

The TUC represents the views of the unions to the Government and others, and gives help on questions relating to particular trades and industries. Full-time officials and various committees do most of this work during the year.

Also the TUC has the responsibility of intervening in disputes and differences between unions and employers, informally if possible, but when necessary a disputes committee is formed.

Many trade unions include what is known as a 'political levy' as a separate part of the union subscription. This means that the political levy is sent to finance the funds of a political party that the union supports – usually the Labour Party. If you want to support union principles but do not agree with its politics, you may 'opt out' of paying the political levy. The trade union representative should make this clear to you before you join.

WHITE COLLAR AND BLUE COLLAR UNIONS

These are general descriptions of professional, supervisory and clerical workers' unions, in the case of white collar unions.

Blue collar unions cover the craftsmen and other manual workers' unions.

FOR YOUR FOLDER

9. TRADE UNIONS

Write these notes in your folder, filling in the missing words and phrases.

1) The trade union representative in a firm is known as the _____.

2) As a trade union member you will be attached to a local _____ of the union.

3) A 'closed shop' agreement means that the employer has agreed not to employ anyone except _____.

4) It is possible to decline to join a union on _____ or conscientious grounds.

5) Any person who does not belong to a union has the right to go to work at his place of employment even though some of his colleagues may try to persuade him not to work by means of _____ which simply means peaceful _____ at the firm's entrance.

6) Workers may be called upon to strike by a shop steward, but until the union's senior officials approve of the strike, it is _____.

7) When a strike cannot be settled by discussion between trade union representatives and management, the facts may be referred to a government body called _____.

8) Two unions which look after the interests of clerical workers are _____ and _____.

9) The separate part of a subscription to a trade union which is sent as a contribution to a political party's funds is known as a _____.

10) It is not compulsory to pay this separate part if you want to support trade union _____ but do not agree with its politics.

11) The initials NUPE stand for _____.

12) The initials GMBATU stand for _____.

13) The initials APEX stand for _____.

14) The initials TGWU stand for _____.

Exercise 11

QUESTIONS ON TRADE UNIONS

1) Explain the meaning of a 'closed shop'.

2) What is the difference between an 'official strike' and an 'unofficial strike'?

3) What is the role of ACAS in connection with strikes?

4) What is the connection between trade unions and the Labour Party? Explain how it is possible to join a trade union and yet not wish to support the Labour Party.

5) When starting work in a firm where there is a trade union which looks after the interests of clerical workers, explain how you would make enquiries about joining.

SECTION B   COMMUNICATIONS AND INFORMATION

CHAPTER 4

The Receptionist

Duties and Appearance

The receptionist's main job is to look after the visitors to a firm. She will, however, have time during the day when there are no callers, to do other work. She may:

- Type
- Operate a switchboard
- File
- Give out brochures and handbooks issued by her firm
- Open and arrange for distribution of mail; receive parcels, and registered or recorded delivery mail
- Help with making tea or coffee for visitors – as it is essential that the reception desk is never left unattended, many firms have vending machines so that callers are able to help themselves to refreshments.
- Be able to give simple first aid, when necessary.

Alternatively, there may be two receptionists – the head receptionist and her deputy – so that the reception desk is never left unmanned.

Visitors to a firm must never be kept waiting unnecessarily. They may go elsewhere if they are, and not return. Valuable business could be lost to the firm.

All large firms (and organisations such as universities, hospitals, colleges, local authorities) have receptionists. In addition, many small firms find their services very useful too – estate agents, accountants, solicitors, as well as doctors and dentists. In fact, almost any office where an appointments system makes the most efficient use of people's time.

A good receptionist should be:

- Polite
- Friendly
- Helpful
- Tactful
- Calm (above all, patient!)
- Neat
- Smart
- Well-groomed (hair, nails, make-up)

- Well-informed about her firm's products, layout and staff, so that she can direct visitors to the right offices, and answer any questions they may ask her.

The receptionist's voice is particularly important; it should be pleasant and clear. Some visitors may be foreigners and have difficulty understanding English.

Reception work is not suitable for shy people. A receptionist must be able to get on easily with strangers.

Generally speaking, an ideal receptionist should be aged 20 or over. She will have sufficient experience by then to be both confident and efficient at her job.

Types of Caller

CALLERS WHO HAVE MADE APPOINTMENTS might include:
- Applicants to be interviewed for vacant jobs
- Sales representatives
- Businessmen from other firms attending meetings
- Visitors from other firms, both in the UK and from overseas.

CALLERS WITHOUT APPOINTMENTS could be:
- People enquiring about vacancies for jobs
- Customers who have come to complain about the firm's goods
- Sales representatives hoping to see the chief buyer or a member of his staff.

REGULAR CALLERS NORMALLY WITHOUT APPOINTMENTS
- Postmen
- Security van drivers delivering cash for wages
- Delivery men from other firms
- Roadline delivery men
- British Rail (BR) delivery men
- Window cleaners, telephone disinfectant service staff, suppliers of pot plants
- People delivering letters and parcels from other firms by hand.

UNEXPECTED CALLERS WITHOUT APPOINTMENTS

These should be asked politely if they would like to write in for one. If they refuse to leave without making an appointment, the receptionist should telephone the secretary of the person the caller is hoping to see, and ask her when an appointment can be made.

Occasionally, callers insist on seeing the person they want without having made an appointment, and refuse to leave. This is where all the tact and patience of the receptionist is required. She should emphasise to the caller that the person he insists on seeing is at an important meeting and will not be available for several hours, or, alternatively, that he has gone to a meeting at another firm. Finally, if the caller still refuses to go, the receptionist should telephone the firm's security police, who will come and escort the caller out, but this is only as a last resort and, if the receptionist knows her job, should not be necessary.

Callers who have to wait because of an unavoidable delay should be looked after in the reception area, offered tea or coffee, and reassured from time to time that they have not been forgotten.

What to do if all else fails!

Greeting Callers and Dealing with Visiting Cards

Using a person's name is friendly and makes a caller feel welcome. The receptionist's name should be either on a brooch pinned to her dress or on a stand in front of her, so that callers can see her name at a glance and use it at once. The receptionist's first question to a caller should be to ask his or her name and then use it. Many businessmen have business visiting cards and will give one to the receptionist. Business visiting cards have printed on them the caller's name, the caller's firm, firm's address and telephone number, and occasionally the caller's home address and telephone number. Sometimes a card also gives information about the firm's products. The information on the business visiting card saves the receptionist asking the caller a great many questions. It also helps her to introduce the caller to anyone in the firm who may not know him.

Usually, business visiting cards (callers' cards) are left with the receptionist and she files them away in alphabetical order of the firms' names. Then, next time a caller comes whom the receptionist recognises, she is able to look up his business visiting card and refer to it for information.

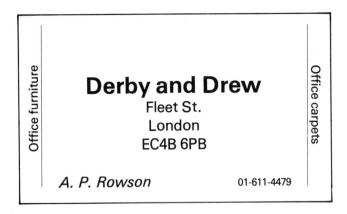

A business card

A card index box is useful for filing business visiting cards. They should be glued or taped to an index card, which makes them easier to handle and find. Business visiting cards form a useful record of callers and can be referred to for names and addresses for sending out advertising material.

Filing a business card

Note that the card on p. 60 is being filed under the name of the firm and not the name of the caller. This is because firms rarely change their names, whereas their employees frequently change their jobs, so it is easier for a receptionist to refer to a firm rather than to someone employed by a firm.

The Receptionist's Desk

In some firms, the receptionist may have a switchboard to look after. In all firms, she will have two telephones: one for internal calls; and the other for external calls. The latest telephones, however, incorporate external and internal lines in one instrument. She may also have a typewriter and a filing cabinet. She will also have her own records, consisting of:

- An index of callers' cards
- Records of callers (callers' register and appointments book)
- A staff 'in and out' book.

Her name may be on her desk in front of her (or on a brooch which she pins to her dress).

She will have a plan of the firm on the wall behind her.

She will also have an organisation chart on the wall. This gives the names of the directors and managers of her firm.

The receptionist's desk should be near to the main entrance of a firm, so that callers are able to find it easily. The picture below shows how an efficient, well-organised receptionist has planned her desk and office equipment.

An efficient receptionist who is well-organised. The VDU may be used instead of an appointments book

FOR YOUR FOLDER

10. THE RECEPTIONIST AND HER DUTIES

Write these notes in your folder, filling in the missing words and phrases.

1) The receptionist's *main* job is to _____ after callers at a firm.

2) When there are no callers, the receptionist may have other duties such as:

    a _____.
    b _____.
    c _____.
    d _____.
    e _____.

3) The receptionist may be given a caller's card from which she can learn the _____.

4) Other information on a caller's card may be _____.

5) The receptionist will file caller's cards (business visiting cards) in alphabetical order of _____ names.

Exercise 12

QUESTIONS ON THE RECEPTIONIST AND HER DUTIES

1) Why is a receptionist important to a firm?

2) What effect might a 'couldn't-care-less' attitude have on callers?

3) Why is it important that a receptionist is well-informed about her firm's layout, products and staff?

4) What are the three different types of caller?

5) What sort of callers who call at a firm regularly would not normally have appointments?

6) Where should a receptionist have her name displayed?

7) Why is it important to use a person's name as soon as possible?

8) What is the correct procedure for dealing with a caller who arrives without an appointment?

9) What are the two important uses of business visiting cards?

10) What information does an organisation chart give?

11) Receptionists are employed by doctors, dentists, hotels, colleges, opticians and veterinaries. What is the ideal age for a receptionist and what type of person should she be?

12) Where should the receptionist's desk be situated?

13) What is the correct way to look after a caller who may have to wait in the reception area for a rather long time?

14) Look at the advertisement below and answer the questions about it.

WANTED: RECEPTIONIST/TELEPHONIST for large firm manufacturing domestic goods. Training will be given on a switchboard. Experience not essential but applicant must be able to type and have a pleasant personality and good telephone manner. Apply in writing to: Personnel Manager, Willis and Lever Ltd, 185 The Parade, Cricksville.

---

a Would this vacancy appeal to you if you were looking for a job?

b Do you think you would be suitable before having had some experience?

c What do you think is meant by a 'good telephone manner'?

d What sort of typing do you think the receptionist would do?

The Receptionist's Reference Books

The receptionist will often need to have reference books to help deal with visitors' enquiries. There is more about this in Chapter 8, especially on p. 189.

The Receptionist's Records

CALLERS' REGISTER

One of the other record books which the receptionist looks after is the *callers' register*. All callers to a firm sign this, with the exception of such callers as postmen and delivery men.

A callers' register shows the name of the caller, his firm or his home address, the time he arrived, who he saw in the firm, and whether he made a further appointment. Opposite is a page from a callers' register, showing the callers at a firm on the morning of 21 November 198—.

Under the heading 'Action Taken' are details about callers who arrived without appointments. This column shows that the usual way to deal with such callers is to ask them to write in for an appointment.

Occasionally, a caller refuses to leave without either seeing the person he wants, or having made an appointment. In either of these cases, the receptionist should telephone the secretary concerned and ask to make an appointment.

Exercise 13

CALLERS' REGISTER

Now rule up a copy of the callers' register page, leaving it blank except for headings, and fill in with the following information. Use today's date.

1) Mr James Brookes of S & J Electronics came at 1030 to see Mr J Ellis, managing director. He made another appointment on his way out for the same time and day next week.

2) Mr S Holmes, Mr A Simpson and Miss W Keene arrived at 1130. They all had appointments to see Mr H Long, the sales manager. All three callers were from Twist, Swindle & Dunnem, Chartered Accountants, Wordsworth Avenue, Champton.

3) Miss T Taplow, Office Equipment Supplies Ltd, Blacking, arrived to see Mr Jones the buyer at 1200, by appointment.

4) Mr C Vernon, Cast Iron Casting Co Ltd called at 1215 in the hope of seeing Mr G Kerr, production manager. He is writing in for an appointment.

CALLERS' REGISTER

DATE 198–	NAME OF CALLER	CALLER'S FIRM OR HOME ADDRESS	TIME OF ARRIVAL	SEEN BY	ACTION TAKEN
Nov. 21	L.M. Parkins	J. Mann + Co. Ltd.	09 00	K. Jones – Buyer	
	Mrs H. Simms	18 Hilary Ave. Worcester	09 45	No appointment	Writing to Personnel Officer with details.
	B.N. Vines	Carson Engineering	09 50	Personnel Manager	
	Miss G.B. Tomkins	44 Scott Cresc. Evesham	10 00	No appointment	Personnel Man's assistant seeing her on 28/11 at 10.00
	Miss K. Lyons	219 Lake Ave. Worcester	10 30	Personnel Manager	
	F. Parkins	Peterson's Export Co.	10 35	Accounts Dept.	Made further appointment to see Chief Cashier 23/11
	Mrs. A. Drew	Wilchester Technical College	11 00	Personnel Manager	
	P. Lester	Perfecta Paper Co.	11 05	No appointment	Appointment made to see K. Jone's assistant
	J.R. Smart	39 Market Place	11 20	No appointment	Writing to Production Manager with details
	Mrs. W. Moxon	Office Equipment Supplies	11 30	Miss B. Burton Typing Pool Supervisor	
	Miss T. Baker	89 The Grove, Droitwich	12 00	No appointment	Writing to Miss Burton with details
	B.M. Townsend	Bellevue Car Hire Co.	12 30	Transport Officer	

65

APPOINTMENTS BOOK

This is used to record all future appointments and is used by the receptionist to see who is expected each day, and also to give future appointments to callers who arrive without one, or who have to make an additional appointment on leaving a firm. Information about appointments comes from secretaries (see p. 24).

A page from the appointments book for 21 November 198— would look like this.

Monday 21 November 198–			
NAME OF CALLER	**FIRM**	**TIME OF ARRIVAL**	**TO SEE**
Mr. L. M. Parkins	J. Mann + Co.	09 00	Mr K Jones
Mr. B. N. Vines	Carson Engineering	09 50	Personnel Manager
Miss K. Lyons	219 Lake Avenue	10 30	"
Mr. F. Perkins	Peterson's Export Co.	10 35	Accounts
Mrs. A. Drew	Wilchester Technical College	11 00	Personnel Manager
Mrs. W. Moxon	Office Equipment Supplies	11 30	Miss B. Burton Typing pool
Mr B.M. Townsend	Bellevue Car Hire	12 30	Transport Officer

Rule up a copy of this page for an appointments book, leaving out the names and other details, and fill it in with the page from the callers' register which you have just completed.

STAFF 'IN AND OUT' BOOK

Another important record book which would be the receptionist's responsibility is a staff 'in and out' book. In this, all staff working in the firm write the reasons for going out of the firm during working hours, with their names, time of leaving and date. They also sign again when they return, writing down the time they returned. This book provides a record of staff absences, so that the receptionist can tell at a glance who has gone out of the firm. It is a much more efficient system than leaving notes or messages, which are easily lost. Where a firm operates flexible working hours, it may not be necessary although it is still useful to know *where* staff have gone, as well as *when*.

Exercise 14

STAFF 'IN AND OUT' BOOK

Following is a page from a staff 'in and out' book for 1 March 198—.

DATE	NAME	DEPT	TIME OUT	TIME IN	REASON

Rule up a similar page and complete it correctly from the following information:

1) Miss R Rhodes, wages, went out to the bank at 0930 and returned at 1000.

2) Miss V Marr, mail room, went to the Post Office at 1100 and returned at 1120.

3) Mr L Moore, buying, left at 1430 to fly to Germany.

4) Mrs W Thompson, personnel, went home ill at 1600.

5) Miss B Crowle, typing pool, left at 1635 for a doctor's appointment.

MESSAGES

The receptionist's duties include taking messages, and passing them on, verbally as well as in writing. It is very important that these messages are passed on immediately. A special message form is a help, as it reminds her not to forget to ask for any vital item of information before the caller has gone.

MESSAGE FORM

Date. . . . . Time. . . . . For. . . . .
From . . . .
Address . . . .
Telephone No. . . . . Extension No. . . . .

Message (telephone/personal—cross out whichever does not apply)

. . . .
. . . .
. . . .
. . . .
. . . .
. . . .
. . . .
Taken by . . . .

Exercise 15

WRITING A MESSAGE

Use the message form on p.67 to pass on the following details. Mrs D Knowles called to see Miss Burton, typing pool supervisor, on an important matter. Mrs Knowles would not make an appointment, but she would like Miss Burton to telephone her at home after 7pm today. Mrs Knowles' address is: 226 Ashtree Avenue, Boyston, and her telephone number is Boyston 886555. Sign the message form yourself, and date it for today, adding the time at which you are writing the message.

PASSING ON MESSAGES

Messages must be delivered as soon as possible. As the receptionist cannot leave her desk, she must ask her relief or her assistant to deliver the messages for her. Alternatively, she may be able to ask one of the firm's messengers to take her messages. Sometimes firms' messengers are young school-leavers, or they can be older, retired men or ex-service men. Their job is to take messages, letters, parcels, etc. around a firm.

If there are no firm's messengers, the receptionist would have to telephone through to the secretary of the manager concerned, and ask her to send someone to collect the message.

A copy of each message should be filed in date order, each day's messages then being arranged in alphabetical order of the *surname* of the person *to whom the message is addressed*. This is in case of a query later on. Carbon copies could be made (on a typewriter or by hand) or photocopies taken of any very important messages.

The Reception Area

GIVING A GOOD IMPRESSION

This is where visitors to a firm wait, either because they have arrived too early for an appointment, or the person they have called to see may be unexpectedly delayed.

It is important that the reception area gives visitors a good impression because it is quite often the first part of a firm they see, and if it is not welcoming and comfortable, they may decide to transfer their business to another firm.

KEEPING TIDY

The first things visitors notice on arrival may well be your own desk and equipment. The receptionist at the top of the page opposite is *not* likely to create a good impression. Can you see why?

How many things can you find wrong with this reception area?

A COMFORTABLE DESIGN FOR THE VISITOR

As well as being warm in winter, cool in summer, well lit and attractively decorated, the reception area should have comfortable chairs for the visitors, and it may also offer amenities such as vending machines for refreshments and cigarettes, toilets, Payphone, coin changing machine, stamp machine and many other conveniences. Overleaf is an assignment on designing a reception area, but first of all here is a picture of what the area near your desk should *not* look like. It is too small, visitors have nowhere to sit, and the receptionist has allowed a telephone conversation to go on for so long that a queue has formed.

A badly organised reception area. How many things are wrong?

Exercise 16

DESIGNING A RECEPTION AREA

Trace the drawing of the reception area opposite, which is carpeted, heated, lighted, but is otherwise almost bare.

Then trace the items below which would help to make a reception area more comfortable and attractive to visitors who have to wait for a short time.

Cut out your tracings neatly and glue them into appropriate places on your drawing. When the glue has dried, colour your reception area suitably.

Then on a separate sheet of paper make a list of everything in your reception area, under the heading 'An Ideal Reception Area'.

The assignment will be graded according to the neatness of your design and how well you make your list. After you have finished this assignment compare your design with that on p. 450.

CHAPTER 5

Telecommunications

Telephones

Telephones come in many shapes and sizes, as you can see below. All telephones used to have dials and make a ringing sound. Nowadays push-button telephones are becoming more common and not all telephones ring — some of them bleep and often the volume of the bleeper can be adjusted.

Making Telephones Mobile

Extra telephone sockets can now be installed quickly by telephone engineers, in homes or offices, for around £30 per socket.

This will be especially useful in offices, because previously the arrangement of the files, desks and other equipment had been governed by the telephone sockets. Now the office layout can be changed and the telephone sockets moved without too much fuss or expense.

A telephone socket

Correct Dialling

According to British Telecom 1000 million calls fail each year, mostly because of misdialling. How often have you had to feel embarrassed and say, 'Sorry I must have the wrong number'? If you follow the following suggestions made by British Telecom you should make fewer mistakes!

Check the number first from your own records or the telephone directory for that area.

Write the number down if it is given to you orally.

Wait for the dialling tone before dialling.

Dial from a written record.

Dial with care. Pull the dial right round to the finger stop and let it return freely.

A selection of telephones available today

Don't pause too long between each figure.

Don't be a dozy dialler! But if you do make a mistake, replace the receiver and start again.

Wait up to 15 seconds for the equipment to connect you and, above all, *concentrate*.

Dial right round to the finger stop

Dial the number very carefully

Correct Keying

'Keying' should lead to fewer mistakes than dialling. It is quicker, because the caller does not have to wait for a dial to return between numbers. When pressing buttons make sure that each button is fully depressed, and be careful to press only one button at a time. Press at a steady rate.

Answering the Telephone and Dealing with Messages

Always pick up the telephone receiver with the hand you do not normally write with. This will make it easier for you to write down a message if you have to!

Preparations for dealing with messages can be made before the telephone even rings.

By the side of every telephone should be:

something to write *on*
something to write *with*.

Better than a writing pad is a pad of telephone message forms, similar to the one on p. 76, so that the headings remind whoever is answering the phone of any questions they should ask the caller before he or she rings off.

It is always better to write messages down, at once, then read them back to the caller so that they can be checked, rather than to try and remember what was said.

After a message has been checked, it must then be taken to the person it is intended for without delay.

A caller may not be willing to leave a message. As an alternative, he could be asked:

● if he would like to phone back later
● if he *would* like to be phoned back — he may suggest a suitable time.

In any case, he must be asked for his name, address (or his firm's name and address), telephone number and extension number, if he has one. The extension number is the number of his internal phone, and if it is known, the caller can ask for it and save the switchboard operator looking it up.

Never let a caller go without finding out who he is and his address.

If his name is a fairly common one, such as Smith or Jones, his address will be essential to identify him. There are a lot of Smiths in any telephone directory!

Exercise 17

TELEPHONE MESSAGES

> *Rule up four copies of the telephone message form overleaf, putting in the headings. Then complete them correctly, with the details in the following telephone messages. Sign the forms yourself.*

1) The Manager of the Swan Hotel, Oxbridge, telephone number 344567, rang up to say that arrangements for the staff dinner on 4 March at 1930 hours are now complete. A room has been booked for

TELEPHONE MESSAGE

FOR Mr. P. Jenkins

DATE Jan. 25th 198-

TIME 1030 hours

URGENT / ~~NON-URGENT~~

TAKEN BY P. Hill

FROM Mrs. P. Barker

TEL NO 436551 EXTN 23

COMPANY NAME Barker and Lane

ADDRESS Highfield Trading Estate
Ruddstoke

Mrs Barker regrets that she cannot call as arranged (at 1130 hours today) as she has been called away unexpectedly.

She would be able to come on Friday 27 January at the same time. Would you please telephone her office to confirm?

P. Hill

30 people. Menus and prices are in the post. The message is for Mr C Bailey of Personnel Department.

2) Mr Vernon, of ABC Group Services Ltd, Milchester, telephone 733552 extension 8, telephoned to say he will be in the neighbourhood on 1 February and would like to see Mr Kendall, Sales Manager, at 1000 hours on that day, if it is convenient. Could Mr Kendall's secretary please confirm, or otherwise.

3) Would Mrs J Grant, Typing Pool Supervisor, please telephone Mrs G Hughes of J V White & Co Ltd, Blandwich, telephone 811356 extension 11, to let her know whether a demonstration of the offset-litho duplicator will be convenient on Monday 31 January at 1200 hours?

4) Miss H Edmonds telephoned to let Mr K Daniels of the Purchasing Department know that she has flu and will not be at work for a few days. She will ring again when she knows definitely when she will be returning to work.

Inside and Outside Calls

Small firms may have one telephone for receiving *outside* (or *external*) calls only. Calls on an outside telephone in a firm should be answered by announcing the name of the firm, first, followed by 'good morning' or 'good afternoon'.

Larger firms will have two telephone systems — one for receiving and sending outside (external) calls and the other for offices to phone each other (internal calls).

Another type of telephone system will deal with both internal and outside calls. The type of call can be distinguished by the tone of the ring.

An *inside* or *internal* telephone should be answered by announcing the name of the office, followed by your own name: 'Sales department, Jane Jackson speaking'; or 'Mr Thompson's secretary speaking'.

In large firms where all outside calls are received by the switchboard operator, she will have given the name of the firm, so an incoming call would be taken by announcing the name of department, office or manager. There is one important thing to remember with an outside call. It is that no caller must be left hanging on indefinitely while the person he wants to speak to is being found. He must be told frequently that he has not been forgotten, and can also be asked if he would like to be phoned back. This saves him wasting time and money.

Telephone Etiquette

WHAT TO DO IF YOU ARE CUT OFF

If you are cut off in the middle of a telephone conversation, replace the receiver, and wait for your caller to dial again, if it was an incoming call. If *you* made the call, you dial again, after replacing the receiver.

ENDING THE CALL

It is considered polite not to conclude a call if you are the person who was *called*. In other words, the person paying for the call should be the one to end it.

A Telephone Style

There are certain *slang expressions* which should never be used on the telephone:

'Hang on'
'Hello' — always name of firm, name of department, or name of boss.

'OK'
'Okey-doke'
'So long!'
'Cheerio!'
'See you!'
'Ta-ta!'
'Hang about a bit.'

Everyone uses some of these during normal conversation, but on the telephone they sound familiar and not very polite.

Neither should callers be addressed as 'dear', 'my dear', 'duck' or 'love' for the same reasons.

Some callers may be inclined to chat unnecessarily, especially if they ring up frequently. Chatting should not be encouraged – 'chatty' callers can be dealt with quite politely by being told that someone else is waiting to use the telephone.

Any telephone conversations which are overheard should never be repeated. They may not be confidential – but in any case should always be treated as if they are.

At the end of a telephone call, thank the caller for ringing and replace the receiver quietly. If you bang it down, it may reverberate in his ear – not pleasant.

When talking on the telephone, speak almost normally, but rather more slowly than usual, holding the receiver so that the mouthpiece is close to your mouth. Remember, it is a small microphone so you must speak directly into it. *Shouting* is no good at all – it merely distorts the sound.

Coping with Indistinct Callers

Sometimes your caller cannot hear you, even though you are speaking slowly and clearly. The line may be 'crackling' or your caller's English may not be very good. There is an internationally recognised way to spell out words, which all telephone operators use called the Standard Letter Analogy or Telephone Alphabet.

TELEPHONE ALPHABET

A	Alfred	J	Jack	S	Samuel
B	Benjamin	K	King	T	Tommy
C	Charlie	L	London	U	Uncle
D	David	M	Mary	V	Victor
E	Edward	N	Nellie	W	William
F	Frederick	O	Oliver	X	X-ray
G	George	P	Peter	Y	Yellow
H	Harry	Q	Queen	Z	Zebra
I	Isaac	R	Robert		

To use the telephone alphabet, you would spell out the word your caller couldn't hear like this:

The word she cannot hear is *parcel*

P – Peter, A – Alfred, R – Robert, C – Charlie, E – Edward, L – London and then repeat the word *parcel*.

FOR YOUR FOLDER

11. ANSWERING THE TELEPHONE

Write these notes in your folder, filling in the missing words and phrases.

1) For recording the most frequently used telephone numbers a _____ is useful.

2) When answering the telephone, pick up the receiver with the hand you do _____ with.

3) By the side of every telephone should be: something to write with, something to write _____.

4) After writing messages down _____ them back to the caller so that they can be _____.

5) After receiving a telephone message and writing it down, it must be taken to the _____ without delay.

6) If a caller is not willing to leave a message, he should be asked to phone back later or _____.

7) Before he rings off, he must be asked for his name, address (or his firm's address) _____ and extension.

8) Never let a caller go without finding out who _____ and his _____.

9) When answering an outside (external) call on a telephone, you should say _____ after the name of the firm.

10) When answering an inside (internal) call in a firm, the name of the office should be given followed by _____.

11) With an outside call, the caller must never be left _____ indefinitely.

12) He must be told frequently that he has not been _____ and can also be asked if he would like to be _____.

13) If you are cut off in the middle of a telephone conversation, _____ the receiver and _____ if it was an incoming call.

14) If it was an outgoing call (you made the call) dial again, after
_____.

15) It is considered polite not to _____ if you are the person
who was called. The person paying for the _____ should be
the one to _____.

Telephone Charges

HOW TELEPHONE CALLS ARE CHARGED FOR

It is possible to dial most calls. Charges for these are recorded
automatically on a meter at the telephone exchange. Charges are based
on:

- Distance between caller and the person to whom he is speaking
- Time of day
- Day of the week
- Length of time the call takes (duration)

A local call is one made within the area around a town or city
extending to about 900 square miles.

A trunk call is a call made outside this area. A trunk call can be
dialled or made via the operator.

Most cities and large towns are now all-figure telephone numbers. This
means that there is a number code which has to be dialled first, before
the number of the person who is wanted on the telephone is dialled. All
the codes are now available in the *Telephone Dialling Codes* booklet.
Before you dial it is very important to check that you have the right
code.

On STD calls (Subscriber Trunk Dialling) there are no 'pips' to show
how long the call has lasted. 'Pips' are only given on trunk calls (long-
distance calls) connected by the operator. These 'pips' can be heard
every three minutes.

Telephone calls are paid for every three months, when an account is
sent to each subscriber (a subscriber is a person who rents a telephone
from British Telecom). This account lists trunk calls, reversed charge
calls separately but adds together STD (dialled) calls. VAT at the current
rate is added to telephone bills. There is also an additional quarterly
rental for the telephone.

Any subscriber who forgets to pay his or her bill is disconnected, after a
warning has been given, and has to pay an extra charge, on top of the
bill for the preceding quarter, before the telephone is reconnected.

Any faults in a telephone system will be repaired by British Telecom
engineers usually without charge. They should be reported clearly and
as accurately as possible from another telephone, giving the number of
the faulty one, to the number given in the *Telephone Dialling Codes*
booklet.

Dialled direct
Inland calls

Approximate **cost** to the customer including VAT   **Time for 5.06p**

		1 min	2 mins	3 mins	4 mins	5 mins	10 mins	
Local	Cheap	5p	5p	5p	5p	5p	10p	8 mins
	Standard	5p	5p	10p	10p	15p	25p	2 mins
	Peak	5p	10p	10p	15p	20p	35p	1 min 30 secs
Calls up to 56 km (35 miles)	Cheap	5p	5p	10p	10p	15p	25p	2 mins 24 secs
	Standard	10p	15p	20p	30p	35p	71p	45 secs
	Peak	10p	20p	30p	40p	51p	£1.01	30 secs
Calls over 56 km (35 miles) connected over low cost routes	Cheap	5p	10p	15p	20p	25p	51p	1 min
	Standard	15p	30p	46p	61p	76p	£1.52	20 secs
	Peak	20p	40p	61p	81p	£1.01	£2.02	15 secs
Calls over 56 km (35 miles) and to the Channel Islands	Cheap	10p	15p	20p	25p	35p	66p	48 secs
	Standard	20p	40p	61p	76p	96p	£1.92	16 secs
	Peak	25p	51p	76p	£1.01	£1.27	£2.53	12 secs
Calls to the Irish Republic from Great Britain and the Isle of Man	Cheap	20p	40p	61p	81p	£1.01	£2.02	15 secs
	Standard	40p	76p	£1.16	£1.52	£1.92	£3.80	8 secs
	Peak	40p	76p	£1.16	£1.52	£1.92	£3.80	8 secs

Exercise 18

THE BRITISH TELECOM CHARGES CHART

1) Make a list of the different types of *inland* call in the chart above. Calculate the cost of the following calls:

2) Three minutes local (peak rate).

3) Three minutes local (cheap rate).

4) Five minutes up to 56 km (35 miles) standard rate.

5) Ten minutes over 56 km (35 miles) connected over low cost routes.

6) Four minutes to the Irish Republic from Great Britain and Isle of Man at peak period.

7) The cost of the above calls includes VAT at 15%. What is the cost of them *without* VAT?

8) How much time is allowed for a local call during the cheap rate period for 5.06p?

9) How much time is allowed for a call over 56 km at peak period for 5.06p?

10) How much time is allowed for a call to the Irish Republic at standard period for 5.06p?

From the charge bands work out the following:

11) Ten minutes at the cheap rate for a local call.

12) Ten minutes at the peak rate for a local call.

13) How much time do you get for 5.6p at standard rate for a local call?

14) How much time do you get for 5.6p at cheap rate for a local call?

15) Five minutes at standard rate for a call over 56 km (35 miles).

16) Five minutes at peak rate for a call over 56 km (35 miles).

17) Five minutes at cheap rate for a call over 56 km (35 miles).

18) Four minutes at peak rate for a call to the Isle of Man.

19) Two minutes to the Isle of Man at cheap rate.

20) Ten minutes to the Irish Republic at standard rate.

HOW TO KEEP TELEPHONE CHARGES TO A MINIMUM

It's not the number of calls that makes the bill high – it's the number of *units* recorded on the meter at the telephone exchange. A unit is measured by the length of the call, the distance between callers, the time of day and the day of the week.

Calls should be kept as short as possible.

Using the operator to make calls increases the cost – dial whenever possible.

Dial carefully – dialling a wrong number can cost a lot of money, when the wrong person answers, from a long distance.

The hour between 0800 and 0900 should be used as much as possible for telephoning. Now that many firms use flexitime, offices are open earlier and calls are cheaper at this time.

The afternoon is the next best time to make calls, especially long-distance ones. This is cheaper than making them in the mid-morning.

The cheapest time for telephone calls at home is on Saturdays or Sundays, or after 1800 hours Monday to Friday.

Note that British Telecom *do not charge* if a caller is cut off or has to re-dial for a wrong number, where the person called answers, *provided* that the operator is called and told. If not, the meter ticks up as usual and the charges go on the bill of the person making the call.

If you want to keep a check on telephone costs as you make each call, you can attach your telephone to a unit like the one below.

How to keep a check on telephone costs

FOR YOUR FOLDER

12. HOW TELEPHONE CALLS ARE CHARGED FOR

Write these notes in your folder, filling in the missing words and phrases.

1) Charges for telephone calls are recorded automatically on a _____ at the telephone exchange.

2) STD means Subscriber _____.

3) On trunk calls connected by the operator _____ are heard every three minutes.

4) A _____ call is one made within the area around a town or city within about 900 square miles.

5) A trunk call can be _____ or made via the operator.

6) On STD calls there are no _____ to show how long the call is taking.

7) Telephone calls are cheapest on Saturdays and Sundays. On weekdays, after working hours, they are cheapest between _____ and _____.

8) On weekdays, during working hours, a telephone call is cheaper after _____ and before _____.

9) Most cities and large towns are now on all-figure telephone numbers. This means that there is a number code which has to be dialled first. All the codes available are in the _____.

10) VAT is _____ to all telephone bills.

TELEPHONE SYSTEMS IN A FIRM

British
TELECOM

BRITISH TELECOMMUNICATIONS

VAT registration no 243 1700 02

BRITISH TELECOM WEST MIDLAND
Service Manager's Office
Providence House
Charles Street
WORCESTER
WR1 2BE
Tel. Worcester (0905) 612311
Or ask operator for Freefone 4521
Telex: 335403 (BT WOR G)
BB FST R7

MR R A DEE
20 LANG AVENUE
STUDLEY
WARKS
B80 7RD

Any call charges not to hand when this bill was prepared will be included in a later bill

See Notes Overleaf	Payment Is Now Due	Telephone number	Date of bill
		STUDLEY 8064	16 NOV 83 (Tax point)

Rental and other standing charges	from	to	£ quarterly rate	£	
	1 NOV	31 JAN	19.40	19.40	

Metered units (See overleaf)	date	meter reading	units used		
	11 AUG	025101			
	7 NOV	025715			
	UNITS AT 4.30P		614	26.40	

```
19 SEP   0.18  LOWER CHARGE
     CAREY    661                         7.43
TOTAL (EXCLUSIVE OF VAT)                 53.23
VALUE ADDED TAX AT 15.00%                 7.98
          TOTAL PAYABLE                  61.21
```

For Office use only

Paid
£

Initials

AX6060
R.P.LTD   PLEASE RETURN THE COUNTERFOIL BELOW WITH YOUR PAYMENT

Exercise 19

THE TELEPHONE BILL

Refer to the bill on p. 84

1) What is the period for which rental will be paid?

2) What is the date up to which the calls are being charged?

3) How many units have been used?

4) What is the price per unit?

5) What is the total cost for the units?

6) What is the total cost without VAT?

7) What is the amount of VAT?

8) What is the total payable?

9) The date of the bill is 16 November. When is payment due?

The Switchboard Operator

WHAT THE DIFFERENT TELEPHONE TONES MEAN

When you pick up a telephone receiver you should hear a low-pitched 'burr-burr'. This tells you that the telephone is working, and that you can go ahead and dial the number you want. This is known as the *dialling tone*.

After you have finished dialling, you should hear a repeated double ring (the *ringing tone*) which tells you that the number you have dialled is ringing.

If you hear a single, high-pitched note, repeated at intervals, you know that the person whose number you dialled is already talking to someone else on his telephone. What you can hear is the *engaged tone* – an engagement ring in fact, but not the sort you can wear on the third finger of your left hand!

If the number you dialled is out of order, you will hear a continuous, high-pitched note. This is the *number unobtainable tone*.

THE PAY TONE

If you hear a series of rapid, high-pitched pips when you pick up your receiver to *answer* the telephone, don't hang up – hang on. This is the *pay tone* and it means that someone is calling you from a public Payphone. You must announce your number as soon as the *pay tone* stops and then give caller time to put his money in. Until he does this, you cannot hear him, but he will be able to hear you.

HOW A SWITCHBOARD OPERATOR SHOULD DEAL WITH CALLS

The switchboard operator deals with all incoming calls (external) telephone calls, re-routing (connecting) them to the person who has been asked for. The switchboard operator also connects the employees in the firm to the number they have asked her for. The exchange which this type of operator uses is called a PMBX (Private Manual Branch Exchange). A cordless PMBX is shown in the picture below. This one has four exchange lines (one for each row) and twelve extensions. (the number of switches in each row) but there are models of other sizes. The operator can either use a headset or a telephone.

An operator using a PMBX switchboard

Answering an external (outside) call. Give the name of the firm, followed by 'good morning' or 'good afternoon'.

The caller then states who he wants (giving the extension number if known). If he does not know the extension number, the operator will look it up from the alphabetical list she has near at hand, and dial it. If it is answered, the caller is connected. If no one answers, she tells the caller, and asks him whether he would like her to try again or prefer to phone back later. If the caller decides to wait while she tries again, and there is a delay of some minutes, the operator frequently comes back to the caller saying 'still trying to connect you' so that he does not think he has been forgotten, or cut off.

Answering an internal (inside) call. This will be someone working in the firm who wants an outside call. The operator will reply 'switchboard' and wait for the caller to tell her the number he or she wants. It is not fair to busy switchboard operators to expect them to look up telephone numbers, except on the rare occasions when it is impossible to find it – i.e. in a part of the country for which there is no directory available. Also, asking for the extension number saves a delay after the call has been answered at the other end. The firm's telephone operator there will be able to put the call straight through.

An automatic exchange is the type which allows employees to dial direct without the operator's help. This is known as a PABX (Private Automatic Branch Exchange). Incoming calls are still routed by the firm's operator. A disadvantage of PABX is that an extension number may be engaged on an internal call but the operator can break in and interrupt. The picture below shows an operator using a PABX system.

A modern PABX switchboard operator

FOR YOUR FOLDER

13. THE SWITCHBOARD OPERATOR

Write these notes in your folder, filling in the missing words and phrases.

1) The switchboard operator answers an external call by saying _____.

2) She answers an internal call by saying _____.

3) PMBX means _____.

4) Internal telephones in firms are _____; that is, employees are able to _____.

5) The most up-to-date types of telephone exchange are _____.

6) When the operator is not able to connect a caller to the person he wants immediately, she will ask him if he would _____ or if he would _____.

LATEST DEVELOPMENT IN SWITCHBOARDS

British Telecom's latest range of switchboards offer even the smallest office a choice of facilities previously found only on large switchboards. These latest small switchboards are often called 'call connect' systems and take up very little space (less than 2 square feet for some systems).

One switchboard automatically routes incoming calls to another extension (if one line is engaged) and repeats the last number dialled, so that if it was engaged, it can be tried again without re-dialling the number.

Each of these small switchboards can be expanded after installation, as the business grows, if required.

LARGER SWITCHBOARDS

The new, up-to-date large switchboards provide the facilities available on the smaller 'call-connect' systems, but in addition, offer faster methods of handling calls so that staff are not waiting around for engaged numbers to be free and many other automatic services such as 'logging' (keeping a record) of all calls.

British Telecom provides training on these switchboards after they have been installed to make sure that the operators (and the office staff) get maximum benefit from the new technology.

A modern switchboard

Payphones

Telephone boxes are a familiar sight all over the country and Payphones have been installed in many large stores, pubs and other buildings used by the general public.

The latest type of Payphone can be used for inland and international calls and when it is out of order the local repair centre is informed automatically.

The coins inserted are held and the amount shown on an illuminated display. As the call proceeds, the amount of credit goes down and a 'bleep' warning is given ten seconds before the credit finally runs out. There is a request displayed to insert more money and a final 'bleep'. The caller is then disconnected unless more money is inserted.

Any money not used at the end of the call is returned to caller.

It is possible to buy (at some post offices, tobacconists and newsagents) slot-in cards, usable only on specially adapted Payphones, installed, at the moment, in some larger towns (usually in railway stations or airports). You simply slot in your card (40 units can be bought for £2 or 200 for £10) and 'key' your number and watch the window which tells you how fast your units are being used.

A modern Payphone

Two-In-One Telephone

There is now available a telephone which is small enough to be placed on a desk and can be switched from ordinary use to a Payphone at the turn of a key.

This is ideal for small businesses such as hairdressers, pubs, wine bars, and shops which want to provide Payphone facilities for their customers or visitors.

It would also be of use in a home where frequent outgoing calls are made by younger members of the family!

The Telephonist's Reference Sources

The following books would be needed by a competent telephonist and Telex operator:

- Local *Alphabetical Telephone Directory*. This lists all the subscribers in the area, in alphabetical order of surnames.

- *Classified Trade Directory* (also called *Yellow Pages*). This lists people and organisations etc. in alphabetical order of their professions, occupations or trades, so that it is possible to find most florists, plumbers, hairdressers or poodle parlours in an area, when their individual names are not known.

- *Telephone Dialling Codes* booklets. These list all dialling codes — both overseas and inland.

- *British Telecom International Guide*. This gives information about overseas telephone services.

- World Atlas. This helps to locate foreign places.

- *Telex Directory*. Telex Directories for other parts of the world.

ALPHABETICAL INDEX

The most frequently used numbers, both internal and external, should be listed for quick reference under the name of the subscriber. An extension number in addition to the external number is useful, too, wherever possible.

The latest British Telecom telephone directory is available on microfiche and the complete UK set of alphabetical telephone directories, including Telex numbers, fits in one small drawer file — saving 15 feet of shelf space. It can be automatically up-dated. It fits almost any type of microfilm viewer.

Exercise 20

THE TELEPHONIST'S REFERENCE BOOKS

In which book would you look to find each of the following?

1) The telephone number of an electrician.

2) The dialling code for Helsinki.

3) The Telex number for Capetown.

4) The cost of a telephone call (standard rate) to Rome.

5) The address of a plumber.

6) The telephone number and address of Mr J K Fowler.

7) Details about a trimphone.

8) The town of Mâcon.

9) The dialling code for Halifax, England.

10) The number to dial to send a telemessage.

   The Classified Trade Directory (Yellow Pages), Telephone Dialling Codes *booklet,* Telex Directory *and the* International Telephone Guide *will be needed for questions 11 – 19*

11) Give the name, address and telephone number of a car hire firm.

12) Give the name, address and telephone number of a watch repairer.

13) What is the minimum charge for an operator-assisted telephone call to Greece?

14) What is the time in Germany when it is 1000 hours in the British Isles?

15) What is the time in Canada when it is 1400 hours in the British Isles?

16) Is there a Telex service from this country to the USA?

17) Give the name, address and telephone number of a kennels.

18) Give the name, address and telephone number of an estate agent.

19) Could a telephone credit card be used for a call to the Netherlands?

Telephone Equipment

TELEPHONE ANSWERING MACHINE

A telephone answering machine can be connected to a telephone to answer calls when the office is closed, and there is no one to answer the telephone.

It makes use of a tape recorder. An incoming call starts the tape, which then plays a pre-recorded message. When the message ends, the set switches automatically to 'record' and the caller has a short time in which to give his name, address, and telephone number, followed by his message. The telephone answering machine then switches itself off until the next incoming call.

This equipment is particularly useful for doctors, veterinary surgeons, and dentists or any one-man businesses. People who wish to make appointments can telephone at any time.

Busy secretaries find a telephone answering machine useful, as it enables them to concentrate on urgent work without constantly being interrupted by the ringing of the telephone. The calls on the tape can be dealt with at a later, more convenient time.

Firms, such as travel agents, often give a telephone number in their advertisements (perhaps a Freefone number) to enable the public to telephone during the evening when their offices are closed, and give names and addresses for brochures advertising holidays to be sent to them.

A telephone answering machine

PUNCHED CARD CALLMAKER

With a punched card callmaker, the card can do the dialling for you. This can be done quickly and it eliminates the possibility of a wrong number. Each card can record up to 16 digits, and numbers are changed by punching a fresh card. An unlimited number of cards can be stored, each with one telephone number.

A punched card

Punching a card

The way to operate the callmaker is quite simple. You lift the handset and when you hear the dialling tone drop the appropriate card into the slot at the front of the callmaker unit. The number will be dialled automatically and the card drops through on to a tray. The picture below shows what a callmaker looks like.

Using a callmaker

TAPE CALLMAKER

A tape callmaker is an alternative to the card callmaker. A magnetic tape stores 400 telephone numbers and each one can have up to 18 figures. Numbers can be altered, added, or removed when necessary. The magnetic tape has a writing surface with an index down the left-hand side. To make a call, the tape is moved until the required entry appears between the two guidelines on the window at the front.

Tape callmaker

DEVELOPMENTS IN CALLMAKERS

The latest callmakers provide a telephone which incorporates a memory that can store up to 10 frequently used numbers of up to 16 digits each. These can be called at the touch of a button. The last number called can also be redialled automatically.

In some models a display shows the number being called or stored in the memory and gives a stopwatch timing of calls. When the telephone is not in use, it may become a digital clock.

A callmaker

Special Telephones

LOUDSPEAKING TELEPHONE

A loudspeaking telephone has a loudspeaker incorporated into the normal telephone dialling arrangement, which can be switched on when a call is being made, so that both speakers in the telephone conversation can be heard by other people in the room. When the loudspeaker is switched off, the telephone conversation is carried on normally, i.e. only the two people speaking to each other can hear.

This telephone is quite different from an intercom, because it is part of an *external* telephone system. An intercom is part of an *internal* telephone system.

Loudspeaking telephone

INTERCOM

Communication from office to office (between the boss and his secretary for instance) is often done by an intercom. The message is relayed though a small loudspeaker so that all the secretary has to do is press a button and then she can hear.

36

The intercom shown has a loudspeaker at the back and a push-button dialling system.

On the top of the next page is the latest type of intercom, which can be left on a desk or picked up and used as a telephone receiver would be used.

TANNOY OR PUBLIC ADDRESS SYSTEM

Loudspeakers are necessary in noisy areas, such as factories, to call people to the telephone, which is situated in a quieter part of the building.

The picture below shows some of the equipment for a public address system (left to right: a microphone for making a call; a telephone for answering a tannoy call; and two types of wall-mountable loudspeakers).

FLASHING LIGHTS

Where the ringing of a telephone disturbs people's concentration (where office workers may be spending most of their time on calculating figures, for example) different coloured lights which flash to indicate that someone is wanted on the telephone, are a noiseless alternative. Each member of staff will know which colour refers to him.

Other users of flashing lights are hospitals, where doctors are called from the wards for emergencies by this system, and in doctors' waiting rooms, where a different coloured light refers to a different doctor.

PAGING

People do move around – to meetings, to other parts of a large building, outside to other buildings, and it becomes very difficult for the telephonist to locate them either to give them a message which may be urgent, or to get them to speak to a telephone caller. One way to make sure that managers and other staff who are frequently away from their own telephones can be contacted is by using 'pocket paging'.

Pocket paging consists of a lightweight receiver, small enough to be carried in a pocket, or hooked over a belt, which 'bleeps' or vibrates when the telephone operator presses the button on the master control which she has close to her switchboard. When the pocket receiver 'bleeps', the person carrying it knows he or she has to go to the nearest telephone as quickly as possible.

The radius (distance) at which pocket paging can be operated from a switchboard is approximately one mile.

Pocket pager

Why would the doctor find paging useful?

RADIO PAGING

This is the system operated by British Telecom. Transmitters are based in most of the large cities such as London, Manchester, Birmingham, Liverpool, forming a national grid which covers most of the UK. The distance over which this system can be operated is about 20 miles.

The British Telecom pager has a display panel which shows numbers up to a maximum of 10, which could show telephone numbers, or be used as a code (agreed with the user) to carry out various instructions — e.g. about prices or which customer to visit next.

CARPHONE

The driver of a car may contact anyone on a telephone by means of a carphone. He presses buttons on the carphone and the call is automatically switched through to its destination.

The car driver can also receive calls direct from any telephone in the UK, he can even contact ships at sea and oil platforms in coastal waters. He can also receive telephone information services (see p. 101).

Pocket paging can be used with a carphone (see p. 97).

FOR YOUR FOLDER

14. TELEPHONE EQUIPMENT

Write these notes in your folder, filling in the missing words and phrases.

1) The switchboard on which the operator deals with *incoming* and *outgoing* calls is a _____.

2) The switchboard on which the operator deals only with *incoming* calls is a _____.

3) Push buttons on a telephone in place of a dial provide a quicker method of dialling and are also _____.

4) A telephone answering machine is particularly useful for _____.

5) A punched card callmaker dials automatically when the punched card is dropped into a slot at the front of the callmaker. This is a quicker method than ordinary dialling and is also _____.

6) A magnetic tape callmaker stores up to _____ numbers.

7) A loudspeaking telephone can be switched on when a call is made so that _____.

8) A trimphone has a bleeper instead of a bell, the volume of which can be adjusted. The dial _____.

9) Communication from office to office (e.g. between a boss and his secretary) is often carried out by means of an _____.

10) In noisy areas a _____ is useful for calling people to the telephone.

11) Where the ringing of the telephone would disturb people's concentration, _____ are often used.

12) When someone moves around a factory a great deal and it is difficult to contact him by telephone _____ is useful.

13) A Payphone is _____.

14) Sending copies of documents in black and white by telephone is possible by a _____.

15) The machine connected to a telephone which records an incoming telephone message is a _____.

16) When the pre-recorded message has finished, the set switches automatically to record and the caller _____.

17) This equipment is especially useful for doctors, veterinary surgeons and _____.

18) People who wish to make _____ can telephone at any time.

19) Firms such as travel agents often give a _____ telephone number to encourage the public to telephone in for travel brochures.

20) _____ uses punched cards which dial telephone numbers automatically.

21) _____ uses magnetic tape which stores up to 400 telephone numbers and dials them automatically.

22) When several people want to hear a telephone conversation at the same time, a _____ is useful, as the caller's voice is amplified.

23) _____ are used on some telephones instead of dials. These have the advantage of _____.

24) They also avoid _____ when dialling.

Exercise 21

TELEPHONE EQUIPMENT

Suggest a suitable item of telephone equipment which could be useful in each of the following circumstances:

1) For a manager who is frequently travelling by car around the UK and receiving (and sending) information about his latest orders.

2) A production manager who spends a great deal of his time in the factory away from his office (the factory is noisy).

3) An office where the workers are engaged on jobs which require great concentration and interruptions are a nuisance.

4) A manager who has to speak often to his secretary in the next office.

5) A supervisor who has to convey instructions to three of his staff from the manager in an office three floors above.

6) A firm which is frequently telephoned after the office is closed.

Telephone Services

ALARM CALL

For a small charge, the telephone operator will ring at any time of the day or night, and go on ringing until the telephone is answered.

This is a useful arrangement when an early train or plane has to be caught, or for an urgent, early appointment.

PERSON-TO-PERSON CALL

A *person-to-person* call does not mean a friendly, chatty telephone call. It is one where there is no charge until the person asked for actually speaks on the telephone (apart from a small, additional charge by British Telecom). A person-to-person call avoids paying for the time wasted trying to find someone who may be out of his office frequently.

FIXED TIME CALL

A fixed time call is a way of making sure that the person called is by the telephone when caller rings. A fixed time call is especially useful for overseas calls, to countries where the time is different from the time in the British Isles.

MESSAGE CALL

A message is recorded and is delivered automatically to a given number at a specified time.

ADC CALL

The caller may need to know how much a telephone call has cost, if for instance, she is telephoning from someone else's telephone. The call must be made through the operator (it cannot be dialled) the operator then asked to ring back at the end of the call and let the caller know the cost. This is known as Advice of Duration and Charge.

TRANSFERRED CHARGE CALLS

Another name for a transferred charge call is a *reversed charge call*. This enables the caller to make a telephone call without payment, but first she must ask the operator to ring the person she wishes to speak to and ask if they are willing to pay for the call. Only when permission has been given will the operator connect the caller. This service is used in some firms by their representatives when they wish to telephone in whilst they are travelling around on firm's business. The switchboard operator would have a list of representatives and also keep a note of the transferred charge calls made.

INFORMATION SERVICES

Information about gardening, weather, motoring, skiing, cricket scores, Stock Exchange prices, tourist facilities, the latest road, rail, sea and air information is available in nine areas of the UK 24 hours a day, seven days a week — this service is called Traveline. The correct time, bed-time stories and even recipes and a hit record can all be obtained over the telephone by dialling the numbers given in your telephone directory.

The services are not free — the charges are the same as for ordinary calls, and the length of the call may be restricted.

FREEFONE

Firms use this method to encourage customers to telephone them and ask for advertising material to be sent to them. A special Freefone number is published in their advertisements in newspapers and magazines, and all that the caller has to do is to ask the operator for the Freefone number. The cost of the call is added to the account of the firm.

TELEPHONE CREDIT CARDS

These are used by businessmen travelling around, who may need to telephone their offices frequently from public Payphones.

Credit cards have a number on them, and it is this number which has to be given to the operator by the caller before he tells her what number he wants. The cost of the call goes on to the account corresponding to the credit card number. It is not necessary to use coins, but as all credit card calls have to go through the operator, they are more expensive.

EMERGENCY CALLS

There are three main emergency services:
- Fire
- Police
- Ambulance

and three other emergency services:
- Coastguard
- Cave or Mountain Rescue Services
- Lifeboat

To call any of the above services, dial 999. The operator will answer and ask which service you want. Then wait until the emergency service you have asked for speaks to you. They will want to know:
- The address of the person requiring help (not necessarily yourself)
- Directions to where they can be found (i.e. if they live in a very long road, it may be helpful to give a landmark such as a pub or church).

If you can keep cool and give helpful directions, this will save the emergency service wasting precious time looking for the house or area.

It is worthwhile practising making a 999 call in the dark – try it with your eyes closed. The figure 9 on the telephone dial is the last figure but one at the bottom of the dial. The last figure is 0. It is also important to remember to turn the dial carefully as far as it will go before dialling again, to make sure you do not dial the wrong number. Get a friend to watch you while you practise, *but leave the receiver on the hook during practice!*

It may one day be necessary to dial 999 in a darkened room and your practice will have been most useful.

One emergency which you do not dial 999 for is if there is a smell of gas. In this case, the Gas Board operate a 24-hour service and their number is in the telephone directory under Gas.

Make a note of it by the telephone, together with numbers for:
- Water Board (in case of leaking pipes)
- Plumber
- Electricity Board
- Nearest doctor
- Nearest hospital with casualty department
- Taxi rank
- British Rail enquiries

FOR YOUR FOLDER

15. TELEPHONE SERVICES

Write these notes in your folder, filling in the missing words and phrases.

1) If it is essential to be woken at any time of the night the British Telecom telephone operator will ring and continue to ring until the telephone is answered. This is known as an _____ call.

2) To avoid unnecessary expense when telephoning someone who may not always be near to his telephone, a _____ call cuts down the cost, as no charge is made (except a small surcharge) until the caller actually speaks to the person he wants.

3) It is possible to make a telephone call without payment, from a Payphone, by asking the operator to ring the number required and to obtain the permission of the person called to pay for the call. This is known as a _____ call.

4) People who travel around and have to make frequent telephone calls to their head office will find a _____ _____ very useful, as this enables them to telephone from a Payphone without

using coins — all they do is to give the British Telecom operator their _____ number.

5) Firms when advertising encourage the public to telephone them and ask for samples, catalogues etc. by using a special number which they can use free of charge. This is called _____.

6) Booking a telephone call for a certain time of day is known as a _____ call.

7) It may be necessary to know how much a telephone call has cost if it has been made from someone else's telephone. The British Telecom operator will ring back and tell caller if an _____ _____ _____ call is asked for beforehand.

8) There are many telephone information services and they cost the same as _____ telephone call. The length of an information call may be _____.

Exercise 22

TELEPHONE SERVICES

Suggest the correct telephone service for each of the following situations:

1) A caller is using a Payphone and discovers he has no money — the call he has to make is an urgent one.

2) A secretary has to telephone New Zealand for her boss and she wants to be sure the person being called will be at his telephone when she puts her call through.

3) A telephone call has to be made to a manager in a firm where he is frequently out supervising the building of new offices.

4) A salesman has to drive to Edinburgh in January and wants to check on the state of the roads in Scotland.

5) A visitor to an office asks if she may use the telephone to make a call to France, and wishes to pay the cost of it before she leaves the firm.

6) A firm wishes to encourage the general public to telephone them free of charge in answer to advertisements.

7) A salesman travelling around the country needs to make frequent telephone calls to his office.

International Telephone Services

It is possible to dial direct by International Direct Dialling (IDD) to most overseas countries. A full list is given in British Telecom's *International*

Telephone Guide, which will be supplied free by dialling 100 and asking for Freefone 2013.

Countries on IDD are also listed in the *Telephone Dialling Codes* booklet.

If IDD is not available, an international call should be made by dialling 100 and asking for 'International Operator' or 'Continental Service' (depending on where the country is).

It is possible to dial direct from public call-boxes or Payphones to many overseas countries, but not all. Countries beyond a certain distance cannot be telephoned from Payphones because the cost would involve putting in too many coins.

International dialling codes are in the *Telephone Dialling Codes* booklet. It is possible to obtain up-to-date lists of international dialling codes by dialling 100 and asking for Freefone 2013. These are supplied free of charge.

For a free demonstration of dialling tones dial 100 and ask for Freefone 2070.

British Telecom's *International Telephone Guide* also gives details of charges for telephone calls abroad, as well as the time differences between the British Isles and other parts of the world. It is known as 'ITG'.

It is possible to telephone ships at sea.

DIALLING INTERNATIONAL CALLS ON IDD

- Write down the *full* number before starting to dial.
- Dial steadily, without long pauses between numbers.
- Be prepared to wait up to a minute before being connected.
- Tones used in other countries are often different from those in the UK.

SPECIAL SERVICES

Transferred charge calls ⎫ Ask the international
Person-to-person calls ⎬ operator to which countries
Credit card calls ⎭ these services are available.

FOR YOUR FOLDER

16. INTERNATIONAL TELEPHONE SERVICES

Write these notes in your folder, filling in the missing words and phrases.

1) IDD is the abbreviation for _____.

2) Countries on IDD are listed in _____ and the *Telephone Dialling Codes* booklet.

3) Calls can be dialled direct from Payphones to certain overseas countries, but not to those beyond a certain distance because _____.

4) The _____ gives the time differences between the British Isles and other parts of the world.

5) A free demonstration of dialling tones will be given if 100 is dialled and Freefone _____ asked for.

6) When dialling calls on IDD, you must write down the _____ number first.

7) Be prepared to wait up to a _____ before being connected.

8) Tones used in other countries are _____ from those in the UK.

Exercise 23

INTERNATIONAL TELEPHONE SERVICES

1) Where are the overseas countries listed to which it is possible to dial direct?

2) If it is not possible to dial direct, how would an overseas call be made?

3) What does 'ITG' stand for?

4) Three special services are available to some overseas countries. What are these services and how would you find out if they were available to the country which you were telephoning?

CONFRAVISION

Confravision is a British Telecom service which links people or groups of people in different cities by television. There are Confravision studios in seven large cities in the UK. These can be booked for discussions to save the expense and time of travelling over long distances.

PRESTEL

Prestel is the world's only Viewdata system. It links television by telephone to 200000 pages of information from an enormous library to which a subscriber can refer at any time, it also supplies up-to-date news.

An electronic 'mailbox' service allows Prestel users to send messages to each other by means of a simple 'keypad', on which a message is tapped out to another Prestel user. The message appears on their screen the next time the television set is switched on.

Gateway allows banks and airlines to plug their computer databases into Prestel.

Television sets have to be modified to allow Prestel to be used, and there are extra charges for this service.

DATEL

Datel enables a computer installed in a firm to communicate with distant sites. Most Datel services can be used to much of Europe, the USA and a number of other countries. Datel (otherwise known as data transmission service) operates over the telephone network.

FACSIMILE TRANSMISSION

Facsimile transmission (Fax for short) is the transmission of a document, picture or letter using the telephone system to reproduce an accurate copy of the original at the receiving end.

1) Place copy in the machine.

2) Switch the machine to 'receive'.

3) Switch machine to telephone line.

4) The machine automatically stops when the document has come to the end. Both sender and recipient then switch back to the telephone and confirm that the document has been received.

Receiving a document by facsimile transceiver

1) Place the document to be sent in the machine.

2) Set the carriage levers to either side of the document.

3) Switch to 'send'.

4) Telephone to the recipient.

Sending a document by facsimile transceiver

Fax works by scanning the original document on the transmitter and electronically encoding its image. The coded information is then sent down a standard telephone line. At the receiving end, another Fax machine decodes the message and prints out an exact 'facsimile' copy of the original document.

Fax is faster than Telex, (see p.109) transmits both words and pictures, and is as easy to use as an office photocopier.

The latest machines are capable of transmitting at speeds of under a minute per document.

A page of urgent information can be sent from London to Aberdeen for about 8½p.

There are several different makes of facsimile transmission machines available for installation in offices.

British Telecom operates a Fax service for use by firms without their own facsimile transmitters (Bureaufax).

The Post Office offers Intelpost (see p. 243), which gives a similar service, but the documents copied are delivered by post or collected.

It is possible to send documents by facsimile transmission to many parts of the world.

Senders (and recipients) of Fax have to have a special 'Fax' telephone number. A directory of 'Fax' numbers is at present being compiled. Firms print their 'Fax' numbers on their letterheading.

Teleprinters and Telex

TELEX AND ITS ADVANTAGES

Telex enables someone to type a message to someone else without posting it. It is like sending a letter by telephone! The typist taps the keys in London for instance and the message can be printed out in Birmingham or a message from Manchester can be received in Milan.

Telex messages are quick — an expert operator is able to transmit at about 50 words a minute. Telex messages are less likely to be misunderstood if in foreign languages, as translations can be made carefully from a written message. Technical information is also received without errors.

Letters may take days, especially those from foreign countries.

Telex messages give a record both for the sender and for the person receiving the message. As the operator types out the message she is sending, it is automatically printed by the teleprinter receiving it. Up to six copies can be produced at once, if required. Black print indicates outgoing messages. Incoming messages (automatically received) are printed in red.

Incoming Telex messages can still be received even after the office is closed, at any time of the day or night, provided the power supply is left switched on and the teleprinter has a supply of paper left in it. This is especially useful for receiving messages from other parts of the world, where the time may be very different from the time in Britain.

Charges for Telex calls are based on distance between Telex subscribers and the length of the message (i.e. time taken to transmit a message). This is the way charges are calculated for telephone calls too.

The units which send and receive Telex messages are called *teleprinters*. They are available for rental. Rental charges include the maintenance of the teleprinter and there is an extra charge for the connection of each new Telex exchange line. Large cities have Telex bureaux where messages may be sent by firms who do not have a teleprinter.

Telemessages (see p. 119) may be sent by Telex.

FIFTEEN STAGES IN SENDING A LETTER AND GETTING A REPLY . . .

Taking dictation

Typing from notes

Checking letter

Signing letter

Taking it to Mail Room

Sticking stamp on

Posting

Transporting

Opening

Reading and dictating reply

Typing a reply

Letter handed back for retyping because of errors

Signing reply

Posting it

Recipient reading reply

. . . BUT ONLY FOUR STAGES USING TELEX

Taking dictation

Transmitting

Receiving message

Sending a reply

110

TELEPRINTER KEYBOARD AND DIALLING UNIT

The teleprinter keyboard is similar to that on a typewriter. What is printed by the operator on her machine is printed at the same time on another teleprinter at the other end of the line. Only capital letters are printed and there are certain special keys:

FIGURES or **FIGS.** After this key has been pressed the machine prints figures or symbols shown on the keys and allows WHO ARE YOU and BELL to be used.

WHO ARE YOU. When this key is depressed, the 'answer back' code, which identifies the other teleprinter operator is printed on both machines.

BELL. When this key is pressed an alarm bell rings on both machines.

LINE FEED. This key moves the paper upwards for the next line of type.

LETTERS or **LTRS.** When this key has been pressed the machine prints the letters shown on the keys as they are operated.

The dialling unit is similar to that of a telephone but there are four additional buttons:

DIAL **CLEAR** **LOCAL** **RESET**

MAKING A TELEX CALL

British Telecom will provide free training for office staff. Here are the basic stages for making a Telex call:

1) The operator presses the 'dial' button by the dial.

2) She dials the Telex number she wants (she has found this in the *Telex Directory*).

3) A green light on the teleprinter shines while it is sending or receiving a message.

4) After the operator has dialled the Telex number, she expects to receive the 'answerback code' of the number she has dialled, which tells her that she is connected to the right number. If a teleprinter is left switched on, it will automatically transmit its 'answerback code'.

5) The operator sends her own 'answerback code' to identify herself.

6) The operator types her message.

7) Identical messages appear on both teleprinters as the call progresses.

8) At the end of the call, the caller sends her 'answerback code' and presses the WHO ARE YOU key to obtain the code of the other machine.

9) The called teleprinter sends its 'answerback code'.

A teleprinter (Telex) operator

10) During the call, either teleprinter operator can press the BELL key, which lights a red lamp on both teleprinters, and also rings an alarm bell. This would be done to call the operator's attention to something in the message which was not clear. The bell would stop and the red light go out when the SPACE bar is pressed.

11) A call can be ended by either operator (either the one sending the message or the one on the machine receiving the message) pressing a button on the dialling unit.

While an operator is being trained, the teleprinter would be switched to local use, which would not prevent incoming calls from being received. The alarm bell and red light would warn that the teleprinter should be restored to normal use if a local call were received during training.

TELEX ABBREVIATIONS

The following abbreviations are recognised all over the world and are used by teleprinter operators sending Telex messages:

ABS   Absent or office closed.
CFM   Please confirm.
COL   Please collate, meaning please repeat. Used for figures in a message, or unusual words.
CRV   Do you receive well or I receive well.
DER   Out of order.
DF   You are in communication with the called subscriber.
EEE   Error.
NOM   Waiting.
NCH   Subscriber's number has been changed.
NR   My call number is _____ or indicate your call number.
OCC   Engaged.
OK   Agreed or do you agree?
R   Received.
RAP   I shall call you back.
RPT   Repeat.
SVP   Please.
TAX   What is the charge? or The charge is _____
W   Words.
WRU   Who is there?
+   End of message.
+ +   End of last message (i.e. there will be no further messages).

REFERENCE BOOKS

When you are operating a Telex you will need the following books:

Telex Directory (UK)
International Telex Directory
Dictionary (Telex messages are *written*, not spoken, so check up on your spelling!)

Exercise 24

WORKING OUT A TELEX MESSAGE

Look at the Telex message below.

1) What does EEE mean in the message?

2) What does CFM mean?

3) JAKVIN LPOOL is the 'answerback code' of the person to whom the Telex message is being sent. Who is JOHNVAL LDN?

4) What does LPOOL stand for?

5) What is LDN?

6) What does COL mean?

7) What do 1400 and 17.1.80 mean?

8) What does SVP mean?

9) Why are 1400 and 17.1.80 included?

10) What does + + mean?

JAKVIN LPOOL

JOHNVAL LDN

ATTENTION MRS K N NORMAN

MAY WE REMIND YOU AGAIN THAT WE HAVE NOT RECEIVED OUR ODRER EEE ORDER 8/543. SVP DELIVER IMMEDIATELY. CFM

1400

17.1.80

COL 8/543 1400 17.1.80 + +

JOHNVAL LDN

JAKVIN LPOOL

SENDING MESSAGES AUTOMATICALLY

Special equipment may be used on a teleprinter to speed up the sending of messages. This special equipment punches the messages on tape, in code, as the operator types them. This tape can then be fed through another machine called an automatic transmitter, which sends the message again at a speed of about 70 words a minute. There are some automatic transmitters capable of sending messages on punched tape at 120 words a minute.

While the teleprinter operator is not busy (during the first part of the morning, for instance) she would have an opportunity to pre-code messages on tape, which would be ready for sending. Sending pre-coded messages is a way of saving time, as they are transmitted more quickly than an operator is able to send them, so that pre-coded messages are cheaper to send.

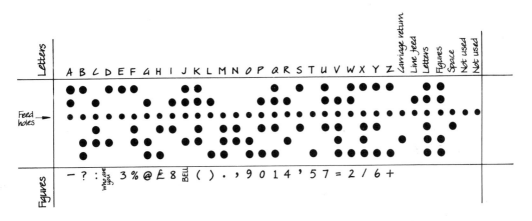

Punched tape code

Below is part of a message on punched tape. Messages can be understood from the punched tape, provided the code is known or is at hand.

115

Exercise 25

CODED TELEX MESSAGES

1) Below is part of another pre-coded message. Using the master code, write down what it says.

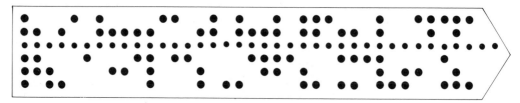

Punched tape

2) Try working out a coded message, perhaps in reply to the message above.

TELEX PLUS

This service is available to all Telex users and saves the operator's time by sending the same message to up to 100 correspondents. It costs 10p extra for each UK message and 20p for an overseas message.

The messages are automatically repeated to each Telex number up to 64 times in 24 hours. Normal delivery time is 2 hours in the UK and countries on direct dialling.

INTERNATIONAL TELEX CALLS

The Telex service is available to many countries throughout the world. It is possible to dial direct to New Zealand and to the United States of America, Canada and Europe.

Telex calls to other countries can be made through the London Telex switchboard operator.

International Telex directories can be bought from the local Telephone Manager's office.

FOR YOUR FOLDER

17. TELEX

Write these notes in your folder, filling in the missing words and phrases.

1) The machine used for the Telex service is called a _____.

2) Teleprinters have a keyboard similar to that of a _____.

3) A teleprinter is for _____ messages not _____ messages. In this way it is different from the telephone.

4) If a teleprinter is left switched on, messages can be received _____.

5) In order to receive messages when the office is closed, you must leave a supply of _____ in the teleprinter.

6) _____ copies can be printed at the same time on a teleprinter.

7) Answerback codes, Telex numbers and details of charges are all to be found in _____.

8) Telex messages can be pre-coded on _____.

9) On the normal teleprinters a message by punched tape can be sent at approximately _____ words a minute.

10) The same message can be repeated to 100 people either in the UK or overseas by the _____ service.

11) The main advantage of a Telex message is that it reaches the person for whom it is intended _____ whereas a letter will take at least 24 hours, probably more if not sent first-class.

Latest Developments in Teleprinters

The latest teleprinters are equipped with:

● Automatic calling, message editing and storage of messages

● A memory of about 4 pages of single line spacing (2500 words — typed)

● Automatic repeating of the same message to several different destinations

● The facility to hold incoming messages in a memory, and re-transmit them

● Storage in the memory for the most commonly used Telex numbers — forming an internal directory.

It is possible to link computers throughout a firm to the teleprinters, and messages can be transmitted direct from the computers. This is having the effect of dispensing with the need for operators to sit all day by teleprinters — most office staff are able to send their own messages.

The appearance of teleprinters is changing. There is often now no dial — calls are selected from the keyboard — and the most comprehensive model now has a keyboard, printer and visual display unit (VDU) with a word processing facility for preparing and editing texts.

Two modern teleprinters from British Telecom

Teletelex

This reproduces the messages with typewriter-quality texts. Offices will be able to send letters (and receive them) between offices instantly 24 hours a day, automatically.

Teletelex will send an A4 page of text in less than 10 seconds — 30 times faster than Telex. The text can then be stored until required and displayed on a VDU or printed.

Many countries will be linked with Teletelex, as well as Europe and the UK.

Telemessages

Telemessages are a British Telecom service. They can be sent only by telephone or Telex, but not handed in at a post office.

To send by telephone — dial 100 (190 in London) and ask for 'Telemessage'.

To send by Telex — consult your Telex directory for the correct number to dial. Type TELEMESSAGE two lines down from your answerback number (see p.112) followed by the address and your message.

The Telemessage service operates to the United States of America and will be extended to other countries over the next few years. The American version of the Telemessage is known as a Mailgram.

The cost for a Telemessage is £3.50 for 50 words (but only £3 before noon). There is no charge for the name and address. The maximum number of words which can be sent is 350. After the first 50 words, £1.50 per 50 words is charged.

There is a specially reduced rate for Telemessages which are sent to a number of different addresses with identical messages. Freefone 2741 gives the details (call to be made during normal working hours). The service to ask for is 'Multiple Telemessage'.

There are Telemessage greetings cards available for special occasions such as weddings, christenings, anniversaries. These cost an extra 50p, but are supplied free with every Telemessage sent before noon on Mondays to Fridays.

Telemessages are delivered by the postman the day after sending, by first post. There is no delivery on a Sunday.

Telemessages are delivered in a bright yellow envelope with three blue stripes across.

A copy of the Telemessage you have dictated will be sent to you, if you ask for 'sender's copy'. A charge of 75p is made.

SENDING A TELEMESSAGE

It is necessary to write out a Telemessage first, before dictating it to the operator, when it is to be sent by telephone.

After drafting, count the number of words in the message, and if the total is more than 50, check to see if unnecessary words could be eliminated to avoid paying an extra £1.50.

Finally, dial 100 (190 in London) and ask for Telemessage. When the operator answers, dictate the name, address and message. You will be asked for your own telephone number. The cost of the Telemessage will be added (plus VAT) to your telephone bill.

(T) Telemessage   British **TELECOM**

BMA1107 LLY6822 PJJ0008 P99 0505PERS   24 OCT 1983/1140

```
                                              43 Cooper Street
                                              Studley
                                              Warwicks   B80 7BR

      TELEMESSAGE      GREETINGS-A             24 October 1983
      MRS T GREEN
      30 LONE ROAD
      PERSHORE
      WORCS



         Dear Sandy

         This is a practice TELEMESSAGE, as a demonstration

         Please keep it for me until Friday

         Love to all


         Gran
```

TO REPLY BY TELEMESSAGE SEE REVERSE SIDE

Exercise 26

TELEMESSAGES

Below are some messages which are to be sent by Telemessage. Re-write them in a suitable form, and work out the cost of each one:

1) Miss Elaine Harrison, 321 Strawberry Fields, Newtonville NC5 8KB.

   Your interview arranged for 14 January is cancelled. Please attend same time 21 January and confirm.

   Personnel Manager Spanmech Engineering Co Lambrove Trading Estate Cardiff.

2) (This is a greetings Telemessage which will be sent during the cheaper period for Telemessages.)

   John Lane 2 High Street Freshley Warwickshire F80 7RB.

   Congratulations on passing your exam. Love from grandad and gran.

3) David Gartside   88 Park Crescent   Abberley   Greatstone   West Midlands G61 WM1.

Strike has been settled. Report for work Monday 9 January 0800.

Jones   Works Manager   Spanmech Engineering Co   Lambrove Trading Estate   Cardiff.

4) Miss Elizabeth Styles   437 Bristol Road   Bridgetown   Liverpool LP1 3HB.

The party planned for Thursday 7 January has been postponed because Tim has 'flu. Another party is planned for a later date but nothing certain has been arranged yet. Tim will be writing as soon as he is well enough. The message is from Tim's mother Mrs Warley of 88 Hamilton Drive   Anychester 4AN 8GO.

5) Messrs Garner & Richards   Norfolk House   Bothampton 3BT 4RT.

The message is from the switchboard operator at Messrs Garner & Richards who is unable to go to work because she has laryngitis and has lost her voice. She hopes to be able to return in about three days' time. Her name is Mrs Lynne Brooks and her address is 5 Upper Cranbrook Road Bothampton.

FOR YOUR FOLDER

18. TELEMESSAGES

Write these notes in your folder, filling in the missing words and phrases.

1) Telemessages can be sent only by _____ or telephone.

2) Telemessages can be sent to any place in the British Isles and also to _____.

3) The cost of a Telemessage is _____ for 50 words.

4) The maximum number of words which can be sent in a Telemessage is _____ words.

5) The cost for the first 50 words is _____.

6) After the first 50 words _____ per 50 words is charged.

7) 'Multiple Telemessage' is the service for Telemessages to be sent to a number of different addresses with _____ messages.

8) A special greetings Telemessage can be sent for no extra charge _____ _____ on Mondays to Fridays. At other times it is _____.

9) Telemessages are delivered by the _____ by _____ post. There is _____ delivery on a Sunday.

10) Telemessage envelopes are _____ yellow with three _____ stripes across.

11) A copy of a Telemessage will be sent to the sender, if 'sender's copy' is asked for. A charge of _____ is made.

12) Before a Telemessage is sent by telephone it is necessary to _____ _____.

13) In London dial _____ for Telemessage service; outside London dial _____.

14) The cost of a Telemessage sent by telephone is added to your _____ bill.

International Telegram

Telegrams may still be sent overseas by dialling 100 and asking for 'International Telegrams'. It is no longer possible to send them from the Post Office.

Exercise 27

CROSSWORD ON RECEPTION, TELEPHONE AND TELEPRINTER

Across

1 A receptionist should be polite and _____ (8)

3 She must not keep callers _____ unnecessarily (7)

7 Callers who have to wait must be _____ after by the receptionist (6)

12 The receptionist must _____ all messages to their destinations at once (4)

14 Callers' cameras, bags, etc. should be placed _____ the receptionist's desk for safety (5)

16 Callers should be escorted _____ and from the offices they are visiting (2)

17 As well as looking after callers, a receptionist may _____ as part of her duties (4)

22 _____ is a telephone service which firms use to encourage the public to telephone them (8)

24 The first impression _____ a firm, is given by a receptionist (2)

26 This should be removed from the ashtrays several times during the day (3)

28 _____ of the regular callers, such as postmen or delivery men, signs the callers' register (4)

29 A receptionist's _____ and nails, as well as make-up, should be immaculate (4)

31 The Health and _____ at Work Act was passed in 1974 (6)

33 (and 21 down) A _____ _____ Call enables a telephone call to be made from a public call box without using coins (7, 6)

36 An _____ call will wake you early! (5)

37 A receptionist must never express _____ to a caller (5)

38 Speak more clearly (do not shout) to telephone callers who cannot _____ (4)

1 Callers' cards must be _____ (5)
2 The staff 'in and out' book should be signed by staff *only* (yes or no?) (3)
4 The first _____ box in reception *must* be checked weekly (3)
5 As well as personal callers, a receptionist will have many callers on the _____ (9)
6 British Telecom ITG _____ gives information about telephone services to countries all over the world (5)
8 Look _____ for callers who may need extra help (3)
9 A receptionist should _____ the answers to almost any questions about the firm she works in (4)
10 The abbreviation for 'editor' (2)
11 French for 'of' (2)
13 It is impolite to callers for a receptionist to _____ while on duty (3)
15 The colour of an outgoing Telex when typed is _____ (3)

18 Any _____ should be written on a specially printed form (7)
19 No one can _____ the importance of a good receptionist to a firm (4)
20 Answer the telephone as soon as it rings – do or don't? (2)
21 See 33 across
22 _____ drill should be practised regularly (4)
23 The Gas Board should be telephoned if there is a smell of gas – _____ 999 (3)
25 A _____ letter is useful for sending confirmation of appointments, or cancelling them (4)
27 Is a receptionist usually a 'he' or 'she'?(3)
30 Appearance _____ less important than a pleasant voice to a telephonist (2)
32 A person who has had an accident may be _____ful, and should be reassured (4)
34 _____ drivers do not sign the callers' register (3)
35 Girl's name (3)

CHAPTER 6

Written Communications

Business Letters

One of the most frequently used ways of passing on information between firms is by business letters. The secretary, shorthand-typist or audio-typist types a business letter from dictation (shorthand notes or on a cassette in a dictating machine see p. 152). Business letters are always typed on good-quality paper and have the firm's name, address and telephone number printed at the top. In addition, there may be an international telegraphic address, a Telex number and a Fax number. The names of the directors may appear at the foot of the letter-heading.

As a business letter is to go from one firm to another, it is very important that the typing is neat and accurate, and that spelling and punctuation is excellent. A firm's first impression of another firm may be from a letter received from it.

SHAW & SHORT LTD
Wholesaler

Whitaker Street
MANCHESTER
M96 8TB

Tel: 432888   Telex: 990 111

Our Ref: PM/JK   25 November 198–

The Sales Manager
Office Equipment Supply Co Ltd
Knightley Road
Bromswood   Lancs
T45 7BC

Dear Sir

Thank you for your letter dated 20 November. I shall be pleased to see you when you call on 1 December in connection with your new model 6000 Word Processing machine and hope that it will be possible for you to arrange several demonstrations to our secretarial staff.

Yours faithfully
SHAW & SHORT LTD

Peter Mason

Peter Mason
Purchasing Officer

PAPER SIZES

A5 paper is half the size of A4.

A5 paper may be used either with the short edge inserted into the typewriter (this is called PORTRAIT) or with the long edge inserted into the typewriter (this is called LANDSCAPE).

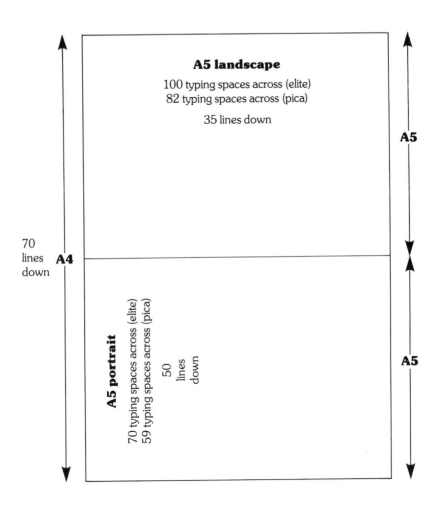

ENVELOPE SIZES

The Post Office sets out sizes for envelopes in the *Post Office Guide* (see p. 207) which they prefer (POP envelopes).

There are three different *shapes* of envelopes which would be kept in a stock of stationery, in varying sizes:

● Pocket, which opens on the short side (see below)

● Banker, which opens on the long side (see below)

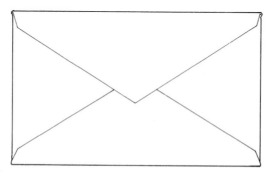

● Window (or aperture) envelopes, which save typing the address on the envelope (see p. 206).

Addressing Envelopes

However carefully a letter is typed, all the effort is wasted if the envelope in which it is posted is wrongly addressed and it is delivered to the wrong place. The Post Office gives very clear directions about addressing envelopes in the *Post Office Guide*, together with a list of abbreviated county names which it will accept. Apart from the shortened names shown in this list, counties should be typed (or written) in full.

A correct postal address normally consists of:

● Name of addressee (the person to whom the letter is being sent)
● Number of house (or name of house if it has no number)
● Name of street, road, avenue or crescent
● District (where this applies)
● Post town
● County
● Postcode

Allow a separate line for each line of the address.

The name of the POST TOWN should be in capitals, as this helps sorting at the Post Office. The postcode should always be typed (or written) on the last line of the address, but if the address is very long, the postcode may be typed after the name of the county leaving at least two spaces between them. The Post Office recommends that addresses should be typed (or written) in the lower part of the envelope (approximately centred) leaving a clear space of not less than 38 mm (1½ inches) at the top of the envelope for cancellation of the stamp and the postmark, as below:

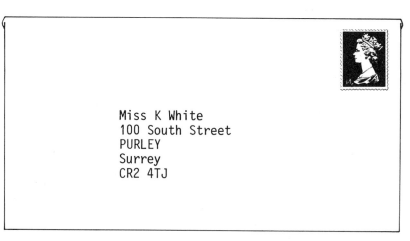

```
Miss K White
100 South Street
PURLEY
Surrey
CR2 4TJ
```

A correctly addressed envelope

FORMS OF ADDRESS

When writing to *individuals*, always give them a title — Mrs, Miss, Ms (when it is not known whether a woman is married or single, or when a woman chooses to be addressed this way), Mr. An alternative (rather out-of-date) title for a man is Esq (abbreviated from Esquire) but this is being used less and less frequently today. When "Esq" is used, it is typed *after* the name.

The titles Dr, Rev (abbreviation for Reverend), Captain, Professor replace any of the titles mentioned above.

Letters after a person's name are typed without spaces in between: JP OBE MP MA. If there is more than one set of letters, they are typed with one space between each set of abbreviations.

Firms should be addressed as Messrs only when their names *do not* include Limited, the abbreviation Ltd, or PLC (Public Limited Company). Firms whose names start with the word "The" or when a title is included in the name — Sir William Watkins & Co — should not be addressed as Messrs.

Postcodes

Every address in the UK has a Postcode, which consists of two groups of letters and figures:

Miss R Black
46 King's Road
Kempston
BEDFORD
MK42 8LA

MK are the letters which direct Miss Black's letter to the area in Milton Keynes where Bedford is situated.

MK42 is the code for Bedford.

MK42 8 describes which part of Bedford the letter has to go to.

MK42 8LA pin-points Miss Black's road.

Machines cannot yet read Postcodes as human beings can, so the mail passes in front of operators who type the Postcodes on the envelopes as blue dots. Electronic sorting machines (Alf — short for automatic letter facer) read the dots at a speed of 16 000 letters an hour, then direct the mail to the receiving areas shown by the outward part of the Postcode (the first group of letters and numbers).

As well as helping the Post Office to speed the mail on its way, Postcodes are used in other ways:

● The Police recommends that property (a bicycle for example) should be marked indelibly with the owner's Postcode and house number so that if it is stolen the owner can be identified easily.

● Postcodes can be used to 'code' files for customers.

● Mail order companies are able to tell which areas bring the most replies to their advertising. Any customer's Postcode gives an immediate key to the area in which he or she lives.

Exercise 28

POSTCODES

Rewrite the following list with the correct Postcode by each town:

Cardiff	LA1 4MD	Edinburgh	GL5 3DY
Gloucester	M32 7LF	Belfast	NR4 7TJ
Norwich	BS6 99K	Plymouth	EH8 8QR
Lancaster	PL4 3AZ	Manchester	BT17 6BH
Bristol	SO9 2UT	Southampton	CF9 4QB

Typing Postcodes on envelopes

Towns 'Without Counties'

Generally, the name of the county in which the post town is situated is necessary on an addressed envelope for sorting by the Post Office. There are, however, some post towns which do not need a county name, as follows:

Aberdeen
Antrim
Armagh
Ayr

Banff
Bath
Bedford
Belfast
Berwick-upon-Tweed
Birmingham
Blackburn
Blackpool
Bolton
Bournemouth
Brighton
Bristol
Bromley
Buckingham

Cambridge
Cardiff
Carlisle
Chelmsford

Chester
Clackmannan
Colchester
Coventry
Crewe
Croydon

Dartford
Derby
Dumbarton
Dumfries
Dundee
Durham

Edinburgh
Exeter

Falkirk

Glasgow
Gloucester

Hereford
Hertford
Hounslow

Huddersfield
Hull

Inverness
Ipswich

Kinross
Kirkcudbright

Lanark
Lancaster
Leeds
Leicester
Lincoln
Liverpool
Londonderry
Luton

Manchester
Milton Keynes

Nairn
Newcastle upon Tyne
Northampton
Norwich
Nottingham

Oldham	Salford	Swansea
Oxford	Salisbury	Swindon
	Selkirk	
Peebles	Sheffield	Torquay
Perth	Shrewsbury	Twickenham
Peterborough	Slough	
Plymouth	Southampton	Walsall
Portsmouth	Southend-on-Sea	Warrington
Preston	South Wirral	Warwick
	Stafford	Watford
Reading	Stirling	Wolverhampton
Redhill	Stoke-on-Trent	Worcester
Renfrew	Sunderland	
Romford		York

County Abbreviations

Abbreviations for county names which the Post Office will accept (other abbreviations cause confusion and should not be used):

Beds	Bedfordshire	Northd	Northumberland
Berks	Berkshire	Notts	Nottinghamshire
Bucks	Buckinghamshire	Oxon	Oxfordshire
Cambs	Cambridgeshire	Salop	Shropshire
Co Durham	County Durham	S Glam	South Glamorgan
E Sussex	East Sussex	S Humberside	South Humberside
Glos	Gloucestershire	S Yorkshire	South Yorkshire
Hants	Hampshire	Staffs	Staffordshire
Herts	Hertfordshire	Tyne & Wear	Tyne and Wear
Lancs	Lancashire	Warks	Warwickshire
Leics	Leicestershire	W Glam	West Glamorgan
Lincs	Lincolnshire	W Midlands	West Midlands
M Glam	Mid Glamorgan	W Sussex	West Sussex
Middx	Middlesex	W Yorkshire	West Yorkshire
N Humberside	North Humberside	Wilts	Wiltshire
N Yorkshire	North Yorkshire	Worcs	Worcestershire
Northants	Northamptonshire		

Exercise 29

ADDRESSES

1) Which of the towns/cities listed in Exercise 28 on p. 128 could be typed in an address without using the name of the county?

2) For which counties are the following the abbreviations?

Leics	Oxon	Middx	Bucks
Salop	Warks	Beds	Lincs
Cambs	Worcs	Northd	Notts

Circular Letters

A circular letter is one of which many copies (sometimes hundreds of thousands) are sent out. Usually, circular letters are sent for advertising purposes, to inform possible customers about 'special offers' or new products to be introduced or new branches of a firm to be opened. The appearance of a circular letter must be of a high standard – it is possible by the use of a word processor (see pp. 156–7) to make each letter appear as if it had been individually typed. The other way of producing circular letters is by a duplicating process – preferably offset-litho which

**OFFICE EQUIPMENT
SUPPLY CO LTD.**

Knightley Road
BROMSWOOD
Lancs
T45 7BC

Telephone : 859333
Telex   : 674231

Date as postmark

Dear Customer

<u>Word Processing Machines</u>

We have pleasure in announcing that we are now in a position
to supply some of the latest range of word processing machines.
Prices and discounts will be sent to you by return, if you will
contact us either by telephone or letter, together with
descriptive leaflets.

This letter has been typed on a word processor, so that you can
judge for yourself the quality of the work produced by it.

Demonstrations of word processors can be arranged to suit your
convenience and, should you decide to buy one, a week's course
of instruction can be organised (which is all that is normally
needed) for any of your staff who may eventually be using the
machine.

We look forward to hearing further from you.

Yours faithfully
OFFICE EQUIPMENT SUPPLY CO LTD

Roy Kingston
Sales Manager

An example of a circular letter

produces good-quality copies. A circular letter does not contain an inside address and may have 'Date as postmark' printed where the date would normally be typed. This ensures that whenever the copies of a circular letter are prepared, they can still be used months later.

Form Letters

Form letters are business letters sent from one firm to another, or to members of the public (e.g. to someone who has applied for a vacancy, giving the time of an interview). Form letters are pre-printed (either by a duplicating process or a word processor—see Chapter 12 and pp. 156–7) on letter headings and are used in offices where a large number of similar letters are sent out and the only information which varies is the name, address and date. The variable information is added by the typist or clerk (it can be added in writing). Form letters save time and can be prepared beforehand during a slack period in an office. The appearance of form letters should be of a high standard as they are to be sent out of the firm. Departments in a firm sending form letters may be:

- Sales Department acknowledging orders (today this is done less frequently than it used to be, because of the cost of postage).
- Personnel Department arranging interviews and advising applicants about the outcome of interviews.

Postcards

These are sometimes sent in place of form letters; as they do not require envelopes, they save time and money. The name of the firm is printed at the top of the postcard, together with the address and telephone number, with a brief message underneath. All that has to be added is the date of sending the postcard and any other short, variable information (the illustration shows that the date of the letter which is being acknowledged has been written in). Postcards require the same stamps as letters, i.e. first or second class.

Customer Relations Department	**Supershops Ltd**
	Supershop House
	Paradise Lane
	Milchester, Devon
	Milchester 7619

Date / 2 June 198 –

Dear Sir/Madam
Thank you for your letter dated . 1 June 198 –
which is receiving our attention.

A postcard message

HALL & GRIFFITH LIMITED

32 Lime Avenue
ELMSTOCK
Oakshire
Telephone Elmstock 36277

Our ref MS/

Date as postmark

Dear Sir/Madam

Thank you for your letter dated
asking for an appointment to see Mr/Mrs/Miss
                      of   Department.

Unfortunately Mr/Mrs/Miss
is away at present and is making no appointments for
several weeks.

Please write again next month if you wish to make
an appointment later.

Yours faithfully
HALL & GRIFFITH LIMITED

M Steele

M Steele
Personnel Manager

A form letter

Compliment Slips

These contain the name and address of the firm, together with telephone numbers and Telex number (if applicable). 'With compliments' is printed on, leaving just sufficient space for a brief message, or the sender's own name and title to be added. The size of compliment slips varies, but is usually about 4″ square. Compliment slips can be used for enclosing with catalogues, price-lists – in fact, anything which is being sent by post where a letter is not necessary but where the recipient must know the name and address of the sender. They save typing letters and are used by many firms whose outgoing mail includes items for which the recipient is not expected to pay – the word 'complimentary' means 'given free'.

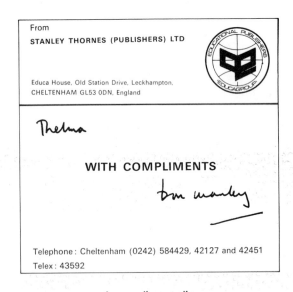

A compliment slip

Memoranda

It is usual to send written communications between offices on memoranda forms called 'memos'. One single 'memo' is a 'memorandum'. All that memos contain (besides the message) is the name of the sender, the name of the recipient, the date and, sometimes, a subject heading. There is no salutation ('Dear Sir'), no complimentary close ('Yours faithfully') and no inside address. It is usual for memos to be initialled, not signed in full, by the employees sending them.

```
MEMORANDUM

To:    Typing Pool Supervisor

From:  Peter Mason, Purchasing Officer      25 November 198-


Subject:   Demonstration of Word Processing Machine

The Sales Manager of Office Equipment Supply Co Ltd will be
visiting the firm on the 1 December to demonstrate a model
6000 Word Processing Machine. I am sure you will be interested
in this demonstration, and if you will telephone my secretary
sometime before the 1 December, she will let you know a
convenient time to see the machine. A later demonstration
can be arranged for members of your staff to see it.

                                    P.M
```

A memo

Circulation Slip or Distribution Slip

A 'circulation slip', or 'distribution slip' (sometimes also called a 'routing slip') is attached to a document that has to be read by a number of employees in turn. It consists of a list of names, and as each person passes on the document to the next on the list he ticks his own name. The document may be a letter which has been received in the incoming mail and has to be seen by more than one person (see p. 202).

Magazine on Word Processors Please read and pass on in order shown below:		
Name	Dept.	Initial/Date
G H Lamb	Buying	GHL, 10/10
Mrs K Potts	Sales	K.P. 11/10
D S Ames	Accounts	
Please return to: R Harris by: 13/10		

A circulation slip

Exercise 30

THE CIRCULATION SLIP

Make a copy of the circulation slip on p. 135 and complete it from the following details:

Miss K Lyons, secretary to the sales manager, has to see the letter *urgently*.

Mr K Samuels, personnel department, can see it at any time before the end of the week.

Mrs B Barton, typing pool, would like to see the letter tomorrow.

Mr V Smart, buying department, must see the letter some time today.

Mrs H English, accounts department, would like to see it the day after tomorrow.

Miss Lyons wants it when everyone else has finished with it.

Assume today is 20 October.

FOR YOUR FOLDER

19. WRITTEN COMMUNICATIONS

Write these notes in your folder, filling in the missing words and phrases.

1) Business letters are always typed on good quality paper and have the firm's name, address, telephone number, Fax number and _____ printed at the top.

2) When an envelope is typed, the name of the _____ should be in capital letters.

3) The Postcode should be shown as the _____ of the address on a separate line if possible.

4) Postcodes are used in the _____ sorting of mail.

5) A circular letter is sent out for advertising purposes, to inform customers about special offers or _____ to be introduced.

6) 'Date as postmark' is sometimes printed on circular letters to ensure that whenever the copies of a circular letter are printed they can still be _____ months later.

7) Form letters are _____ and are used by firms when a great many similar letters are sent out.

8) Departments using form letters might be _____ for acknowledging orders or personnel department for arranging _____ and advising applicants about the _____.

9) Postcards are sometimes used for brief communications instead of form letters. As they do not need _____ they save time and money.

10) Compliment slips are often enclosed with items such as catalogues and price-lists where a letter is not necessary but recipient must know _____.

11) Written communications between offices in a firm are _____.

12) When a document is sent from one employee to another in a firm a _____ is often attached.

Meetings

TYPES OF MEETING

Business meetings in firms are usually informal and attended only by a few managers. A notice of a meeting may be sent out on a memo, which also sets out the purpose of the meeting. A manager's secretary may be present to take notes of what is discussed and decided at the meeting, which she later types out and distributes to those who attended the meeting.

A more formal type of meeting is one attended by the shareholders of a company. The chairman of the company often takes charge of this meeting ('chairs' it) and notes ('minutes') of the meeting may be taken by the company secretary (see pp. 4 – 5).

The topics for a committee to discuss are set out beforehand in the form of an agenda, which is sent round to committee members about a fortnight before each meeting, together with the date, time and place of the next meeting, by the secretary. The secretary and the chairman discuss the agenda beforehand and agree the items.

In many firms, the social club has a committee elected by the members of the club. This committee meets regularly to arrange functions for the members. The members of the social club also elect a chairman, secretary and treasurer to act as 'officers' of the club. At the committee meetings, the secretary takes notes for the 'minutes' (the minutes are a record of the proceedings of the committee meeting). The treasurer looks after the money spent by the club and also any money received. The job of the chairman is to make sure that the committee meetings are businesslike and orderly and that the topics to be discussed are dealt with sensibly.

Most clubs and societies (drama, cricket, sports, etc.) elect a committee to conduct their business for them. Every year there is a meeting which can be attended by all members, when the chairman, secretary and treasurer are elected. This is the AGM (Annual General Meeting).

The officers are usually elected by ballot – votes are marked on separate slips of paper by each voter and then placed in a ballot box. This is a 'secret' method – no one knows how anyone else has voted. At some meetings voting may be by a show of hands.

Below is an example of a combined agenda and notice of meeting for a social club:

COMMITTEE MEETING OF THE MIDCHESTER MANUFACTURING COMPANY SOCIAL CLUB

to be held in the Committee Room of the Midchester Works Canteen at 2000 on Thursday 20 November 198—.

AGENDA

1) Apologies for absence
2) Minutes of last Meeting
3) Matters arising out of the Minutes
4) Correspondence
5) Treasurer's report
6) Secretary's report
7) To discuss sports programme for summer 198—
8) To discuss raising of subscriptions
9) To discuss Christmas pantomime
10) Any other business
11) Date and time of next Meeting.

Jane March
Secretary

An agenda is always set out in roughly the same order. In the agenda illustrated items 1, 2, 3, 4, 5, 6 would be dealt with before other matters for discussion. 'Any other business' allows committee members to raise questions on items not on the agenda. This is where the chairman's tact and firmness are needed so that the meeting does not go on too long. The date and time of the next meeting are always decided before the meeting is concluded. The only exception to this may be an Annual General Meeting, where it is not possible to decide as far as a year ahead.

MINUTES

'Minutes' are a record of what was decided at a meeting. They are usually kept in a Minute Book and signed by the chairman of the committee at the next meeting. Copies of Minutes are circulated to committee members after each meeting. It is the secretary's job to make notes of what has been decided during a meeting and then type (or write) them out as soon as possible after the meeting.

MINUTES of the Meeting of the Committee of the Midchester Manufacturing Company Social Club held on Thursday 20 November 198— in the Canteen at 2000.

Present: J Allan (Chairman)
          P Carter   L Williams
          H Jones   G Ziebarts

1)	APOLOGIES	There were no apologies for absence
2)	MINUTES	The Minutes of the Meeting held on Thursday 23 October 198— were approved and signed by the Chairman
3)	MATTERS ARISING	There were none
4)	CORRESPONDENCE	The Secretary read a letter from Mr H Moore who has left the firm and regrets that he has to resign from the Committee. It was agreed that a letter should be sent to Mr Moore to thank him for all his help with the work of the Committee
5)	TREASURER'S REPORT	This had been circulated and was accepted
6)	SECRETARY'S REPORT	This had been circulated and was accepted
7)	SPORTS PROGRAMME FOR 198—	A sub-committee was formed who agreed to deal with the preliminary arrangements for this. The sub-committee consists of P Carter, H Jones and L Williams
8)	RAISING OF SUBSCRIPTIONS	It was agreed to defer discussion of this until the Annual General Meeting in February 198—
9)	CHRISTMAS PANTOMIME	As last year's Christmas pantomime had not been successful financially and in fact had made a loss it was agreed not to go ahead with one for 198—
10)	ANY OTHER BUSINESS	Concern was expressed by several members about the fall in membership of the Social Club and it was agreed to advertise in the Works Magazine as soon as possible to try and interest new employees in the Club
11)	DATE AND TIME OF NEXT MEETING	This was fixed for Thursday 18 December at 2000 in the Works Canteen.

Signed . . . .
Chairman
18/12/8—

FOR YOUR FOLDER

20. MEETINGS

Write these notes in your folder, filling in the missing words and phrases.

1) Officers of an organisation are usually the chairman, the treasurer and the _____.

2) The job of the chairman is to make sure that committee meetings are businesslike and _____.

3) Topics for a committee to discuss are set out beforehand in the form of an _____.

4) The meeting for all members of an organisation, when the chairman, secretary and treasurer are elected, is the _____, held once a year.

5) Officers are usually elected by _____ (slips of paper are marked by each voter and placed in a box).

6) Minutes are a record of what was _____ at a meeting.

7) It is the _____ job to take the Minutes at a meeting.

8) Business meetings in a firm are usually _____ and attended by only a few _____.

9) A notice of a business meeting may be sent out on a _____.

10) A manager's secretary may be present to take notes of what is _____ and decided at a meeting.

11) A more formal type of meeting is one attended by the _____ of a company.

Exercise 31

ASSIGNMENTS FOR MEETINGS

1) Form a club and then hold an Annual General Meeting, electing by secret ballot a committee, treasurer, secretary and chairman.

2) Hold a committee meeting, after drawing up a suitable agenda.

3) Discuss what should be included in the Minutes, after the meeting during which the secretary takes notes of what is discussed.

4) Make out an agenda for the next meeting.

Charts and Graphs

There are many different ways of presenting information — one of them is by speaking (telling people some facts) — and there are many different ways of acquiring information (hearing, seeing, touching, tasting and smelling).

Seeing something usually has a more lasting impact than hearing the same thing described. Therefore, if information is important to a large number of people, it is better to present it to them where they can see it than simply to tell them.

In offices, charts and graphs are commonly used in order that information will be not overlooked.

Let us consider a company called Thingums PLC which makes and sells a product called 'Thingamajig'. It is sold in the UK as well as overseas (exported). The home market (in the UK) is divided into four areas: North, South, East and West.

The overseas (export) market is divided into two areas: Europe and Africa.

Two departments in Thingums PLC are the production department (responsible for making the product) and the sales department (responsible for selling it). Each department keeps its own records, as will now be described.

TABULATIONS

Below is a list of quantities of Thingamajigs sold in the home market over the last nine years. The information will be presented in different ways.

Year	Regional Sales				Total sales
	North	South	East	West	
1	2780	2840	3150	1680	10 450
2	2820	3250	3180	1950	11 200
3	2950	3200	3250	2050	11 450
4	2750	2950	3100	2050	10 850
5	2900	3000	3200	2080	11 180
6	3200	3350	3000	2000	11 550
7	3300	3500	3070	2000	11 870
8	3250	3000	3100	2130	11 480
9	3200	2800	3100	2150	11 250

A tabulation

The table of figures you have just read is known as a tabular presentation or 'tabulation'. To understand the figures takes time and is not easy. To compare, the figures region by region is also quite difficult and requires great concentration to see what has happened in relation to the total sales.

LINE CHARTS

A line chart presents the information by means of a straight line, the length of which is an indication of the difference in the values of the figures being used. The lines can be vertical or horizontal.

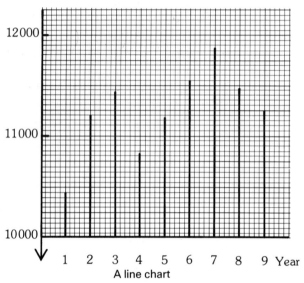

A line chart

If we record the total yearly sales over the past nine years, we see that the lowest figure is 10450 and the largest is 11870, a difference of 1420, so that if our scale covers 2000 it will be enough for this chart.

It is important when using graphs and charts that the scale is appropriate for its purpose.

The line chart above shows the following:

● There seems to be a 'cycle' of two good years followed by two poorer ones.

● The best sales year was the seventh year.

● After two good years, in the second and third years, sales dropped back for the fourth and fifth years.

● Sales picked up again in the sixth and seventh years.

● There was another drop in the eighth and ninth years.

● There have been two poor years in the eighth and ninth years, therefore should production and advertising be increased in anticipation of a better year for the tenth year?

142

BAR CHARTS

These are similar to line graphs except that the line becomes a rectangle of appropriate length. Bar charts may be vertical or horizontal, in the same way as line graphs.

Shown below is a bar chart recording the total sales figures of Thingamajigs over each of nine years.

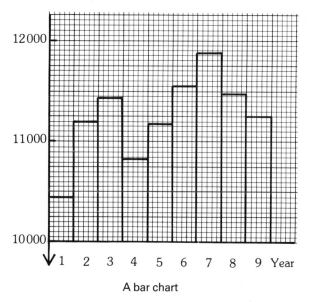

A bar chart

It would be difficult, but not impossible, to incorporate the sales figures in the various regions on the same line chart as the total sales. There is, however, a method which allows the regional sales figures to be shown on the same chart as the total sales figures. This is by means of a graph which is simple and easy. An example of this graph which most people see when they are patients in hospitals is an ordinary temperature chart.

143

With regard to the sales figures, as mentioned earlier, the total figure varies between 10450 and 11870, whilst the regional sales figures vary between 1680 and 3500.

These varying figures are plotted on the vertical line of the chart and it would seem therefore that the vertical line ought to be long enough to cover any quantity from say 1500 (just below the lowest figure of regional sales) to 12000 (just above the highest figure of total sales).

We can get over this by putting a break or zigzag in the vertical line at least big enough to be noticeable. This simple device will enable us to cover both lots of figures without difficulty. The break or zigzag in the vertical line tells an observer that the scale is not continuous — this is made clear by an arrowhead at the bottom of the vertical line when the scale does not start at zero.

Further, since we are going to draw lines on our graph which will mean different things, they ought to be different from each other. Normally, they would be in different colours with a 'key' or 'legend' stating what each colour represents, but if copies are to be sent round a firm, they will often be in black and white and the lines will have to be varied, again with a 'key' to show what each 'pattern' represents.

A line graph

At the foot of page 144 is a line graph (with zigzags and key). It indicates the total sales each year for the last nine years together with regional area sales in the same period.

The scale of the line graph is not continuous.

It will be seen that north and south regions seem to cause the bulge in total sales, whereas east and west regions sales seem to be fairly steady without much variation up or down.

As an alternative to the line graph above, we could use a double scale as shown in the graph below. The disadvantage of this type of scale is that if the values are close to each other, the lines are difficult to separate and the eye is confused, so the mind does not take in the differences and their significance.

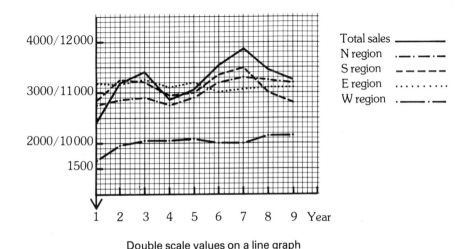

Double scale values on a line graph

PIE CHARTS

Pie charts are often used to illustrate relative quantities, proportions or percentages. A pie chart gets its name because a circle is used as the basic shape and the circle is divided up into segments which show the relative sizes of things to each other.

Whereas a tabulation or line chart, bar chart or line graph can show information at a glance, a pie chart shows information at one stage only. In using a pie chart to show the proportion of sales in each region in a year, it would be necessary to have a separate chart for each year, i.e. nine separate pie charts for nine years' information.

A small calculation is required to work out:

● What percentage of the whole, each region has

● How many degrees each percentage represents

(As you know, there are 360 degrees in a complete circle.) When this has been done, we can then mark out that number of degrees on our circle, by using a protractor.

We will take years 7 and 9 as our examples, and we can produce the pie chart below.

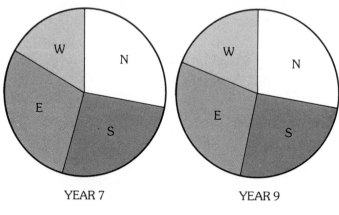

A pie chart

The segments of the pie chart could be completed in different colours, but if copies are required these will be in black and white (unless spirit duplicating is used – see pp. 269 – 72). Therefore different shading will be required for each segment.

Pie charts are normally used for information purposes rather than comparison. As you can see, it is difficult to observe the differences in regional sales between the two years — but we know there are some from the previous graphs.

YEAR PLANNER

One type of chart in common use is a year planner, which incorporates the weeks and months of the year, usually along the top of the chart, with spaces down the side of the chart.

One of the uses to which such a chart is put is planning staff holiday weeks. Other uses could be for training, conferences, exhibitions, room reservations in hotels and guest houses, representatives' and service engineers' engagements.

Opposite is part of a planning chart illustrating its use as a holiday rota indicator for the staff in an office. Normally, such a chart would cover a whole year and a one-year planner could be used for more than one purpose, but to show its general form and general use only, a portion of the chart is shown.

HOLIDAY ROTA 198–													
	MAY		JUNE				JULY					AUGUST	
	21	28	4	11	18	25	2	9	16	23	30	6	13
N.E. Body			◯	◯							◯		
J. Smith					◯				◯	◯			
L.B. Jones	◯	◯	◯										
R. Foster						◯	◯					◯	
J. Earle						◯						◯	◯

A planning chart

The reservation indicators could be of different colours and/or shapes in sticky paper or hatched lines.

PICTOGRAMS

Instead of using a line to show information on a graph, it is sometimes effective to use a symbol or series of symbols to connect the various points on the graph.

Similarly for bar charts, symbols may be used to show values instead of a rectangle.

Making these pictograms requires the ability to draw the symbols and to be consistent. They are often used in Government statistics mainly because they look more interesting and are easily recognisable.

The birth rate could be shown as a line of storks.

Beer production could be represented by barrels.

How the Government spends our money could be shown by a pile of coins divided up, so much for defence, education, social services etc.

Numbers of cars registered over the years could be shown by a line of cars.

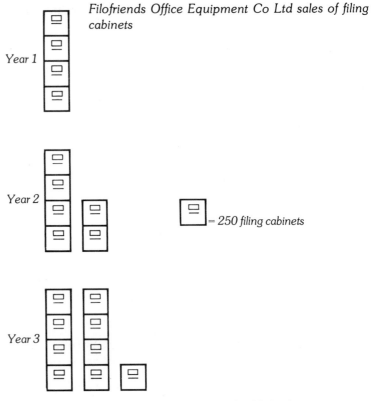

Filofriends Office Equipment Co Ltd sales of filing cabinets

= 250 filing cabinets

A pictogram showing filing cabinet sales from a supplier expanding his business

FOR YOUR FOLDER

21. CHARTS AND GRAPHS

Write these notes in your folder, filling in the missing words and phrases.

1) In offices charts and graphs are commonly used in order that _____.

2) Figures are sometimes shown in table form, known as a tabulation. To understand figures in a tabulation takes time and is not _____.

3) A line chart presents information by means of a _____.

4) The lines can be vertical or _____.

5) It is important when using charts and graphs that the _____ is appropriate for its purpose.

6) _____ charts are similar to line graphs except that the line becomes a rectangle of appropriate length.

7) Different information can be shown on the same graph by means of _____.

8) A pie chart gets its name because _____.

9) Pie charts are often used to illustrate _____.

10) Pie charts show information at one _____.

11) For planning staff holiday weeks, conferences and exhibitions a chart in common use is a _____.

12) Instead of drawing lines to show information on a graph, it is sometimes effective to use a chart made up of symbols called a _____.

13) These symbols are often used in Government _____.

Exercise 32

CHARTS AND GRAPHS

For the first two questions look at the pictogram opposite.

1) How many filing cabinets were sold in Year 2?

2) How many more filing cabinets were sold in Year 3 than in Year 1?

3) The average temperature per month in degrees Celsius over the six months April to September was as follows:

April	13	May	18	June	21
July	22	August	24	September	22

Draw a line graph to show these temperatures.

If the vertical line of your scale does not start at zero, do not forget to show this.

4) Draw a line chart to show the information given in the pictogram on p. 148.

5) Of the new cars sold in the UK in a particular year:

Company A sold 30%.

Company B sold 28%.

Company C sold 24%.

European imports accounted for 10% of sales.

The remainder were imported from other countries.

Show the above information by means of a pie chart.

6) On a certain day the temperature in degrees Celsius in the following towns and cities was as follows:

Athens	11	Beirut	25	Belgrade	0
Cardiff	8	Hong Kong	23	Stockholm	5
Tokyo	15	Lisbon	18	Sydney	20

Arrange the above in order lowest to highest and draw a vertical bar chart to illustrate this information.

7) The sales staff of J Evans PLC are arranging their holidays. Draw a part of a suitable chart to illustrate who is going to be away and when.

The holiday dates are weeks commencing Monday:

J Bray	28 May	23 July	30 July
M Smith	11 June	18 June	25 June
N Poole	18 June	9 July	16 July
D Evans	28 May	4 June	23 July

8) Draw a line graph showing the export sales of Whatsits over the past 8 years:

Year 1	100	Year 2	180	Year 3	230
Year 4	280	Year 5	390	Year 6	500
Year 7	520	Year 8	510		

Comment upon the situation which your graph has shown.

9) H B Cardgrove has a piece of equipment which is loaned out for display at various exhibitions. It is in great demand. Bookings during a typical two-month period are as follows:

Birmingham	6 June	Norwich	11 July
Cardiff	20 June	Bristol	13 June
Swindon	27 June	Lincoln	18 July
Kings Lynn	25 July	Cambridge	4 July

Assume each exhibitor borrows the equipment for a week. You need not concern yourself about transport.

How could a record be kept of these bookings which would be effective and very easy to follow? Illustrate your answer.

10) Five products of a company identified as A, B, C, D and E are shown to contribute to total turnover as follows: Product A 33%, B 40%, C 8%, D 15%, E 4%.

Draw a pie chart to illustrate these figures.

11) Draw a line chart showing the amount which each of the five products in the previous question contributed to turnover. The figures in thousands of pounds are:

A 33, B 40, C 8, D 15, E 4.

12) The chart below shows the monthly sales figures in thousands of a certain item.

(a) In what month was the highest number sold? How many?

(b) Was the build-up to peak sales as sharp as the fall in sales?

(c) How many were sold in October?

(d) What was the lowest quantity sold and in what month?

(e) Between what two months was the highest growth in sales recorded?

(f) Could the graph indicate sales of ice cream or winter coats? Give reasons for your answer.

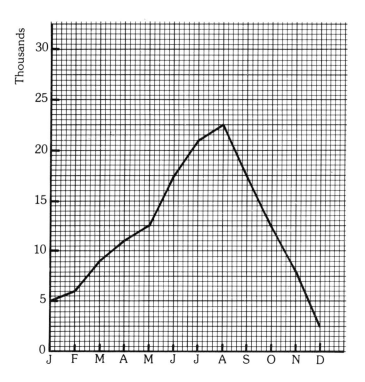

CHAPTER 7

Office Machinery

There are lots of different machines in offices. The telephone is one which we have already looked at, and later on in the book we will be looking at copiers and duplicators. What we are going to look at now are machines which help to put communications on to paper (typewriters and so on) and machines which process information (calculators and computers).

Audio-typing

One area in which the use of two pieces of equipment is combined is that of audio-typing. The typist listens through headphones to a pre-recorded cassette or tape and types what she hears. She can stop or start the recording by use of a pedal, thus leaving her hands free for typing. A competent audio-typist develops a technique which allows her to listen to quite long phrases, and type them back very quickly. She must also have a very good standard of English, as she has no 'copy' to look at. Her spelling and punctuation have to be very accurate indeed.

Foot control

Earphones

A dictating machine

Recording media used on dictating machines may be:
- belts or sleeves
- tapes
- cassettes
- sheets
- wire
- discs.

Magnetic media can be re-used. Non-magnetic media is used once only and then discarded. It is cheaper than magnetic to buy, but more expensive in the long term.

ADVANTAGES OF AUDIO-TYPING

The workload can be spread among several audio-typists

Cassettes, sleeves, tapes etc. can be posted

Time is saved while a secretary is typing from one audio machine and her boss is dictating on to another.

DISADVANTAGES OF AUDIO-TYPING

Audio-typing requires intense concentration and is tiring for long periods

The dictator's voice may be indistinct and difficult to hear

A great deal of background noise is often recorded also – many rooms in firms are far from sound-proof

Loss of personal contact between boss and typist or secretary

Recording media is difficult to keep entirely confidential – copies are easily 'dubbed'

Tapes are cleared when finished (if magnetic) and all records are lost – shorthand notes could be referred to later, long after the notes have been transcribed, if necessary.

CENTRALISED AUDIO-TYPING

With centralised audio-typing several dictating machines are in one room and the dictation is put on in offices in several parts of the firm. The tapes are then taken to the central audio-typing unit by messengers or direct tube. Centralised audio-typing often forms part of the typing pool (see p. 13).

BANK SYSTEM

In a bank system the manager has a microphone only in his office (sometimes like a telephone) and when he wants to dictate he dials a code and starts dictating after receiving a signal to say the machine is free. The tape is then taken to an audio-typist to be transcribed.

TANDEM SYSTEM

Yet another arrangement is the tandem system. Each typist has two dictating machines and can type from one while the other is available to record dictation. If she has any queries, she can telephone the person dictating to ask him what he said or even play back part of the tape to him, so that he can listen and explain. The 'tandem' system is used by many firms because it means the typist has some contact with the person dictating and feels the work is less impersonal.

A dictating machine cannot take over the role of the secretary, who is able to think for herself and use her own initiative. Ideally, a good secretary should be able to write shorthand *and* use audio-typing equipment.

Stenotyping

Stenotyping is a system of recording speech on a special machine. It is used as an alternative to writing shorthand – the machine prints the letters instead of the operator writing shorthand symbols with Biro or pencil. The notes still have to be typed back (transcribed) on a typewriter in the same way as shorthand notes have to be 'transcribed'.

The British stenotyping machine is called a Palantype.

The operator of the Palantype uses phonetics instead of spelling the words in the ordinary way; that is, she writes down the words as they sound.

Stenotyping is used for court reporting where speakers are reported as they make their speeches – this is 'verbatim' reporting.

Stenotyping can also be used by secretaries and shorthand-typists in offices instead of shorthand.

It may soon be possible to combine stenotyping with computers (pp. 165 – 7) or word processors (see pp. 156 – 7) by using it as an 'input'.

Typewriters

There are two main kinds of typewriter in general use in offices –

154

electric and manual. In addition, there are what are known as 'special-purpose' typewriters which are used in offices where the work is highly specialised.

MANUAL TYPEWRITERS

There are three different kinds of manual typewriter:

- Standard length carriage used in most offices (14")
- Specially long carriage for typing wide documents
- Portable typewriters – extra light to carry so that they can be moved easily.

Manual typewriters are cheaper than electric typewriters, they need no power point, and are much less heavy than electric machines.

ELECTRIC TYPEWRITERS

These produce very good-quality work, when used by a well-trained typist, because of the evenness of touch. It is not possible to 'bang' too hard on electric typewriters. They are less tiring than manual typewriters for this reason, and also because of the 'repeater' keys on the machine – usually for underscore and fullstop. The carriage return is automatic, too, and helps to speed up the typist.

Some electric typewriters will produce more carbon copies than manual machines (a manual will produce about six). With very thin carbon and typing paper, an electric machine, with pressure adjusted to maximum, may produce up to 12 carbon copies. Some electric typewriters also 'justify' the right-hand margin – that is, they automatically space out the letters in the line of type so that the right-hand margin is exactly even, similar to right-hand margins in books. This greatly improves the appearance of the typing.

It is also possible to change the typeface on some electric machines – by means of a removable 'golfball' on which the characters are mounted or by means of a moulded segment. These interchangeable typefaces enable the typist to change the 'pitch' of her machine (i.e. the number of characters the machine produces per inch – pica is 10 and elite is 12) and also provide a different type-style for display work. In addition, some foreign languages (Russian for example) have different characters and an interchangeable typeface would have to be used for these.

Up to the present, electric typewriters which have been in general use have keyboards and carriage movements driven by an electric motor – the action is mechanical.

ELECTRONIC TYPEWRITERS

It is now possible to buy a truly electronic typewriter – the keyboard is controlled from an electric impulse through a circuit board (with silicon

155

'chips'). The weight of an electronic typewriter is about half that of an electric typewriter, and repairs are much easier and quicker to carry out, as it consists of only seven components, each of which can be replaced when necessary. The faulty part can be repaired and stored by the mechanic until required to repair another faulty machine.

The electronic typewriter is almost identical in operation to an electric typewriter except that it has a small 'memory' of eight characters which can be used to:

- backspace
- correct automatically
- adjust layout of headings.

The touch required on an electronic typewriter is feather light – even less than on the traditional electric typewriter.

The price of the two machines is almost the same.

The typing element is called a 'daisy wheel' because it is shaped like the petals on a daisy – there are no type bars or typeface. The 'daisy wheel' is interchangeable to give different pitch and characters.

MEMORY TYPEWRITER

This can store up to 200000 characters (about 200 pages of A4 typing). The characters are not just the letters printed on the paper, but also include instructions to the machine regarding line spacing, headings, etc. A copy of each letter or document stored in the memory must be kept in a folder so that it is possible to refer to them for reference and retyping when required.

WORD PROCESSOR (OR TEXT PROCESSOR)

This is the more sophisticated development of the memory typewriter, where the storage of the typed material is outside the machine and may be on magnetic card or floppy disks (called 'floppy' because they are limp). A word processor also has a visual display unit (VDU)' on which the typist can see what she is typing as she does it. It is printed out only when text and layout are satisfactory. Whole sections can be moved out, revised, added, deleted or enlarged. Only the new material will need to be retyped. On some word processors a high-speed independent 'printer' (a typewriter without a keyboard) prints out the work once it has been approved, from the memory, at 500 words per minute without possibility of errors – a perfect 'top' copy every time.

A word processor will produce all the repetitive work of a typist – circulars, reports, minutes, legal documents, much faster and with complete accuracy, and of a sufficiently high quality to be suitable for sending out to other firms or organisations.

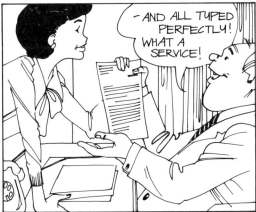

To operate a word processor efficiently and make use of all the facilities which it can offer requires a course of training followed by practice under the supervision of an experienced operator. Keyboards on word processors are standard as far as the letter keys are concerned, but have in addition special 'command' or 'instruction' keys that have to be learnt by the word processor operator. One of the disadvantages of word processors at present is that the 'command' keys are different on *every* make of machine — and there are a great many makes. An operator with experience on one machine would have to be retrained before being able to use another make of machine.

Some operators find the VDU causes eyestrain and headaches — frequent short rest periods are necessary.

MICROWRITERS

A Microwriter (trade name) is a small word processor which can be held in the hand. It has a keyboard with six *blank* keys, which are designed around the hand. Each finger has its own key. Characters are produced by pressing *combinations* of keys down together. The manufacturers claim that it is quick and easy to learn to operate it.

The Microwriter can be attached to a printer, telephone modem, Telex, cassette recorder for storage of text, computer and VDU.

A Microwriter

As the copy is typed, it is stored on a 1600 word memory (about five pages of A4 paper). Once there, it can be recalled on to the moving display at any time, allowing corrections or insertions to be made. Plug into a printer or electronic typewriter and the copy is turned into neatly typed text.

The Microwriter could be very useful to managers for letters, memos, reports, speeches, notes and has the advantage of being fully portable.

TYPEWRITER FOR THE HANDICAPPED

A typewriter with a single-handed keyboard has been developed to meet the needs of people who have to use a keyboard with one hand.

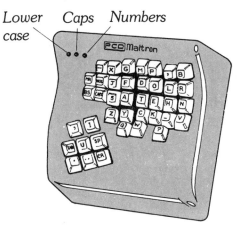

Indicators for

Lower case *Caps* *Numbers*

Single-handed (right-handed) keyboard for the handicapped courtesy of PCD-Maltron Ltd)

FOR YOUR FOLDER

22. STENOTYPING, AUDIO-TYPING, TYPEWRITERS, WORD PROCESSORS

Write these notes in your folder, filling in the missing words and phrases.

1) Stenotyping is the system of taking down shorthand by _____.

2) Audio-typing is listening through headphones and _____ what has been recorded.

3) Audio-typists must have accurate typing with good speeds and excellent _____.

4) Audio-typing is useful because it spreads the work evenly among typists but has the disadvantage of _____.

5) Recording media may be tapes, cassettes or _____. Recording media are easily _____.

6) Manual typewriters may be standard, long-carriage or _____.

7) Electric typewriters produce good quality work and are less tiring for the typist to use than a manual typewriter because of the _____ on the electric machine and also because it is not possible to _____ on an electric machine.

8) Some electric typewriters have interchangeable typefaces which enable the typist to change the pitch of the machine and also provide a _____ _____ for display work.

9) An interchangeable typeface could also be useful for typing in a
_____ language.

10) Keeping the right-hand margin absolutely straight is known as
_____ it.

11) The latest electronic typewriter has a small memory of
_____ characters and a 'daisy wheel' _____
element.

12) A memory typewriter can store up to 200 000 characters (about
_____ pages of A4 typing).

13) A word processor has a visual display unit (VDU) and stores the
material in its memory on magnetic card or _____.

14) A word processor will produce all the repetitive work of a typist —
circulars, reports, minutes, _____ of a sufficiently high
quality to be sent out to _____.

15) The disadvantages of word processors are the possibility of eyestrain
and headaches from the VDU and _____.

16) The Microwriter is a small, hand-held _____.

Supplies for the Typewriter

RIBBONS

Typewriter ribbons are made of nylon, silk, cotton, or carbon. Nylon
and silk ribbons produce work of very good appearance but carbon
ribbons produce the best imprint of all. The finer the fabric, the sharper
the imprint. Unfortunately, carbon ribbons can be used once only and
so are very expensive. Two-colour ribbons are available (called bi-
chrome) usually red and black, and correcting ribbons, which switch
from normal black to white, so that the error is typed over in white,
made invisible and the correction typed over again in black. Lift-off
ribbons can be used on all self-correcting typewriters (electric and
electronic) that have provision for fitting the tapes, but they are
suitable only for correcting errors made with carbon ribbons.

COPYHOLDERS

Many typists are trained to stand their textbooks and notebooks upright
on copyholders and prefer to continue to use them in the office.
Complicated work is assisted by accurate line-by-line reading and some
copyholders are electrically operated by means of a foot-controlled
switch.

Using an illuminated copyholder

CONTINUOUS STATIONERY ATTACHMENT

This is fitted to the back of a typewriter (see below) and enables the forms (which are in sets with interleaved carbon or NCR perforated between each set) to be fed into the machine and torn off as completed. A continuous stationery attachment saves the typist's time as each set of documents is ready in the typewriter when the previous one has been completed.

A typewriter with a continuous stationery attachment

Typist's Accessories

ERASERS

These are available in many shapes and sizes, from the pencil type, which can be sharpened to keep a fine erasing point, to the larger rectangular one which has a soft pencil rubber and a hard typewriter rubber combined.

ERASER SHIELDS

These are placed over the word to be corrected so that only the letters to be replaced are erased. Eraser shields are made of clear plastic.

An eraser shield

LIQUID AND PAPER CORRECTIVE

These are available in many colours, including white, so that the colour of the letterheading and/or typing paper can be exactly matched.
The error is 'painted' over, allowed to dry and then retyped.

The carbon copy must, of course, be erased in the normal way – if it is 'painted' out also, time must be allowed for it to dry. This way of correcting errors is very neat and effective *if* it is carried out carefully and gently.

Correcting fluid in use

162

BACKING SHEETS

These can be supplied with scales showing the typing lines and inches along the top. They help to show the typist when she is nearing the bottom of her page. Backing sheets also protect the platen (roller) from wear and tear and improve the appearance of the work. The 'fold-over' top of a backing sheet helps to keep carbons and carbon copies level when the typist is feeding them into her machine.

A scaled backing sheet

The Care of the Typewriter

A typewriter is an expensive and complex piece of machinery and should be looked after by the typist, whether it is her own portable, which she uses at home, or an electric typewriter she uses in an office.

Here are some guidelines:

1) Switch off and unplug an electric or electronic typewriter at the end of the day. Switch off when not in use, during the day.

2) *Always* cover a typewriter after use, to keep out the dust.

3) Remove dust daily (preferably first thing in the morning) especially underneath, because this rises into the machine and clogs it.

4) Rub out carefully on manual and electric machines, moving the carriage (using the margin release) so that the bits of rubber dust fall on to the desk and not into the type basket. *Do not rub out* if using an electronic machine — use the lift-off corrective ribbon or, remove typing from machine, paint over liquid corrective, allow to dry and retype.

5) Use a backing sheet when single copies are being typed — this improves the look of the typing as well as protects the roller (platen) from wear and tear.

6) To move a typewriter, *lift from underneath,* not by the carriage, and move both margins to the centre so that the carriage will not slide along.

7) Never leave a typewriter near the edge of the desk, where it could be accidentally knocked off by a passer-by.

8) Never leave a typewriter near a hot radiator — this will dry out the oil in the machine.

9) Clean the typeface on a manual or electric typewriter with a stiff brush and white spirit, once a week. This will remove the surplus ink which will eventually clog the typeface. On an electronic typewriter, use specially impregnated cleaning paper. Clean finger marks off the machine with spirit and dust with a soft brush where rubber dust has collected on a manual or electric machine. Wipe the platen with a duster dampened with spirit.

10) *Do not oil* a typewriter — leave this to a trained mechanic. Surplus oil in a machine can ruin typing and is difficult to get rid of.

11) Always call in a trained mechanic to repair faults — *don't* try to mend them yourself.

FOR YOUR FOLDER

23. TYPEWRITER ACCESSORIES AND SUPPLIES

Write these notes in your folder, filling in the missing words and phrases.

1) Typewriter ribbons are made of nylon, silk, cotton or _____.

2) Carbon ribbons produce the best imprint of all but can be used _____.

3) Apart from carbon ribbons, the best work is produced by _____ and _____.

4) Bi-chrome ribbons are _____ usually black and red.

5) Correcting ribbons can be switched from black to _____ so that the error is made _____ and can be retyped.

6) Copyholders are used to keep work upright and some are _____ operated by means of a foot-controlled switch.

7) A continuous stationery attachment enables sets of forms, perforated between sets, to be _____ and torn off when completed.

8) A useful accessory when correcting an error is an _____ which enables the typist to rub out only the incorrect letters she has mistyped.

9) Liquid and paper correctives are painted over errors, allowed to dry and then the correction is retyped. Carbon copies must be erased by rubbing out – if 'painted', time must be allowed for the corrective to _____ .

10) Backing sheets are available with scales showing typing lines and inches along the top. They may also have a 'fold-over' top which helps to 'feed' _____ and _____ level into the typewriter.

Computers

WHAT DO THEY DO?

Computers are electronic machines which can:
- store information. This information is called *data*.
- sort out the data and, if required, perform calculations. This is called *data processing*.

In the office the computer may be used for:
- working out the payroll
- accountancy
- stock control
- market research
- production planning

TYPES OF COMPUTER

There are three types of computer:
- *Mainframes* are large machines which would be used, for example, by banks.
- *Minicomputers* are much smaller and are now being used in many offices.
- *Microcomputers* are even smaller. They are used increasingly at home and on desk tops in the office. The sequence of operations in an automatic washing machine is programmed by a *microprocessor*, and this too can be thought of as a sort of microcomputer.

A computer 'terminal' consisting of 'input' (keyboard) and 'output' (VDU)

165

COMPUTER HARDWARE

A computer has five main parts:

- *the input.* Here information is put into the computer. This may be typed in at a keyboard or inserted in the form of printed cards, paper tape, magnetic tape, magnetic discs or characters in magnetic ink. (This last type of input is used on cheques so that they can be sorted by banks' computers.)
- *the central processing unit.* This contains the parts of the computer which process the data.
- *the memory.* This is where information is stored in the computer.
- *the output.* This is where information comes out of the computer. It may appear on the screen of a *visual display unit (VDU)*, be printed out on paper by a *line printer,* or presented in a number of other ways (for example, on tape, microfilm or discs).
- *the backing store.* Information which is not actually being processed in the computer can be kept in a special backing store. Magnetic tapes can be kept in special cupboards, for example, which are kept at a constant temperature.

COMPUTER SOFTWARE

Once a computer has been assembled from electronic components, it is unable to perform any task until it is given a set of instructions to follow. These instructions, which are stored in the computer's memory, are known as the *software.* The word *program* refers to a part of the instruction set, usually those parts of the software that are regularly used or changed. The part of the software that allows us to have control and make changes of any kind is known as the *operating system.*

An example of a program in a simple computer language known as *BASIC* could take the form:

```
10   INPUT "ENTER TWO NUMBERS"; A,B
20   C = A+B
30   D = A-B
40   PRINT "THEIR SUM IS: " ; C
50   PRINT "THEIR DIFFERENCE IS: " ; D
60   END
```

This listing could either be typed directly into a computer by a *programmer* (the keyboard operator), entered on tape, cards, via a telephone link or in many other ways. The computer operating system controls how programs may be entered. Old programs may be removed from the computer and stored for future reference in a variety of forms, such as paper tape, magnetic tape or printed paper. All such pieces of equipment for inputting or outputting information are part of the hardware and are known as *peripherals.*

USING THE COMPUTER

Training is required for the operation of sophisticated computers, but skills for simple computers can be readily acquired at home on a range of machines known as *home computers*. These usually have a QWERTY keyboard, like any ordinary typewriter, for inputting programs and they connect to a television set for output.

Extra keys may be present on the keyboard depending on the complexity and range of functions of the computer. Large computers, such as those owned by large companies, universities etc., are known as *mainframes* and can be so big that they occupy entire buildings. These mainframes need several trained staff to control all the functions and to maintain the upkeep of the equipment.

Calculators

Machines for adding have been used since the seventeenth century. One of the first machines capable of dealing with money columns was the Burroughs, produced in 1888. The cash registers largely in use until a few years ago were a development along the same lines. Modern calculators which carry out very complex mathematical calculations, as well as simple addition, subtraction and multiplication, have become smaller and cheaper due to the development of the 'silicon chip'. Pocket calculators are used everywhere today – in schools, colleges, offices, shops and home. The slimmest pocket calculator is no larger than a pocket diary, and there is even one with an alarm and a clock which prints a message when the alarm rings, to remind the person awoken where he has to go!

A pocket calculator

In offices, it is often useful to have a slightly larger, heavy-duty calculator to stand on a desk. It is also necessary when working with figures to have a record of the total, and some calculators print-out the calculation in addition to showing the answer in the display unit.

The larger calculators can be plugged into the mains, or operated from batteries, some of which are rechargeable by being left plugged in overnight.

A calculator with print-out

The latest type of small calculator is 'solar-powered' – in other words, its battery is recharged by exposure to sunlight or artificial electric light.

Small pocket calculators may unfortunately be easily picked up and stolen, so they must be carefully stored away in locked cupboards in offices after use.

Calculators (the ones capable of the more complicated calculations) are sometimes described as 'pocket computers'. This is wrong – the essential difference between a computer and a calculator is that a calculator cannot work out sums by logic, i.e. produce an answer by selecting figures from a 'chain' whereas a computer is able to do so, from information stored in its 'memory'.

A large desk-type calculator

FOR YOUR FOLDER

24. COMPUTER AND CALCULATORS

Write these notes in your folder, filling in the missing words and phrases.

1) The sorting out of information in a computer is called _____ _____.

2) A computer may be used in the office for working out the payroll, accounting, stock control, market research and _____.

3) A set of instructions fed into a computer is called a _____. The person who writes this is called a _____ and his first task is to produce a _____ _____.

4) Programs are referred to as _____ and the computer equipment is called _____.

5) The five main parts of a computer are: the input, the central processing unit, the _____, the output and the backing store.

6) The input into a computer may consist of punched cards, paper tape, _____ tape or characters in _____ ink.

7) Information for the computer may appear on a screen called a _____ _____ _____ or printed on paper by a _____ _____.

8) The three types of computer are _____, _____ and _____.

9) Modern calculators carry out very complex mathematical calculations and have become smaller and cheaper due to the development of the _____.

10) The latest type of calculator is solar-powered – its battery is recharged by _____.

11) When it is necessary to have a record of figures used in a calculation a calculator with a _____ is essential.

12) Computers and calculators both work out sums, but only a computer can work out the _____ – this is the essential difference between them.

13) Calculators should not be called '_____ _____'.

Exercise 33

TYPEWRITERS, WORD PROCESSORS, COMPUTERS AND CALCULATORS

1) Compare the 'bank' system of audio-typing with the 'tandem' system and explain the disadvantages and advantages of each.

2) 'An audio-typist does not need such a high standard of English as a shorthand-typist.' Do you agree with this statement or not? Give your reasons.

3) Compare the work of a shorthand-typist with that of a stenotypist.

4) Electronic typewriters are the first of the typewriters to be controlled by silicon chips. Compare an electric typewriter with an electronic typewriter.

5) What are the advantages of a word processor?

6) Does a word processor have any disadvantages? If so, what are they?

7) Explain the advantages of copyholders and continuous stationery attachments.

8) Describe a Microwriter.

9) List points to be observed in the care of a manual typewriter: (a) daily, (b) weekly, (c) when it is faulty.

10) What effect has the microprocessor (the silicon chip) had on computers?

11) How is information stored in a computer produced when required?

12) Compare pocket calculators with computers.

CHAPTER 8

Finding Out

Reference Books in General

'Finding out' is simple if you know which reference book to look in, and how to use reference books.

All public libraries have a good selection of reference books in a separate section. They are not to be taken out on loan because:

- They are usually large, heavy and awkward to carry
- They are expensive and librarians cannot afford to run the risk of losing them
- They have to be always available.

Reference books have to be replaced as soon as a new edition becomes available, because out-of-date facts are misleading and worse than useless.

HOW TO USE REFERENCE BOOKS

Check the contents list first, to verify that it is the right book for the information required. The contents list is at the beginning of a reference book, and is easy to find.

After you have found the topic you want in the contents list, turn to the index. This is at the back of a reference book, and is an alphabetical list of topics, very often divided by sub-headings in heavier type.

When using an index, remember that the item you are looking for may be under a different word with the same meaning (a 'synonym'):

'Car' may be under:
- Automobile
- Motor vehicle
- Motor car

so if you cannot find what you are looking for at once, try to think of another word with a similar meaning, and see if it is indexed under that.

While looking up information in a reference book, place slips of paper in between the pages which you want to go back to, as you work through the book. This makes it much easier to turn back later and recheck. Remember that many reference books have over a thousand pages!

OTHER WAYS OF HELPING THE USER

Some reference books have attached book marks in the form of ribbons or cards.

Others may have tabs on the edges of pages as 'signposts'.

Edge printing is often combined with different coloured pages.

There may also be a 'thumb' index.

A bookmark

A thumb index

Coloured pages

Tabs

FOR YOUR FOLDER

25. HOW TO USE REFERENCE BOOKS

Write these notes in your folder, filling in the missing words and phrases.

1) Reference books are not lent to borrowers by public libraries because they are expensive and (mostly) very _____ and must always be _____.

2) Reference books need frequent replacement because the information *must* be _____.

3) At the front of all reference books is a _____ which lists the topics dealt with in the book.

4) At the back of all reference books is an _____ which is a detailed alphabetical list of all the facts in the book.

5) To help readers to find the information they need, some reference books have attached _____ in the form of _____.

6) While looking up information in a reference book, it is helpful to mark the pages with _____ as you go through the book.

7) Some reference books have different coloured pages with _____ to help the user.

8) _____ are given by tabs on the edges of the pages.

9) Another way of guiding the user of a reference book is by _____.

10) When using a reference book, remember that the item you are looking for may be under a different word with the same meaning – a _____.

General Knowledge

'General knowledge' means a knowledge of facts covering a wide range of topics. It is impossible for any one person to know everything, but a lot of information can be looked up in an encyclopaedia which consists of a book or series of books with topics arranged in alphabetical order.

Encyclopaedias contain information about people, events, places and modern technology. Because of their size, it is only possible to up-date them every few years, and so are soon out of date regarding facts concerning people, events and technology. Also, because encyclopaedias are so comprehensive, they cannot give detailed information on each subject – or they would be enormous!

It is necessary to use specialised reference books if detailed information is needed about one particular subject. These specialised reference books will be dealt with later.

The largest encyclopaedia is *Encyclopaedia Britannica.* It consists of about thirty separate books and is packed with all sorts of facts and figures. Although very good, it is probably too big and too expensive to keep handy in your office. You may, however, find the *Britannica* in your local library.

A small, compact one-book encyclopaedia which is published annually, and is therefore nearly always more up to date than the larger multi-volumed encyclopaedias, is *Pears' Cyclopaedia. Pears'* is divided under three main headings: Everyday information (dictionary, foreign phrases, commercial phrases and legal notes); Events, famous people, government and international organisations; Home and Personal (medical dictionary, gardening, sports, pets, and cookery).

Another general reference book published annually, is *Whitaker's Almanack.* This contains information about *every* country in the world, as well as statistics regarding imports and exports, revenue, population, production and industry in the United Kingdom. *Whitaker's* also contains information about the Royal family and members of the peerage, the House of Commons, the Law Courts, and the police and armed forces.

Pears' and *Whitaker's Almanack* provide nearly all the information which may be needed on a general basis, in an easily portable up-to-date form. They have also another advantage – compared with the large encyclopaedias, they are relatively cheap. As well as reference books, general information can be obtained from the reference section of the central libraries in large cities by telephoning or writing. *The Daily Telegraph* maintains an information section at its library at 135 Fleet Street, London, where letters or telephone calls will be dealt with by expert staff.

Prestel

Prestel is British Telecom's two-way computerised service. It gives useful information on a television screen to anyone who has a modified set and a telephone. Users call their local Prestel Centre via their normal telephone line. Prestel supplies news and information from an enormous library, and one of the many useful information services Prestel utilises is in connection with vacancies for jobs. Eventually, Prestel will become international (see p. 106).

FOR YOUR FOLDER

26. GENERAL KNOWLEDGE

Write these notes in your folder, filling in the missing words and phrases.

1) Knowledge of facts covering a wide range of subjects is called _____ knowledge.

2) The most comprehensive encyclopaedia containing general knowledge is the _____.

3) General knowledge reference books are up-dated only every few years and are thus soon _____.

4) If detailed information is required on any subject a _____ is required.

5) A small single-volume encyclopaedia which is published annually is _____.

6) Another general reference book which is published annually is _____.

7) Information is obtainable from other sources than books. The British Telecom's two-way computerised information service is called _____.

8) One of the most useful information services the above supplies is in connection with _____.

9) The national newspaper which runs its own information section is the _____.

10) The _____ _____ of libraries in large cities will answer queries by letter or on the telephone.

Usage of English

A dictionary is essential both for the spelling and for the meanings of words.

A small dictionary is better than no dictionary at all, but, to be really useful, a dictionary should be as large and as comprehensive as possible. The smaller dictionaries do not give derivatives – that is, all the different words which come from one 'root' word – and are not so much help with the spelling or the meaning.

The *Concise Oxford Dictionary* (COD), *Chambers' Twentieth Century Dictionary,* and *Collins Dictionary of the English Language* are all excellent, comprehensive dictionaries. In addition to spelling and definitions, a dictionary may give the following information:

- Pronunciation
- Whether the word is slang, vulgar, or old-fashioned
- Abbreviations
- Foreign words and phrases
- Common English forenames
- Correct ways to address titled people.

As guides for spelling common words, three small books which can be very useful are: *The Little Oxford Dictionary, The Oxford Mini-dictionary* and the *Collins Gem Dictionary of Spelling and Word Division.*

A dictionary gives several words with the same meaning (synonyms) but a greater selection is given in *Roget's Thesaurus.* The word 'thesaurus' means a 'treasury'. *Roget's Thesaurus* is a 'treasury of words', which has words arranged in groups according to meaning. It is thus much more comprehensive than a dictionary. Using the *Thesaurus* gives you an idea of how rich the English language is.

566. STUDENT

.1 NOUNS student, pupil, scholar, learner, studier, educatee, trainee, *élève*[Fr]; inquirer; self-taught person, autodidact; auditor; monitor, prefect, praepostor [Brit]; —log *or* —logue.

.2 disciple, follower, apostle; convert, proselyte 145.7.

.3 self-taught man, autodidact.

.4 school child, school kid [informal]; schoolboy, school lad; schoolgirl; preschool child, preschooler, nursery school child, infant [Brit]; kindergartner, grade schooler, primary schooler, intermediate schooler; secondary schooler, prep schooler, preppie [informal], high schooler, schoolmate, schoolfellow, fellow student, classmate.

.5 college student, collegian, collegiate, varsity student [Brit informal], college boy or girl; co-ed [informal]; seminarian, seminarist; *bahur* [Heb], *yeshiva bocher* [Yid].

.6 undergraduate, undergrad [informal], cadet, midshipman; underclassman, freshman, freshie [informal], plebe, sophomore, soph [informal], upperclassman, junior, senior.

567. SCHOOL

.1 NOUNS school, educational institution, teaching institution, academic *or* scholastic institution, teaching and research institution, institute, academy, seminary, *Schule* [Ger], *école* [Fr], *escuela* [Sp].

.2 public school, common school, district school; union school, regional school, central school, consolidated school; private school; day school, country day school; boarding school, *pensionat* [Fr]; finishing school; dame school, blab school; special school, school for the handicapped; night school, evening school; summer school, vacation school; correspondence school; extension, university extension; school of continuing education, continuation school; platoon school; progressive school; free school, nongraded school, informal school, open classroom school; alternate *or* alternative school, street academy, storefront school, school without walls.

.3 [Brit terms] provided school, council school, board school; voluntary school, nonprovided school, national school, charity school.

.4 preschool, infant school [Brit], nursery,

A facsimile page from *Roget's Thesaurus*

To help with difficult points of grammar, *Fowler's Modern English Usage* is of great assistance. It helps to decide whether to put in an apostrophe or not, for instance, and whether to use 'principle' or 'principal' when the meaning is 'most important'.

Urdang's *Mispronounced, Misused and Misunderstood Words* gives guidance about spoken as well as written English.

A *Dictionary of Acronyms and Abbreviations* by Eric Pugh explains all those terms in common use such as NATO and SALT which are words in themselves – just in case you've forgotten what NATO and SALT stand for.

176

FOR YOUR FOLDER

27. USAGE OF ENGLISH

Write these notes in your folder, filling in the missing words and phrases.

1) For meanings of words a _____ is essential.

2) For another word with the same meaning (a synonym) a _____ is useful.

3) A _____ helps with pronunciation.

4) For assistance with awkward points of grammar, _____ would be useful.

5) If you were not sure you were using the word with the right meaning _____ would help.

6) The different words which come from one root word are called _____.

7) Three good dictionaries are _____, _____ and _____.

8) The definition of a word is the _____ of a word.

9) The book to use to check whether a word is out of date is a _____.

10) The book to use to check the spelling of the plural of a word is _____.

11) A collection of first letters of words used as a word is an _____.

12) The reference book to look up the above is _____.

Exercise 34

USE OF *WHITAKER'S ALMANACK, PEARS' CYCLOPAEDIA* AND *ROGET'S THESAURUS*

You will find the answers to the following questions in Whitaker's Almanack.

1) What is the population of Nottingham?

2) When was the Union Jack first used (with the cross of St Patrick)?

3) What does it cost to visit the Stock Exchange in London?

4) Name the six states of Australia.

5) Where is the headquarters of the Waterways Board?

6) Where is the Bank of England?

7) To whom is the George Cross awarded?

8) Where is Hadrian's Wall?

9) When was the word 'Parliament' first used?

10) Where is the Foreign Office?

You will find the answers to the following questions in Pears' Cyclopaedia.

11) What is Lamaism?

12) Who were the Iceni?

13) What is a 'lace-wing'?

14) What is another name for 'aster'?

15) What took place in Caernarvon Castle on 1 July 1969?

16) Who lost his head in 1649?

17) When was President Kennedy assassinated?

18) What took place on 1 April 1973?

19) What time did the sun rise and set on 27 December 1970?

20) What is the capital of Massachusetts?

The answers to the following questions will be found in Roget's Thesaurus.

21) Find a synonym for 'angry'.

22) Find a synonym for 'lazy'.

23) Find a synonym for 'likable'.

24) Find a synonym for 'dress'.

25) Find a synonym for 'expert'.

26) Find a synonym for 'smelly'.

27) Find a synonym for 'impecunious'.

28) Find a synonym for 'well-behaved'.

29) Find a synonym for 'naughty'.

30) Find a synonym for 'kind'.

People

Information about famous people in this country is given in *Who's Who* (published annually).

International Who's Who lists famous people all over the world. There are several other *Who's Who's* giving specialised information – *Who's Who in Education* is an example.

Information about famous people who have died is given in *Who Was Who* and in the *Chambers' Biographical Dictionary* (prominent people all over the world).

People who have titles are listed in *Debrett's Peerage* and *Burke's Landed Gentry*.

Other specialised directories include:

Medical Register – doctors
Dentists' Register – dentists
Army List
Navy List } – lists of officers serving and retired
Air Force List
Crockford's Clerical Directory – clergy in the Church of England only
Directory of Directors – approximately 40 000 company directors with a list of their appointments
Black's Titles and Forms of Address – how to write and speak to titled people.

Exercise 35

USE OF *WHO'S WHO, INTERNATIONAL WHO'S WHO* AND *BLACK'S TITLES AND FORMS*

The answers to the following questions will be found in Who's Who.

1) What does Frank Muir list as his hobbies?

2) What are Mrs Thatcher's first names?

3) When did Lord (Harold) Wilson get married?

4) Who is Thomas Neilson Risk?

5) What does Denis Norden list as one of his hobbies?

6) What is the address of Patrick Moore, astronomer?

7) When did Lord Olivier marry Joan Plowright?

8) When did Dame Margot Fonteyn become President of the Royal Academy of Dancing?

9) Who is Brigid Brophy?

10) To which school did Lord Carrington go?

The answers to the following questions will be found in International Who's Who.

11) When was Dino de Laurentis born?

12) Who is Rosella Falk?

13) What did Naum Gabo publish in 1962?

14) When did Princess Grace marry Prince Rainier of Monaco?

15) Who is Edward Gierek?

16) When was Stefan Askenase born?

17) When was Charles Edward Barnes born?

18) What is Paul Clark's middle name?

19) Who is George Biddle?

20) When was the Hon. John Robert Nicholson born?

The answers to the following questions will be found in Black's Titles and Forms of Address.

21) If you spoke to the Queen, how would you address her?

22) How would you address an envelope to a retired Bishop?

23) What is the correct complimentary close on a letter to a Duchess?

24) Do the younger sons of a baronet have any form of title?

25) What does BAO stand for?

26) How would you address an envelope to an Archdeacon?

27) How would you speak to a Justice of the Peace when he is presiding on the Bench in Court?

28) What does 'Cantab' stand for?

29) What is the correct pronunciation of the name Knyvett?

30) If you were talking to Princess Anne, what would you call her?

Places and Travel

Books which could be useful for information on places and travel include:

- a large atlas — gives information about climate, products, population, terrain, rivers, oceans, lakes, boundaries, principal cities
- road maps — essential for car drivers
- *A – Z street maps* are available for most large cities in the British Isles
- *AA* or *RAC Handbooks* (free for members only) contain useful maps, information about hotels, ferries, distances between cities, population
- bus and train timetables

Large street maps are available in many libraries and are useful for strangers visiting cities.

ABC Railway Guide ABC World Airways Guide ABC Shipping Guide	They are essential for planning journeys. They contain detailed information about trains, ships, flights and are issued every month.
ABC Hotel Guide	This is a supplement to ABC World Airways Guide and is published twice-yearly, every January and June. It gives a comprehensive list of the main hotels all over the world.
ABC Travel Guide	This is issued quarterly and contains all the information necessary for travellers by air – about inoculations, vaccinations, visas, currency.
Hints to Businessmen	This is free, and is produced by the Department of Trade. It contains advice on consulates, hotels, customs and visas.
Statesman's Yearbook	Contains current information on countries of the world and international organisations.

Exercise 36

USE OF TRAVEL REFERENCE BOOKS

The answers to the following questions will be found in the AA Handbook.

1) Which is the hotel in Worcester with the best food according to the AA?

2) Which is early closing day in Chichester?

3) Which day is market day in Ironbridge?

4) What is the distance from Keswick to London?

5) Which hotel in Spalding has rooms with private baths?

6) What are the licensing hours in Cambridge on weekdays?

7) What time is last post on Friday in Hereford?

8) Which county is Fleetwood in?

9) What is the population of Abberley?

10) Which restaurant in Buckingham meets the AA's Approved Standard?

The answers to the following questions will be found in the ABC Rail Guide.

11) What is the charge for sending luggage in advance from any British Rail Station in Great Britain (collection, conveyance and delivery)?

12) Is it possible for a passenger to insure himself or herself when travelling by rail?

13) Is it possible for a passenger to insure his or her luggage when travelling by rail?

14) What is the maximum age for a child to travel free on a train?

15) What is a 'Rover' rail ticket?

16) What are Motorail services?

17) Give one special facility for handicapped passengers.

18) What is the extra charge for reserving a seat on a train?

19) Is it possible to reserve a seat on a train by telephone?

20) If you were travelling by train to Bournemouth from London, at which station would you catch your train?

21) What is the telephone number for Passenger Service Information at Euston station?

22) What is the time of the first train from Charing Cross for Canterbury?

23) Is there a train on a Monday at 0427 from St Pancras to Barnsley?

24) What is the first train after 1200 from Coventry to London on a Saturday?

The answers to the following questions will be found in the ABC World Airways Guide.

25) What were the Bank Holidays in China last year?

26) What is the address of Air Tasmania?

27) Codes are used in the *ABC World Airways Guide* for cities. Which city has the code letters BRS?

28) Which city has the code letters BHX?

29) Flight Routing No 500 flies between which cities?

30) Flight Routing No 796 flies between which cities?

31) What is the name of the currency used in Poland?

32) What is the flying distance between Paris and Washington, DC?

33) What is the name of the Soviet airlines?

34) Air Nuigini is the national airline of which country?

35) What is the name of the currency used in Malaysia?

36) What were the Bank Holidays in Luxembourg last year?

37) What is the flying distance between Belgrade and Vienna?

38) Which city has the code letters COV?

39) Of which airline is 001 the code number?

The answers to the following questions will be found in the ABC Shipping Guide.

40) What is the Paris address of the CTC shipping line?

41) How many sailings are there on European Car Ferries between Great Britain and the Channel Islands?

42) How long does it take to sail between Folkestone and Calais by Sealink?

43) What is the address of Sealink UK Limited?

44) Which shipping line owns the *Chrissi Ammos*?

45) Has the ship *Adabelle Lykes* air-conditioned accommodation?

46) What is the address for the shipping office of Paquet Cruises?

47) Do Paquet Cruises carry cars?

48) Which countries do Paquet Cruises sail between?

49) What are the ports in Saudi Arabia?

50) Are there any shipping lines which operate in either of these ports?

51) What is the name of the shipping line which sails to Itea?

52) What type of ship is the *Bugel Eussa*?

53) What is the address of the Stena Line?

54) Which shipping line owns the *Queen Elizabeth 2*?

The answers to the following questions will be found in The Statesman's Yearbook.

55) What does USSR stand for?

56) What was the old name for Thailand?

57) Name the chief religion and currency in Chile.

58) When did India become a republic?

59) Which church in Sweden has the most members?

60) Who discovered the Fiji Islands?

61) Where are Andorra and Liechtenstein?

62) How many islands go to make up Japan?

63) When was the Declaration of Independence made by America?

64) When did the last Russian Emperor abdicate?

London→Reading→Swindon→Gloucester→Cheltenham Spa

Mondays to Saturdays

Station			125	125	125	125	125	125	125	125	SX
			Ⓨ	⚬	Ⓨ	Ⓨ	Ⓨ	Ⓨ	Ⓨ	Ⓨ	⚬
Paddington	d	—	0725	0835	0935	1035	1205	1335	1435	1535	1627
Reading	d	—	0753	0903	1003	1103	1203	1403	1459	1603	1658
Swindon	d	0730	0848	0942	1042	1142	1300	1442	1542	1642	1740
Kemble	a	0745	0903	0957	1057	1157	1315	1457	1557	1657	1755
Stroud	a	0801	0919	1013	1113	1213	1331	1513	1613	1713	1810
Stonehouse	a	0806	0924	1018	1118	1218	1336	1518	1618	1718	—
Gloucester	a	0819	0937	1031	1131	1231	1353	1531	1631	1731	1827
Cheltenham Spa	a	0833	0953	1045	1153	1245	1409	1545	1647	1820	1842

Mondays to Saturdays

Station		125		125	125	125	125	125	125	125
		SO	SO	SX			SX	C	D	E
		Ⓨ	⚬					Ⓨ	Ⓨ	
Paddington	d	1625	1727	1742	1835	2000	2140	2340	2350	2355
Reading	d	1649	1759	1729	1903	2024	2208	0007	0024	0029
Swindon	d	1742	1840	1837	1942	2102	2248	0050	0105	0200
Kemble	a	1757	1855	1851	1957	2118	2303	0106	0120	0230s
Stroud	a	1813	1910	1905	2013	2134	2319	0123	0136	0255s
Stonehouse	a	1818	1915	1910	2018	2139	2324	0128	0141	0305s
Gloucester	a	1832	1930	1923	2034	2152	2337	0141	0155	0325s
Cheltenham Spa	a	1851	1951	1937	2048	2205	2350	0155	0225h	0345s

Sundays until 1 January

Station				125		125	125	
Paddington	d	—	0940	1036	1435	1620	1835	2100
Reading	d	—	1021	1109	1508	1652	1903	2124
Swindon	d	0955	—	1235	1550	1734	1945	2210
Kemble	a	1025	—	1305	1605	1753	2000	2225
Stroud	a	1050	—	1330	1621	1808	2016	2241
Stonehouse	a	1100	—	1340	1626	1813	2021	2246
Gloucester	a	1120	1305	1400	1644	1830	2034	2259
Cheltenham Spa	a	1140	1245	1420	1656	1851	2104	2312

Sundays from 8 January

Station		125	125	125	125	125		125	125
		Ⓨ	Ⓨ						
Paddington	d	0805	0845	1130	1135	1435	1820	1835	2100
Reading	d	0843	0919	1204	1213	1508	1852	1903	2124
Swindon	d	0919	1000	1236	1255	1550	1734	1945	2210
Kemble	a	—	1015	—	1310	1606	1753	2000	2225
Stroud	a	—	1031	—	1326	1621	1808	2016	2241
Stonehouse	a	—	1036	—	1331	1626	1813	2021	2246
Gloucester	a	0958	1051	1317	1346	1644	1830	2034	2259
Cheltenham Spa	a	—	1120	—	1400	1658	1851	2104	2312

Information

Times shown in heavy type (e.g. **2050**) represent through services: those in light type (e.g. 0040) indicate connecting services and passengers are advised to enquire where to change trains.

This folder shows the complete service between

London, Reading, Swindon
and
Kemble, Stroud, Stonehouse, Gloucester, Cheltenham Spa.

Other timetables give the service between stations in each group.

Notes

C   Monday night/Tuesday morning to Friday night/Saturday morning
D   Saturday night/Sunday morning from 7/8 January
E   Saturday night/Sunday morning until 31 December/1 January. Special bus connection from Newbury.
SX   Saturdays excepted
SO   Saturdays only
125   Service scheduled to be operated by InterCity 125 for all or part of journey

Catering available for whole or part of journey:
Ⓨ   Hot dishes to order, also buffet service of drinks and cold snacks
⚬   Drinks and cold snacks

Adapted from British Rail timetable by kind permission — not now in operation!

Exercise 37

USING A RAILWAY TIMETABLE

Refer to the timetable on p. 184, then answer the following questions:

1) What does SX mean?

2) What do *a* and *d* mean? (They are not mentioned in the notes but you should be able to work them out!)

3) What time does the earliest train leave Paddington on a weekday that goes to Cheltenham?

4) On most of the trains from Paddington to Cheltenham you need to change at a particular station. Which one?

5) What is the first through train on a Saturday from Paddington to Cheltenham?

6) If you wanted to get to an afternoon appointment on a Sunday in Cheltenham at 2.40 pm, what train would you need to catch from Paddington (a) before 1 January, (b) after 8 January?

7) What significant advantage does the 2000 train have over the 2140 (apart from being earlier)?

8) If you got on the 1627 to Stonehouse and then looked at this time-table what would you do?

9) If you caught the 0940 on Sunday before 1 January you would arrive in Cheltenham at 1245. True or false?

10) '125' means

    A There is a limit of 125 seats on the train

    B Service scheduled to be operated by Intercity 125 for all or part of the journey.

    C The distance from Paddington to Cheltenham is 125 miles

Travel Arrangements

The first step in arranging a business trip is to draft an itinerary based on the places to be visited and the time to be spent at each one. This is just as important (and useful) for a day's visit to London as it is for a fortnight's visit to Singapore.

An itinerary is a programme of travel arrangements which gives dates and times of arrival and departure for a person about to undertake a journey. In addition, names, addresses and telephone numbers of hotels are given if the traveller's journey involves staying away from home.

The method of travel has to be decided (and although these days it is usually air for an overseas trip) it may occasionally be combined with road or sea for various reasons. In any case, periods of relaxation must be incorporated into a long trip, to avoid over-tiredness and to allow the traveller time to write reports and meet people unofficially.

When the itinerary has been approved, hotel and flight reservations are made together with arrangements for transport to and from the airport and hotel. Copies of letters (or Telexes) making hotel bookings should be placed into a travel folder, so that there is no question of a misunderstanding on arrival.

Travel documents include passport, any visas necessary, health certificates and insurance. These should all be placed in a separate wallet together with tickets and currency, so that they are available for the journey. A small amount of the currency of each country to be visited (or stopped in, however briefly) is necessary, if only to buy a cup of coffee and a newspaper. Traveller's cheques are essential for large sums of currency , but they are not very useful for paying for small items.

Lastly, when all reservations have been confirmed, the itinerary can be retyped in its final form. If the trip is to be a long one, separate itineraries should be typed for each day (or even half day) on A6 card so that they can be slipped into pocket or handbag for quick reference.

Mr J K Haldane's visit to London 10 May 198—	
0700	depart Hereford Station
0957	arrive Paddington Station, London
1030	J K Tonkins & Co Ltd, Uxbridge Road, Shepherd's Bush. Telephone: 879331 Meeting with Mrs Pauline Tedder, Company Secretary
1300	J K Tonkins & Co Ltd Lunch with Directors in the Board Room
1530	Twist Dunnem & Swindle, Solicitors, 107 High Street, Ruislip. Telephone: 333241 Meeting with Miss L Carr
1700	depart Paddington Station
1945	arrive Hereford
2100	The White Hart Hotel, Hereford Dinner with Mr and Mrs G Barnes

An itinerary

FOR YOUR FOLDER

28. MAKING TRAVEL ARRANGEMENTS

Write these notes in your folder, filling in the missing words and phrases.

1) An itinerary is a _____ of travel arrangements which gives dates and times of _____ and departure for a person about to undertake a _____.

2) The first step in arranging a business trip is to draft an _____.

3) Travel documents for an overseas journey include passport, any visas necessary, _____ and insurance.

4) Traveller's cheques are essential, and also a small amount of the _____ of each country to be visited is necessary, to pay for small items such as a cup of coffee or a newspaper.

5) If the trip is to be a long one, _____ itineraries should be typed for each day or half-day on _____ card so that they can be slipped into pocket or handbag for quick _____.

Exercise 38

PLANNING AN ITINERARY

Work out an itinerary for Ms Diana Devinson for Thursday next (give the date). She is going to Cheltenham by train, but she wants to leave Paddington as late as possible. (See the timetable on p.184.) Rearrange the times of her appointments, train arrivals and departures in the correct order:

Ms Devinson is having lunch at the Cotswold Grange, five miles from Cheltenham station, with Mr J K Haldane, at 1245.

After lunch (at 1430) she will tour round Haldane's Hosiery Works, which will be followed by tea at the Hosiery Works at 1600. Tea is likely to finish at 1630 and there is a train to Paddington at 1728.

THE LONDON UNDERGROUND

Lines

| VICTORIA | CENTRAL | CIRCLE | DISTRICT | METROPOLITAN | NORTHERN | BAKERLOO | PICCADILLY | JUBILEE |

East London Section

Under Construction

◯ Interchange with other Underground Lines

✦ Interchange with British Rail

■ Exhibition Service only

† Open during Monday to Friday rush hours only

Certain Stations are closed at Weekends and during Public Holidays

Exercise 39

THE LONDON UNDERGROUND

1) You are at Euston Station and want to get to Charing Cross. Which underground line would you take?

2) Which line would you take to get from Charing Cross to Tower Hill?

3) From Tower Hill, which line would you take to Liverpool Street Station?

4) From Liverpool Street Station, what lines would you take to get back to Euston and where would you change?

5) From Victoria Station which line would take you to King's Cross?

6) From King's Cross, how would you get to Edgware?

7) From King's Cross, how would you get to Euston?

8) From Paddington, how would you get to Oxford Circus?

The Telephonist's Reference Books

The telephonist will find many of the books mentioned in this chapter useful, but she will also need to refer to the books listed on p. 90.

The Receptionist's Reference Books

Many of the books mentioned in this chapter will be useful for receptionists, but she may need additional books, pamphlets and magazines to help deal with visitor's enquiries. These may include:

● Local guides to the area
● A map of the local area
● Local bus and train timetables
● A brochure on the firm's activities for visitors' information
● Egon Ronay's *Just A Bite* (cheap meal guide).

Books in the Mail Room

The Post Office Guide is a 'must' in the mail room and several other books will be needed too. We shall deal with these in Chapter 9.

Miscellaneous Reference Books

Willings Press Guide	Contains a list of all British, and principal European periodicals and newspapers, together with the addresses and telephone numbers of the publishing offices.
Books in Print	Lists all books available with title, publisher, author and price.
Hansard	Is the official report of Parliamentary proceedings and contains a 'verbatim' (word for word) account of debates in Parliament.
Keesings Contemporary Archives	Contains information on current events, updated each week.

Exercise 40

USE OF *WILLINGS PRESS GUIDE*

1) How many publications are there for chess players?

2) How many publications are there for people who keep horses, or are interested in them?

3) How many newspapers are published in Suffolk?

4) What are the names of the newspapers published in Cambridge?

5) What are the names of the newspapers published in Southall?

6) What is the address and telephone number of the head office of the *Kentish Times?*

7) What is the address and telephone number of the head office of the *Newcastle Journal?*

8) How often is *Kempe's Engineers' Yearbook* published?

9) How often is the *Police Gazette* published?

10) Is the general public able to buy the *Police Gazette?*

A Final Hint

If you cannot find the information in the book you think should contain it, try somewhere else. Not all dictionaries have the less usual words and not every encyclopaedia will tell you who Sweeney Todd was. Just keep trying different possibilities – and if you really do get stuck, your local library is there to help!

Exercise 41

CHOOSING THE RIGHT REFERENCE BOOK

In which reference book (or books) would you look to find the following information:

1)   The meaning of an abbreviation you do not understand?

2)   Regulations controlling the type of Christmas present to a friend in Kuwait?

3)   How to address a letter to Lord Carrington?

4)   The name and address of a manufacturer of squash racquets?

5)   The number of votes the Labour Party were given in the last General Election?

6)   The meaning of the word 'misrule'?

7)   The actual name of Pope John Paul II?

8)   At least four other words with the same meaning as 'calm'?

9)   Which day is market day in Barnard Castle?

10)   The population of Montevideo?

11)   The telephone number and address of all the firms in Newcastle-upon-Tyne manufacturing rope?

12)   The departure and arrival times of a train from Plymouth to London?

13)   Whether Chile is mountainous or flat and its climate?

14)   The telephone dialling code for Brussels?

15)   Information about the growing of silk?

16)   Whether to use 'further' or 'farther' in a piece of written English?

17)   What UNESCO means?

18)   Information about a large firm in your town?

19)   The newspapers and magazines published in Carlisle?

20)   Information about an event which took place last week and was the subject of much discussion on radio, television and in the national newspapers?

Exercise 42

GETTING INFORMATION FROM THE RIGHT REFERENCE BOOK

The answers to the following questions will be found in a dictionary, Who's Who, Black's Titles and Forms of Address, Post Office Guide, International Telephone Guide, Roget's Thesaurus, Willings Press Guide, the AA Handbook or the RAC Handbook.

1) Who is Roald Dahl?

2) How should the envelope be addressed which contains a letter to the Duchess of Kent?

3) Is it possible to send saccharin to Albania?

4) What day each week is there a cattle market in Loughborough?

5) What is the correct pronunciation of the word 'mnemonic'?

6) What is the meaning of 'mnemonic'?

7) Find as many other words as you can with the same meaning as 'mnemonic'.

8) Who are the publishers of *Woman's Weekly*?

9) Where was Edward Heath born?

10) If you were speaking to the Dean of Westminster, what would you call him?

11) What would be the time in Greenland when it is 1400 in this country?

12) When did Glenda Jackson appear on TV as Elizabeth I?

13) How far from London is Paignton?

14) How much does *Sporting Life* cost?

15) *L'Express* is a Swiss newspaper. How often is it published?

16) What are the several different meanings of the word 'mite'?

17) Who is Peter de Polnay?

18) Is it possible to send a Telex message to Wake Island?

19) If you were speaking to Princess Margaret, what would you call her?

20) Where would you write about advertising in *Honey*?

21) When did John le Carré write *Tinker Tailor Soldier Spy*?

22) What is the population of Lymm?

23) What does the abbreviation 'cdv' mean?

24) Which are the only football pools coupons which are allowed into Sarawak?

SECTION C DEALING WITH PAPERWORK

CHAPTER 9

The Mail Room

The Room Itself

Most firms large enough to be divided into departments have a mail room where letters and parcels are delivered by the postmen, and where all outgoing mail is stamped, or franked, before being taken to the post office or post box for collection. Staff working in a mail room are trained by a supervisor and are efficient and (eventually) experienced, so that mail is dealt with promptly, both incoming and outgoing.

A well-organised mail room will contain scales (two types) for weighing both letters and parcels, franking machine, possibly other equipment for dealing with large quantities of outgoing mail, as well as mail room accessories and reference books for the staff to use to deal with any queries. Shelves and tables should be arranged to make it easier for the staff to carry out sorting incoming mail, and placing outgoing mail into the various categories ready for posting.

The illustration below shows one way in which a mail room could be arranged, and this is similar to a layout recommended by the Post Office for efficient handling of mail. The Post Office is extremely anxious that firms should organise their mail competently, as this makes the work of Post Office staff simpler.

A well-arranged mail room

Incoming Mail

Mail arriving at a firm may include many different documents besides letters. There may be invoices, quotations, estimates, orders, applications for jobs and advertising material. It is very important to open and distribute the mail to the different departments without delay, so that the office staff and managers are able to make a start on their day's work. In a large firm, mail room staff may take it in turns to come in before other office workers in order to make sure that all the mail has been taken round to the departments by the time the office workers are ready to start. In a small office, the manager may open and deal with the letters himself.

One type of letter would never be opened except by the person to whom it is addressed. This is a letter marked 'Personal', 'Private' or 'Confidential', which would be placed on one side and handed over to the addressee unopened as soon as possible.

Styles of addressing a confidential letter

In order to be certain that mail is in an office early in the morning, some firms arrange with the Post Office to rent one of the Post Office Private Boxes at a delivery office. Letters and packets may be collected at any time from a private box, except on Sundays, or days when the Post Office does not deliver. Firms using this service are given a number by the Post Office to use as part of their address. The Post Office makes a yearly charge for private boxes. A similar arrangement is possible for a private bag, into which a firm's mail is sorted at the delivery office, and which can be collected by the firm using it on normal Post Office delivery days. A charge is made by the Post Office for private bags, too.

If a firm has no private box or bag at the Post Office's delivery office, mail will be delivered in the normal way by a postman to the reception desk of the firm, and mail room clerks will collect it from there using trolleys if there is a large quantity of letters and packets.

A Post Office Private Box

OPENING MAIL

As it is so important to open and distribute the mail quickly, following a daily routine ensures that it is done efficiently:

1) 'Face' envelopes (i.e. turn envelopes so that address is the right side up and the right way round). While doing this, take out any envelopes marked 'Private' and place them on one side, unopened, for delivery with the opened mail.

'Faced' mail

2) In some firms, it is usual to divide incoming mail into first and second-class, opening the first-class mail first, as it is (generally) more important. Second-class mail is a slower and cheaper service, normally taking two days to deliver. First- and second-class postal services are known as the 'two-tier' system.

3) Open envelopes by slitting *both* long edges. This can be done with a paper knife, or, more quickly, with an electrically operated letter opener.

A paper knife

An electrically operated letter opener

The electric letter opener removes a very narrow strip or 'sliver' of paper from the edge of an envelope, so narrow that it is unlikely to damage the contents, but in order to make sure that this does not happen, the envelope must be tapped on the desk so that the contents drop to the bottom of the envelope. Slitting both long edges makes it easy to check very quickly that nothing has been left accidentally in the envelope. Some mail rooms keep opened envelopes for a few days in case of queries. The address or postmark on the envelope may be useful.

Nothing left in the envelope!

4) Unfold letters, or other documents, smoothing them out flat, and apply a date-stamp, taking care not to stamp over any of the typing or writing on the paper. Some firms use a stamp which automatically prints the time on the document as well as the date. Dating incoming mail is an

important check on when it was actually received in the mail room. An envelope marked 'Private' would be date stamped on the (unopened) envelope.

Examples of date-stamps. The one on the right is an automatic date-stamp

5) Some letters, or documents, may have enclosures attached to them, or folded with them. Enclosures may be: catalogues, price-lists, leaflets, samples, photographs, cheques, stamps or postal orders. If they have not been attached to the letter, they should be stapled to it at the top left-hand corner. Pins and paper clips are not suitable as they have a tendency to catch on to other papers by mistake. Photographs may be kept together with paper clips but it is advisable to protect a glossy surface from direct contact with a clip.

If there is more than one sheet of paper in an envelope (a continuation sheet to a letter, or enclosures) make sure they are kept together — once separated, it may be difficult to tell to which letter they belong.

A long-arm stapler

A stapler

Letters containing money in any form should have the amount and the initials of the person opening the letter in pencil at the foot of the letter – this helps as a check in case of any later query. In some firms a remittances book is used into which all money received is entered before being taken to the cashier or the mail room supervisor. An entry in this book shows the date of receipt for each sum of money, the person or firm who sent it, and the amount. It also shows whether the money was received as a cheque, postal order or cash, and the signature of the person who recorded the information. The money goes with the opened letter and is eventually passed on to the cashier in the accounts department.

DATE	SENDER	REMITTANCE	AMOUNT £ p	SIGNATURE
198–				
June 1st	M.L. Mann and Co. Ltd	Cheque	20—00	P. Fox
June 1st	Mrs F. Hopkins	P.O.	2—00	P. Fox
June 2	Messrs. Page & Vines	Chq.	49—75	S. Smith
June 4	Mr H.M. Harrison	Cash	10—00	S. Smith
June 4	Miss G. Manson	P.O.	5—00	J. Johnson
June 5	P.K. Engineering	Cheque	97.44	J. Johnson

A page from a remittances book

Exercise 43

THE REMITTANCES BOOK

Copy a remittances book page and rule it up.

Using today's date, enter the following remittances which have been received with this morning's mail. Initial the entries yourself.

Mrs O Marsh enclosed a postal order for £5.50
Miss K Neale enclosed a cheque for £10
Messrs Lang and Dunn enclosed a cheque for £50
Mr P Barnes enclosed £45 in notes
Mr F Pearce enclosed a cheque for £9
Miss M Knowles enclosed a postal order for 50p
Mrs R Frost enclosed 45p in stamps
Messrs Nash and Grimes enclosed a cheque for £34.75.

A register of incoming mail may be kept by a small firm; in most large firms this is no longer the practice.

Missing enclosures should be noted in pencil and initialled at the foot of the letter by the person opening it. It is easy to tell, in most cases, whether a letter should have an enclosure by a quick glance, as there are several ways in which a typist or secretary may indicate that something is attached to a letter:

a 'Enc.' (which is the abbreviation for 'Enclosure') typed at the bottom left-hand side of a letter.

b A small label with 'Enc.' or 'Enclosure' printed on it, affixed to the letter. Some firms instruct their typists and secretaries to stick a label on the envelope, too, as an extra check. Enclosure labels may be numbered, for reference when replying to the letter.

c The symbol / typed in the left-hand margin alongside the sentence which refers to the enclosure.

d Three dots typed in the left-hand margin alongside the sentence which refers to the enclosure.

e The enclosures are listed at the bottom of the letter.

c and **d** are used less frequently than **a**, **b** or **e**.

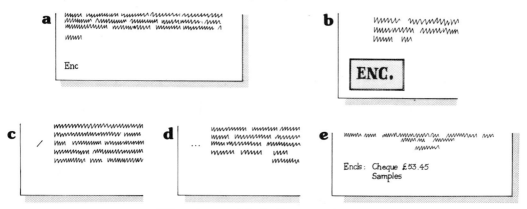

Different ways of indicating an enclosure

Distributing Mail to Different Departments

While sorting the mail, the mail room clerks will be looking for the following to help them to decide where to send it:

● 'For the attention of (followed by name)'. This would be typed under the inside address on a letter immediately *over* 'Dear Sir'.

● The letter may have a subject heading typed underneath 'Dear Sir'.

● There may be a reference at the top of the letter. This is usually the initials of the sender of the letter followed by the initials of his typist or secretary.

If the letter does not contain any of the above information, it will be helpful to read it through quickly.

Not all letters come by post. Some are delivered by firms' messengers and are inter-departmental. This is known as internal mail and, if confidential, may be enclosed in large envelopes which are printed with lines for the name of each recipient so that after opening the name is crossed out and the next name written underneath. Letters between offices, departments and even branches of the same firm, are known as 'memos' (see Chapter 6).

An envelope for internal mail (holes show whether it is empty or not)

Parcels may arrive later in the day, as may mail which has to be signed for in the presence of the postman. Into this latter category will come registered letters and recorded delivery. There is more information about these Post Office services in the next chapter.

It may be the responsibility of the mail room supervisor to arrange for a letter to be seen by more than one person, if the letter mentions several topics. She could arrange for this to be done by:

- asking a typist to type a copy with several carbon copies
- photocopying it
- sending the letter to each person or department accompanied by a routing slip (see p. 135).

The choice of which method to adopt would depend on the urgency with which the letter had to be circulated. Photocopying is the quickest and most accurate, but it is also the most expensive. Carbon copies are the cheapest but the typist may make a mistake which could be serious. This method is slow, too. A routing slip also may take time as some people on the list could hold on to the letter thus delaying its progress round to the others on the list.

A trolley

Wire letter trays

Pigeon holes. Note that the letters are laid flat

FOR YOUR FOLDER

29. INCOMING MAIL

Write these notes in your folder, filling in the missing words and phrases.

1) Mail arriving at a firm may include (besides letters) applications for jobs, orders, advertising material and _____.

2) It is very important to distribute the mail to the different departments without delay so that the _____ are able to make a start on _____.

3) In a large firm, mail room staff may _____ in order to make sure that all the mail has been distributed by the time the office workers are ready to start.

4) The type of letter which would *never* be opened in the mail room is marked _____ or _____ or _____.

5) In order to be certain that the mail arrives at offices early in the morning some firms arrange with the Post Office to rent a _____ at a delivery office.

6) Sorting incoming mail starts with removing any marked 'Private' and _____ the envelopes containing the remainder of the mail.

7) Envelopes should be slit (either by paper knife or electric letter opener) along both _____ so that it is easy to check very quickly that _____.

8) When envelopes have been opened and contents removed, the letters or other documents should be _____ or _____ on a suitable blank space.

9) Enclosures should be _____ to the letters.

10) If the enclosure is money in any form (a remittance), the amount should be _____ and the initials of the person opening the letter in pencil at the foot of the letter.

11) In some firms a _____ book is used to enter all money received and is taken to the cashier or mail room supervisor.

12) Missing enclosures should be _____.

13) It is easy to tell whether there should be an enclosure with a letter by 'Enc.' typed at the foot of the letter,/in the left-hand margin, a small label with 'Enc.' or 'Enclosure' printed on or _____.

14) To help them sort the mail, mail room clerks will look for 'For the attention of _____, subject heading or _____.

15) Not all letters come by post. Some are from other departments and are known as _____ mail.

16) Parcels, registered mail and _____ may arrive later in the day.

17) Useful items for dealing with incoming mail are: stapler, trolley, wire letter trays, pigeon holes and _____.

Exercise 44

INCOMING MAIL

1) Describe the 'two-tier' system of mail delivery by the Post Office.

2) Explain how you would deal with a letter which should have been accompanied by a cheque and the cheque was not in the envelope.

3) How can you quickly make sure that a letter does not have an enclosure?

4) Describe how you can decide where to deliver a letter.

5) How should all money be dealt with in incoming mail?

6) List some equipment for dealing with incoming mail.

7) Why is it necessary for staff dealing with incoming mail to arrive before other office staff?

8) There are several ways of arranging for more than one person to see a letter. Which is

a quickest?
b cheapest?
c (in your opinion) most efficient (ignoring cost)?

9) Why are opened envelopes sometimes kept for a few days before being destroyed?

10) How could a mail room clerk make absolutely sure that she/he had left nothing in an envelope by accident?

Outgoing Mail

Mail for posting may arrive at any time during the day, but the afternoons are the busiest times in the mail room, and to avoid a sudden rush of mail, a system of regular collection from every department should be organised. Trays marked 'Outgoing Mail' placed where the messenger from the mail room can conveniently collect the mail at frequent intervals ensures that letters for posting are dealt with promptly. The mail room may also state a final collection time, after which no mail will be accepted for that day. This will avoid mail room staff having to stay late to deal with a last-minute rush and will ensure that Post Office collection times can be met.

In some firms, letters are sent to the mail room already folded and inserted into envelopes, with a pencilled '1' or '2' in the top right-hand corner, to show whether the letter has to go by first or second-class post. It will still be necessary to weigh a letter if it is bulky or seems heavier than the maximum weight allowed by the Post Office for minimum first-class or second-class postage. An addressee receiving a letter without enough stamps on it has to pay the postman the missing amount of postage (second-class) plus 10p so the sender will not be popular!

A letter with insufficient postage

205

Other letters which must be weighed are letters going abroad, whether by airmail or 'surface' mail. Airmail is expensive, and special thin paper and envelopes cut the cost down. There is also an airmail letter form (of A4 size) available at post offices which is the cheapest way to send letters by air. This is called an 'aerogramme'. 'Surface' mail is carried by train, ship or van, and is cheaper than airmail but slower.

In many firms, letters and other documents are sent to the mail room accompanied by correctly typed envelopes, and the mail room clerk's job is to fold and insert the letters into the envelopes. While she is doing this, she should:

- check by looking at the letter to see if there should be an enclosure. If the enclosure is missing, the letter should be placed on one side and later returned to the sender.
- if there is an enclosure, attach it to the letter by stapling or, if not suitable, paper-clip. Pins should never be used as the person opening the envelope may receive a sharp jab.
- check that letter has been signed.
- check that inside address is the same as that on the accompanying envelope. If not, again put letter and envelope on one side for querying either with sender or mail room supervisor. 'Window' or 'aperture' envelopes are often used by firms to avoid the possibility of sending a letter to the wrong person or firm.

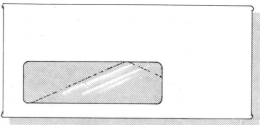

A window envelope. This envelope has a transparent panel

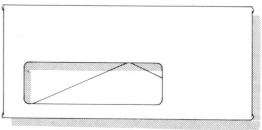

An aperture envelope. 'Aperture' is another word for 'space'. This envelope has space through which the address on the letter can be read

- fold the letter so that it fits the envelope with as few creases as possible. This is not as easy as it sounds, and most mail rooms have a special way of doing it. Some firms print their letterheading with small marks near the edges which indicate where the letter has to be folded.

- place the letter (with enclosure if there is one) into a suitably sized envelope and seal. The Post Office prefers envelopes to be within certain sizes (90 mm × 140 mm and 120 mm × 235 mm). These are known as POP envelopes (Post Office Preferred).
- weigh the letter if bulky (it may need extra postage) or if it is addressed to a country overseas.
- affix correct stamps and place letter into one of the following three categories:
    (i) *Inland* – anywhere in the British Isles
    (ii) *Overseas* – both airmail and surface mail
    (iii) *Registered Post or Recorded Delivery* – for which a receipt has to be obtained from post offices. They cannot be posted in a letter box (see pp. 229-30).

BULKY LETTERS

It is important not to cram too much into a small or flimsy envelope. It may break open in the post and the contents may not reach their destination. Sometimes the Post Office will rewrap broken packages with special tape.

For sending long documents (say 200 sheets of A4) a zip-up plastic bag can be very useful. The zip is held down by a stud and the address and postage information are placed in special slits. Such a bag will only be sent if it is likely to be returned, of course. An alternative is the padded bag (or Jiffy bag).

This...   or this...

will avoid the Post Office having to use this brown adhesive tape...

Post Office	P144 Date Stamp	Post Office	P144 Date Stamp
Found open or damaged and officially secured		**Found open or damaged and officially secured**	
Arrivé ouvert ou avarié et remis en état		Arrivé ouvert ou avarié et remis en état	
Initials _____	480169	Initials _____	480169

FOR YOUR FOLDER

30. OUTGOING MAIL

Write these notes in your folder, filling in the missing words and phrases.

1) The busiest time of the day in the mail room is the _____.

2) An instruction to the mail room about affixing a first-class or second-class stamp to a letter is by _____.

3) Letters which should be weighed to check if any extra postage is needed are airmail, surface mail and _____ letters.

4) Any letter which is under-stamped is penalised by the Post Office. The postman has to collect the amount underpaid (second-class rate) plus _____ from the unfortunate recipient!

5) Before placing a letter into an envelope and sealing it, the mail room clerk should check enclosures (if any), signature on letter and _____.

6) _____ envelopes are often used by firms to avoid the possibility of sending a letter to the wrong address.

7) POP (Post Office Preferred) envelopes are envelopes which the Post Office prefer to be within _____.

8) After envelopes are sealed, outgoing mail should be divided into three main categories – inland, overseas and _____.

Stamps

Stamps need to be kept dry and free from damage in a special book. Later we shall learn about the franking machine, but it is always a good plan to keep a few stamps for an emergency, such as when the franking machine has broken down and you need to send out an urgent letter.

Using a stamp book

The Postage Book

A postage book gives a detailed record of all letters, packets and parcels posted. An example is shown below.

STAMPS BOUGHT	NAME AND TOWN OF ADDRESSEE	STAMPS USED	DETAILS
£ P		£ P	
20. 00	21 June 198–		
	F. Jones Ipswich	17	
	L. Naylor Cardiff	17	
	P. Knight Coventry	34	Rec. delivery
	S. Singh Calcutta, India	42	Airmail
	K. Wilson & Sons Ltd Reading	1. 16	Reg. letter
	J. Ross & Co Ltd Hove	17	
	A.B. Rowe & Co Rugby	3. 10	Parcel
		5. 53	
	Balance c/f	14. 47	
20. 00		20. 00	
5. 53	22 June 198–		
14. 47	Balance b/f		

Exercise 45

THE POSTAGE BOOK

Copy the postage book above and use it to make entries for the questions below. Using Postal Rates leaflets, work out the correct postage.

1) Stamps bought £25. Use today's date.
   First-class letter D Smythe, Canterbury
   First-class letter L Barnett, Coventry
   Second-class letter M Mole, Stoke-on-Trent
   Parcel weighing 2 kg (Rate) to V Scott
   Parcel weighing 3 kg (Rate) to M Mason
   Airmail letter to C Dunsford, Madras, India: 30 g
   Registered letter (value of contents £350)

   Total the stamps used, find the balance, and bring it forward to the next day.

2) Copy the postage book above. From an up-to-date Postal Rates leaflet, find the correct postal rates for the following and enter them in the postage book:

209

Recorded Delivery letter (second-class) to P Tomkins, Hull
Recorded Delivery letter (first-class) to Messrs T Price, Rugby
Registered packet to J K Brown & Co Ltd, Sutton – value £375
Airmail packet to Montreal, Canada – weighing 110 g
First-class letter to Johnson, Bromsgrove
First-class letter to Hill, Redditch
Second-class letter (weighing 150 g) to Dawson, Cambridge.

THE RECORD OF STAMPS

A simple record of stamps is used in some firms as a check on the number of stamps used each day. Details of correspondents are omitted.

STAMPS BOUGHT	DATE	STAMPS USED	
£ P			£ P
15. 00	21 June 198–	30 @ 13	3. 90
		40 @ 17	6. 80
		10 @ 4	40
		Balance c/f	11. 10
			3. 90
15. 00			15. 00
3. 90	22 June 198–	Balance b/f	

Mail Room Equipment

A FRANKING MACHINE

A franking machine prints in red the value of a stamp on an envelope, postcard or label, as well as the date and time of posting, the place of posting, licence number of the machine, and an advertising slogan, if

A franking machine

Setting the postage rates

Franking a label

required. It saves the time spent on keeping a record of stamps used, as well as the trouble of sticking stamps on envelopes, parcels and packages.

Franking machines may be purchased or hired from the manufacturers. A licence to use the machine must first be obtained from the Post Office. There is no charge for this. The Post Office also sets a meter on a

Franked envelopes, one with an advertising slogan and the other a franked label (no advertising slogan). Labels would be affixed to parcels or letters too bulky to go through a franking machine

franking machine in accordance with the amount of money paid to them and then seals the meter. Each time an envelope, postcard or label is franked, this meter deducts the amount used – it is a 'descending' meter as the figures shown decrease. There is a second meter on a franking machine which increases or 'ascends' with each franked impression – this one is called an 'ascending' meter as the figures increase, showing the amount of postage used. A *franking meter control card* has to be sent to the Post Office every week, showing the reading of these two meters, even though no postage may have been used. Franking machines are lockable so that they cannot be used dishonestly. The mail room clerk whose responsibility it is to look after a franking machine has to reset the date each morning, and make sure the roller which holds the red ink making the impression does not need reinking. She also has to watch the 'descending' meter carefully, so that more money could be paid to the Post Office and the meter reset well before it is due to run out. A well-organised mail room will have a supply of postage stamps available in case the franking machine breaks down.

FRANKING MACHINE CONTROL CARD

Licensee . . . .
Meter Office
(as shown on Record Card) . . . .

Machine (or Meter) No . . . .

Setting or Recording Unit . . . .
I certify that the following particulars in respect of the above described machine for

week-ended . . . . are correct:—

	ALL MACHINES	LOCKING MACHINES	ALL MACHINES
	Reading of Ascending Register	Reading of Descending Register	Last entry in col. "Total Deposits" or "Total Settings" on Record Card
	(Totalisator)	(Credit Meter)	
Mon.			
Tue.			
Wed.			
Thur.			
Fri.			
Sat.			

NOTE 1. Whether or not the machine has been used, this card must be posted on Saturday, or on Friday if no postings are made on Saturday.
NOTE 2. The daily entry must be made on completion of each day's postings.

Signed . . . .

. . . . 19 . . . .

Franked mail or 'metered mail' as it is also called, can by-pass Post Office facing and cancelling in the Post Office sorting office, often catching earlier trains and planes. Because such mail saves the Post Office time, it has to be posted in a special way – either handed in over the counter of a post office, tied in bundles and 'faced' or posted in a letter box in a special envelope for franked mail.

If an envelope or label has the wrong value franked on it by mistake, it should be kept and returned to the Post Office (when the franking machine meter is taken for resetting would be a suitable time). A refund will be given less five per cent of the value franked.

Some firms still like to keep a record of outgoing mail, even though there is a franking machine in use, and this record will just consist of names and addresses of recipients of letters and parcels.

Larger franking machines incorporate equipment for sealing envelopes as well as stacking them after they have been franked.

A modern franking machine

The latest franking machine (above) has a remote meter resetting system, which allows postage to be bought by 'phone. There is no need for visits to the Post Office — postage credit is reset in seconds.

FOR YOUR FOLDER

31. THE FRANKING MACHINE

Write these notes in your folder, filling in the missing words and phrases.

1) A franking machine prints in red the value _____ on an envelope, label or postcard.

2) It also prints the date and time of posting, the place of posting, licence number of the machine and an _____ (if required).

3) A franking machine saves the time taken to stick stamps on envelopes, parcels and packages, and on keeping a _____ of stamps used.

4) Labels are franked and used for _____.

5) Franking machines may be _____ or hired from the manufacturers.

6) The Post Office issues a _____ (free of charge) for the use of franking machines.

7) Every week a franking machine _____ has to be sent to the Post Office.

8) A well-organised mail room will have a supply of _____ available in case the franking machine breaks down.

9) Another name for 'franked mail' is _____.

213

10) Franked mail is dealt with more quickly by the Post Office because it by-passes facing and _____.

11) Franked mail has to be posted in a special way — either handed in over the counter of a Post Office, tied in 'bundles' and 'faced' or _____.

12) If an envelope or label has the wrong value franked on it by mistake it should be kept and returned to the Post Office. A refund will be given less _____.

FRANKING MACHINE CONTROL CARD

A franking machine control card is required weekly by the Post Office as a check that the franking machine is operating correctly, and also as a safeguard in case of fire or theft.

The franking machine control card below has been completed from the following details:

Name:	Jones & Williams Bros
Meter office:	Cardiff Post Office
Unit:	1p
Machine number:	H1202
Number of units purchased:	42000 ⎱ at commencement of week
Number of units used:	34602 ⎰

Monday	used	3286
Tuesday	used	1908
Wednesday	purchased	5000
Wednesday	used	972
Thursday	used	2234
Friday	used	1451

FRANKING MACHINE CONTROL CARD

Licensee.. JONES + WILLIAMS BROS LTD

Machine (or Meter No.).. H 1202   Setting or Recording Unit...... 1p

Meter Office (as shown on Record Card). CARDIFF POST OFFICE

CHECK DATE DAILY

I certify that the following entries for the above machine for the week ended..are correct and that the correct date has been shown on each day's posting

Put initials in column below to show date has been changed		ALL MACHINES	LOCKING MACHINES	ALL MACHINES
		Reading of Ascending Register (Totalisator)	Reading of Descending Register (Credit Meter)	Last entry in col. "Total Deposits" or "Total Settings" on Record Card
	Mon.	37 888	4112	42 000
	Tue.	39 796	2204	
	Wed.	40 768	6232	47 000
	Thur.	43 002	3998	
	Fri.	44 453	2547	
	Sat.			

NOTE 1. Whether or not the machine has been used, this card must be posted on Saturday, or on Friday if no postings are made on Saturday.

NOTE 2. The daily entry must be made on completion of each day's postings.

Signed.. E. Ford

12 December ...198..

Post Office Examining Officer's initials..............................

Exercise 46

THE FRANKING MACHINE CONTROL CARD

Make a copy of the franking machine control card below and complete with the following details. State the balance of credit at the end of the week.

Name: Dobey and Sons Ltd
Meter office: Andrew Post Office, Portsmouth
Unit: 1p
Machine number: 6258
Number of units purchased: 80000 ⎫ at commencement of week
Number of units used: 71880 ⎭

Monday	used	1236
Tuesday:	used	3864
Wednesday	used	1150
Thursday	purchased	10000
Thursday	used	1896
Friday	used	1978

FRANKING MACHINE CONTROL CARD

CHECK DATE DAILY

Licensee...

Machine
(or Meter No.)............................... Setting or Recording Unit...............................

Meter Office
(as shown on Record Card)...

I certify that the following entries for the above machine for the week

ended..are correct

and that the correct date has been shown on each day's posting

Put initials in column below to show date has been changed		ALL MACHINES Reading of Ascending Register (Totalisator)	LOCKING MACHINES Reading of Descending Register (Credit Meter)	ALL MACHINES Last entry in col. "Total Deposits" or "Total Settings" on Record Card
	Mon.			
	Tue.			
	Wed.			
	Thur.			
	Fri.			
	Sat.			

NOTE 1. Whether or not the machine has been used, this card must be posted on Saturday, or on Friday if no postings are made on Saturday.

NOTE 2. The daily entry must be made on completion of each day's postings.

Signed...

....19........

Post Office Examining Officer's initials.......................................

215

Parcels

When you pack parcels, it is very important to make sure that you use strong, suitable, boxes. Every year the Post Office has to repack large numbers of parcels which become unfastened in the post and lose their contents. Parcels should be clearly addressed, with a stick-on label as well as a tie-on label, and should also have the name and address of the sender on the outside as well as the inside.

A parcel shedding its contents

A parcel correctly wrapped and labelled

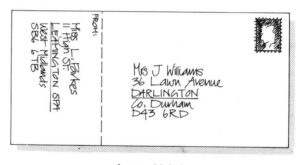

A parcel label

Whenever possible, a strong box is preferable to wrapping paper (supermarkets nearly always have cardboard boxes which they will supply free of charge) especially if the article to be sent is heavy.

Plenty of packing material — shredded paper is ideal (see p.218) or crushed newspaper or any sort of crushed scrap paper — should be placed around the contents.

For small items, padded bags give protection, especially for books, whose corners may be damaged in the post if unprotected.

When a box or padded bag is not available, use corrugated paper wrapped in strong brown paper.

Anything breakable should be marked clearly with the words **FRAGILE — WITH CARE**, and the Post Office will try to take extra care when handling the package.

Self-adhesive tape should be used along all sides of a parcel and, in addition, string should be firmly tied in at least two directions, knotting tightly where the string crosses.

The *Post Office Guide* gives full information about articles which may *not* be sent by post.

FOR YOUR FOLDER

32. PACKING PARCELS

Writes these notes in your folder, filling in the missing words and phrases.

1) Parcels should be clearly addressed, with a tie-on label and a _____.

2) The name and address of the sender should be on the _____ as well as the outside.

3) Whenever possible a strong box is preferable to _____.

4) Plenty of packing material should be placed around the contents. Crushed newspaper, scrap paper or _____.

5) For small items _____ give protection.

6) Anything breakable should be marked _____ and the Post Office will try to take extra care when handling the package.

7) Self-adhesive tape should be used along _____ of a parcel and in addition, _____ should be firmly tied in at least two directions, knotting tightly where the _____.

8) Full information about articles which may *not* be sent by post is in the _____.

217

Packing for Special Parcels

Large maps, plans, unframed pictures should be rolled and packed in a cardboard tube, securely sealed at both ends.

Small quantities of leaflets, brochures, exam papers should be packed in a padded bag or special bag (see below) as ordinary manilla envelopes are not strong enough for heavy contents.

Photographic prints must be placed between sheets of cardboard in an envelope marked **DO NOT BEND.**

Umbrellas and fishing rods (anything long and thin) should be packed between two strips of wood, wider and longer than the article and wrapped in corrugated paper and brown paper and marked **DO NOT BEND**.

Special packing

Liquids in tins or bottles should be surrounded by polystyrene chips or sawdust (this will absorb the liquid if there should be a breakage) and packed in a strong box.

Pictures in frames should be sandwiched between stout pieces of hardboard and wrapped in corrugated paper and strong brown paper.

Flowers must be packed in a strong box in layers separated by damp moss to keep the flowers fresh. If no moss is available, damp tissue paper or even damp newspaper will provide some humidity for the flowers.

Anything sharp (scissors, knives for example) are only accepted by the Post Office if the edges or points are properly protected so that they cannot cause damage when being handled. Heavy cardboard should be used inside a cardboard box.

Exercise 47

CHOOSING THE CORRECT PACKING FOR PARCELS

Describe the best way to pack the following for posting:

1) A china figure

2) A walking-stick

3) A bottle of expensive perfume

4) Holiday photos

5) A bunch of daffodils

6) A framed picture of a wedding group

7) A thick, glossy magazine

8) A small but heavy metal box

9) A large plastic toy

10) Ten large heavy books

11) Scissors

12) A golf club

REDUCED RATES FOR COUNTY PARCELS

Many firms deliver to customers located within a few miles and the Royal Mail offer a reduced rate for distribution within specified areas — usually a group of counties. These Royal Mail areas are listed in the *Royal Mail Postal Rates* leaflet (inland) and shown on a special map.

If many parcels are sent a considerable saving can be made by checking and making use of the county rate (see p.220).

County Parcels service is not available in the London area.

BULK POSTING OF PARCELS

There is a reduction in price for sending large numbers of parcels by post regularly — a lower rate for more than 30 parcels a week, and special terms for more than 200 a week, on a regular basis.

COMPENSATION FEE

This is the Post Office service which is for parcels over a certain weight containing valuables, for inland post only. The maximum amount of compensation paid is scaled according to the amount of fee paid.

Details of Registered Post, Recorded Delivery and Compensation Fee (CF Parcels) are in the Postal Rates (Inland) leaflets obtainable at all post offices free. These are updated after each change of postal rates.

Parcel Post

Weight not over	National rate	Area rate	Weight not over	National rate	Area rate
1 kg	£1.30	£1.10	7 kg	£2.65	£2.45
2 kg	£1.67	£1.47	8 kg	£2.80	£2.60
3 kg	£2.00	£1.80	9 kg	£2.95	£2.75
4 kg	£2.20	£2.00	10 kg	£3.10	£2.90
5 kg	£2.35	£2.15	22½kg*	£3.95	£3.75
6 kg	£2.50	£2.30			

*Parcels over 10 kg and up to 22½kg are accepted at most post offices.

The Area rates apply as follows:

County Parcels

For parcels posted and delivered within a group of postal counties as shown below

1   Avon/Gloucestershire/Somerset/Wiltshire
2   Staffordshire/Warwickshire/West Midlands/Worcestershire
3   Bedfordshire/Leicestershire/Northamptonshire
4   Derbyshire/Nottinghamshire
5   Cambridgeshire/Lincolnshire/Norfolk/South Humberside/Suffolk
6   Dyfed/Gwent/Herefordshire/Mid-Glamorgan/South Glamorgan/West Glamorgan
7   Cheshire/Lancashire
8   Cumbria/Dumfriesshire/Kirkcudbrightshire/Wigtownshire
9   Northern Ireland
10 Berwickshire/East Lothian/Fife/Kinross-shire/Midlothian/Peeblesshire/Roxburghshire/Selkirkshire/West Lothian
11 Aberdeenshire/Banffshire/Kincardineshire
12 Argyll/Arran/Ayrshire/Bute/Clackmannanshire/Coll/Colonsay/Dunbartonshire/Gigha/Iona/Islay/Jura/Lanarkshire/Mull/Renfrewshire/Stirlingshire/Tiree
13 Angus/Caithness/Canna/Eigg/Inverness-shire/Morayshire/Nairneshire/Perthshire/Rhum/Ross-shire/Skye/Sutherland
14 Cleveland/Co Durham/Northumberland/Tyne & Wear
15 North Humberside/North Yorkshire/South Yorkshire/West Yorkshire
16 Berkshire/Buckinghamshire/Oxfordshire
17 Dorset/Hampshire/Isle of Wight
18 East Sussex/Kent/West Sussex
19 Clwyd/Gwynedd
20 Powys/Salop
21 Cornwall/Devon
22 Barra/Benbecula/Harris/Lewis/North Uist/South Uist
23 Orkneys
24 Shetlands

For parcels posted and delivered within a single postal county as below

25 Surrey
26 Middlesex
27 Hertfordshire
28 Essex
29 Merseyside (including South Wirral)

Area price concessions do not apply to London postal districts

CASH ON DELIVERY (COD)

Under this service the cost of the article delivered can be collected by the postman from the recipient. This sum is then sent to the sender of the parcel by means of a special order. All parcels must be registered. It is a service often used by mail order firms and mentioned in their advertisements in newspapers and magazines. Anyone sending an order does not enclose a remittance, but pays the cost of the goods received to the postman delivering the parcel.

OTHER SERVICES FOR PARCELS DELIVERY

As well as the Post Office, parcels may be delivered by:

● British Rail — station-to-station service and Red Star.
With both these services the parcel must be collected by the addressee from a station. Red Star is the faster service of the two.

● Private carrier services — there are many of these listed in *Yellow Pages*.

Delivering parcels is not a 'monopoly' of the Post Office as is the delivery of letters.

Private firms delivering parcels may be cheaper than the Post Office service, may be quicker, too, and will usually accept larger and heavier parcels than the Post Office limits permit (the Post Office limit is usually $22\frac{1}{2}$ kg).

FOR YOUR FOLDER

33. PARCELS DELIVERY SERVICES

Write these notes in your folder, filling in the missing words and phrases.

1) The Royal Mail has a reduced rate for parcels delivered within a few miles. These areas are listed in the *Royal Mail Post Rates* leaflet (inland) and the service is known as ＿＿＿＿＿＿＿.

2) If many parcels are to be sent a saving can be made by ＿＿＿＿＿＿＿ posting.

3) The maximum weight for a parcel is ＿＿＿＿＿＿＿.

4) The name of the service which allows a parcel to be delivered to the recipient and payment made to the postman is ＿＿＿＿＿＿＿.

5) The Post Office service which is for parcels over a certain weight containing valuables (inland post only) is ＿＿＿＿＿＿＿.

Other Mail Room Equipment

SCALES

Traditional scales look like the two below on the left, but many firms are now using electronic scales like those below on the right. Electronic scales can be used for letters and parcels and by pressing the right keys you can work out the weight and postage for mail to anywhere in the world. Every time postal rates change, though, you need a new 'microchip' from the Post Office — they will arrange an exchange for you.

Parcel scales

Letter balance

Electronic parcel and letter balance

ADDRESSING MACHINES

An addressing machine may be linked to folding and inserting equipment, or used on its own.

Addressing machines are used by firms who send out a great deal of mail regularly to the same people — mail order firms, football pools,

No 123987X

Mr D Shepherd
8 Billing Close
WIGTON
Cumbria
CA7 8WL

charitable organisations — and plates with the names and addresses on are typed (or duplicated) ready for use. Each name has a code, which is also printed on the envelope when the addressing machine plates are used.

Addressing machines are now being replaced by word processors (see p. 156) or computers (p. 165) where lists of names and addresses can be stored in the memories.

FOLDING MACHINES

A *folding machine* will fold the letters and documents to be inserted into envelopes. A *folding and inserting* machine also inserts the letters into their envelopes.

This...

or this...

saves all this...

COLLATORS

Collators (like the ones below) are useful for sorting numbered papers into sets.

A horizontal collator   A vertical collator

STRAPPING MACHINES

A machine such as the one below helps make a package or parcel secure without the hard work involved with using string. Twine is wrapped around the package tightly and securely, a knot is made and the ends cut — all within two seconds!

A strapping machine

MAIL ROOM SUNDRIES

Small items used in a mail room are known as mail room sundries. A list of these sundries is as follows:

- Brown paper — for wrapping parcels
- Clear adhesive tape — to use instead of string. (Fold the end of the tape *back* after cutting a piece off — this makes it easier to find the end next time you need the tape!)
- Corrugated paper — for packing breakables
- Envelopes — POP sizes
- Gummed paper strip — also to use instead of string
- Paper knife — if there is no electric letter opener
- Scissors
- Sponge moistener — for moistening stamps and envelopes
- Roller moistener — does the same job
- Sealing wax — for sealing registered packets
- String

MAIL ROOM REFERENCE BOOKS

The *Post Office Guide* gives very clear and detailed instructions about parcelling everything, from musical instruments to umbrellas, and an up-to-date copy should be in every mail room for reference, not only in connection with parcels, but for information about postal rates and services to every country in the world. Separate leaflets (red for inland and blue for overseas) are issued by the Post Office after each change in postal rates. These give more detailed information than the *Post Office Guide*. The *Post Office Guide* may be bought from large post offices, the leaflets are free.

Other books useful in the mail room include:

- A large atlas
- A local *Classified Trade Directory (Yellow Pages)*
- Telephone Directories

- A-Z Street Maps
- Postal Addresses and Index to Postcode Directories
- Postcode Directories — (all these may be supplied on microfiche — see p. 315).

FOR YOUR FOLDER

34. MAIL ROOM EQUIPMENT

Write these notes in your folder, filling in the missing words and phrases.

1) To avoid sticking on stamps and keeping a postage book, many firms use a _____.

2) Parcels can have the value of a stamp affixed by using a _____ franked by this machine.

3) Many firms now use _____ scales for letters and parcels.

4) For sorting numbered papers into sets a _____ is useful.

5) In a very large mail room a folding and inserting machine folds and _____ into the envelopes.

6) Firms sending a great deal of mail regularly to the same people find _____ machines useful.

7) A letter that has been through one of these machines will often be easy to recognise because there is a _____ above the name on the envelope.

8) A _____ machine saves a lot of work tying up parcels with string.

9) Small items used in the mail room are known as _____.

10) These could include brown paper, clear adhesive tape, corrugated paper envelopes _____ sizes, gummed paper strip, paper knife, scissors, sponge moistener, roller moistener, sealing wax for _____ and string.

Exercise 48

OUTGOING MAIL

1) Explain how the mail room clerks would know whether a sealed letter has to go by first-class or second-class mail.

2) What arrangements should be made by the mail room supervisor to try and avoid a 'rush' of mail in the afternoon, and also to make sure that collection times are met?

3) What are the four important steps to check before folding a letter and placing it in an envelope?

4) Which letters have to be taken to the Post Office and a receipt obtained for them?

5) A franking machine saves time and trouble in the mail room. What would be the duties of a mail room clerk, every day, if she were in charge of a franking machine?

6) How is the postage paid for when a franking machine is used?

7) How is franked mail posted?

8) Apart from saving time in the mail room, franked mail has another advantage. What is it?

9) What is the reference book in the mail room which lists trade and professions alphabetically?

10) Why is the *Post Office Guide* so important in the mail room?

CHAPTER 10

Inland and Overseas Mail and Post Office Services

Information from the Post Office

It is most important for any office employee who has the responsibility of dealing with the despatch of mail to have a thorough knowledge of the Post Office mail service, and the regulations covering the despatch of mail.

The *Post Office Guide* and up-to-date Post Office leaflets giving the cost of stamps and the postage rates in the UK and overseas are obtainable at most large post offices. The leaflets are free but you must pay for the *Post Office Guide*.

Inland Mail

'Inland mail' refers to letters, packets and parcels posted to destinations in the British Isles.

For letters and parcels there is a two-tier system, meaning that the sender may choose to send them first or second-class. First-class post is dearer but arrives at its destination (usually) within 24 hours. Second-class post is cheaper, but slower, and it may take up to 4 days, depending upon when it is posted (e.g. a letter posted on Friday with a second-class stamp may not arrive at the address of the recipient until the following Tuesday).

POSTCODES

This code is used by the Post Office to speed the sorting of mail in its sorting office. It is important that the correct postal code is written (or typed) on envelopes, parcels and packets or delivery may be delayed (see p.128).

CERTIFICATE OF POSTING

This is a way of making sure that an important letter has actually been posted (and not still in someone's pocket!). The service is free and the letter has to be handed in at a post office for the counter clerk to complete and stamp a receipt. (It must *not* be posted in a letterbox.)

This receipt, when taken back to the office, is proof that the letter has been posted, and when. Delivery of the letter is made by the postman in the ordinary way (through a letterbox) and no receipt form has to be signed by the recipient.

RECORDED DELIVERY

With this method, the Post Office issues a receipt on a yellow slip to the person posting the letter and also authorises the postman to collect a signature from the recipient, so that proof of posting and delivery is provided. Recorded Delivery is suitable only for letters and packets containing important papers – not valuables, because compensation is very limited. Papers suitable for sending by Recorded Delivery could be: passport, birth certificate, examination papers, legal documents – anything which could cause a great deal of inconvenience if lost.

REGISTERED POST

When anything valuable (up to a certain size and weight) has to be sent by post, it should be sent by Registered Post. Compensation is paid according to the amount of fee paid. Letters and packets sent by Registered Post are handled with special security measures by the Post Office and separately from ordinary mail. The counter clerk at the post office gives a receipt and the postman obtains one from the addressee. Registered post is for inland post only – valuables being sent abroad by post are sent by another Post Office service.

A letter or packet to be sent by Registered Post should be in a strong envelope, obtainable at post offices. These envelopes, already stamped with first-class postage are available in three sizes.

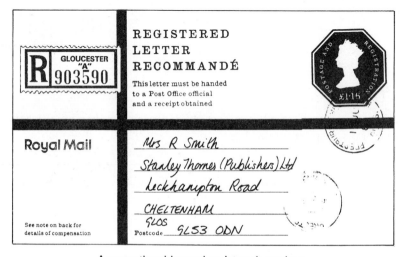

A correctly addressed registered envelope

CONSEQUENTIAL LOSS INSURANCE

A registered letter or packet may be insured against loss, damage or delay by taking out Consequential Loss Insurance cover. An example of loss to the user of a postal service could be a winning competition entry failing to arrive before closure date, a passport lost in the post, samples delayed causing loss of sales. When posting a registered letter (or packet) for which this extra insurance is required, ask at the Post Office for a Consequential Loss Insurance cover note. Fill this in with exactly the same name and address as on the packet and buy stamps to affix to the amount of cover required:

up to £1000	£0.45
up to £2500	£0.60
up to £5000	£0.85
up to £7500	£1.10
up to £10000	£1.35

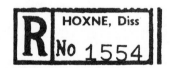

Label for consequential loss insurance

The cover note will be initialled and date-stamped by the counter clerk in the Post Office and should be kept in case a claim is made later on.

Consequential Loss Insurance is also available for COD service (see p. 221) and Special Delivery service (see p. 241).

ADVICE OF DELIVERY

By completing an Advice of Delivery form (obtainable from any post office) advice of delivery will be sent to you for either Recorded Delivery or Registered Post.

Fees for advice of delivery: (requested at time of posting)   20p

(requested after time of posting)   50p

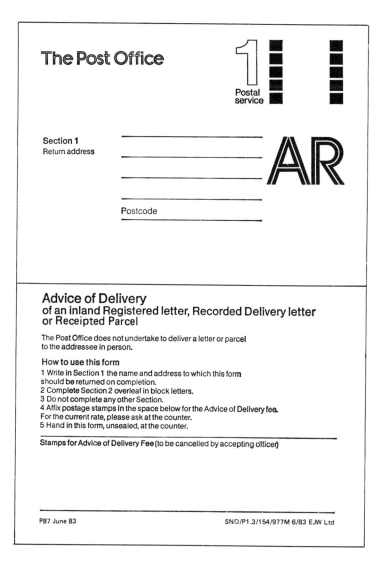

REDIRECTION SERVICE

The Post Office will redirect mail from an address which you have left to your new address.

A week before leaving, a Royal Mail redirection form has to be completed and handed in at the post office nearest to the *old address*.

You may select periods for redirection of:

- 1 month (£2.25)
- 3 months (£5.50)
- 12 months (£13.00)

The normal period for redirecting mail from a Poste Restante address (see below) is one month only.

Redirection service is for letters only. Normally, parcels will be returned to sender, unless the Post Office is notified separately (on the form) that parcels are to be redirected also.

Special Post Office Services

POSTE RESTANTE

This is a Post Office service which enables people on holiday or businessmen travelling around to collect their letters even when they are not sure where they will be staying. Letters must be addressed as follows:

Mr K Matthews
Poste Restante
Post Office
TUNBRIDGE WELLS   or
Kent
TW9 1AJ

Mrs E Holder
(to be called for)
Post Office
TUNBRIDGE WELLS
Kent
TW9 1AJ

BUSINESS REPLY SERVICE

This service is used by firms who wish to obtain replies from customers without putting them to the expense of paying postage. Business Reply forms may be in the form of a postcard, envelope, folder or gummed label.

The envelope etc. is posted in the normal way but without a stamp.

Business Reply forms may be first or second-class (they are marked with a large 1 or 2).

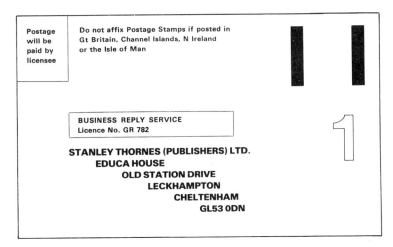

Business Reply envelope first-class

The service may be used by anyone who obtains a licence. The form to obtain a licence is available at main post offices. Postage on Business Reply forms is paid by the firm receiving the mail (the *licensee*). The service cannot be used in the Irish Republic and a Business Reply form cannot be redirected (unless extra stamps are added).

FREEPOST

A firm who wishes to obtain a reply from a customer without putting him to the *expense of paying postage* may include in his address the word 'FREEPOST'. The reply bearing this word can then be posted in the ordinary way but *without a stamp*. The firm sending the letters pays the postage to the Post Office. The letters will be sent by second-class post only.

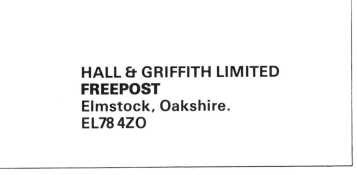

A Freepost envelope

A licence from the Post Office is needed to use the 'Freepost' service, available from main post offices. As with the Business Reply service, redirection is not permitted (unless extra stamps are added).

FOR YOUR FOLDER

35. MAIL SERVICES

Write these notes in your folder, filling in the missing words and phrases.

1) 'Inland' mail refers to letters, packets and parcels posted to destinations in the _____.

2) A Certificate of Posting is a way of making sure that a letter has actually _____. A receipt is obtained from the counter clerk at the Post Office and the letter must not be posted in a letterbox.

3) The mail service suitable for sending important papers (not valuables, because compensation is very limited) is _____.

4) Valuables sent by post should be sent by _____. Compensation is paid according to the amount of fee prepaid.

5) Extra insurance may be taken out by paying for _____.

6) When you move office, letters will be redirected to a new address if a _____ form is completed and handed in at a post office nearest to the _____ address.

7) The Post Office service which allows people on holiday or business-men travelling around to collect their mail is the _____.

8) The two services which enable users to post letters without paying for stamps are _____ and _____.

OTHER ITEMS ON SALE AT POST OFFICES

The following are available for sale at most post offices:

● Postnotes (notepaper, stamp and envelope all combined, first-class postage pre-paid, size 297 mm x 210 mm).

● Envelopes with first and second-class stamps.

● Books and rolls of stamps (first and second-class).

Overseas Mail

PARCELS

Parcels should be labelled clearly and should always have the sender's name on the outside as well as the inside. The country to which the parcel is being sent should be clearly shown. An airmail label is necessary where airmail is being used. There is a choice between air and surface mail.

The maximum size for a parcel being sent overseas is 1.05 m in length and 2 m in length and girth combined but to many countries the limits are now 1.5 m length and 3 m length and girth combined. The maximum weight is 20 kg to most countries but some will only accept up to 10 kg. On the otherhand some countries will accept up to 22.5 kg. The weights and sizes to each country are given in the *Postal Rates Overseas Compendium*.

The Post Office has a scheme of insurance for parcels going overseas which will provide compensation in the event of loss. There are also other supplementary services such as Express Delivery, Cash on Delivery and Franc de Droits (payment of overseas customs charges by sender). If goods weigh less than 2 kg, they can be sent via the letter service. If the goods need to be sent very quickly then there is International Datapost, which is available to a growing number of countries for items up to 15 kg (see p. 239). If Datapost is not available then there is Express Delivery or Swiftair for items less than 2 kg.

CUSTOMS

All packets and parcels posted to an overseas destination require a declaration label describing the contents. This applies to both airmail and surface mail. The reason for this declaration is to inform the customs officers in the country to which the parcel is sent what it contains — on some articles a tax has to be paid by the recipient and this tax is known as 'duty'. Duty is imposed on some goods to discourage people from sending them, the idea being that if the goods are manufactured in that country, the inhabitants want to sell their own and prevent foreign goods of similar type competing with them. Gifts may be allowed in duty free in certain countries if described on the label as 'gifts'. The *Post Office Guide* gives full details of regulations to all the countries of the world.

For letter packets, there is a green label, if the contents are less than £50 in value and a white form for goods in excess of that value. For parcels, the white form is used in most cases along with a despatch note. In other cases a combined declaration/despatch note is used. VAT labels will be needed if the goods are over £10 in value and other forms may be required depending on destination. The documentation for Swiftair is the same as letters and Datapost the same as parcels.

CUSTOMS DECLARATION

DECLARATION EN DOUANE   (NON-ADHESIVE)   PP 70 B

BEFORE COMPLETING THIS FORM YOU SHOULD READ CAREFULLY THE INSTRUCTIONS OVERLEAF
AVANT DE REMPLIR CETTE DECLARATION LIRE ATTENTIVEMENT LES INSTRUCTIONS AU VERSO

1. Name and address of sender	2. Sender's reference, if any
Nom et adresse de l'expéditeur	*Eventuellement numéro de référence de l'expéditeur*

3. Name and address of addressee
Nom et adresse du destinataire

4. Place a cross (X) here if the contents of the packages are a gift
Faire ici une croix (X) s'il s'agit d'un cadeau

5. The undersigned certifies that the particulars given in this declaration are correct
Le soussigné certifie l'exactitude des renseignements donnés dans la présente déclaration

6. Place and date
Lieu et date

7. Observations

8. Signature

9. Country of origin of the goods *Pays d'origine des marchandises*

10. Country of destination *Pays de destination*

11. Total gross weight *Poids brut total*

.................*lbs*................*ozs*

12. Number of items *Nombre d'envois*	13. Detailed description of contents *Designation détaillée du contenu*	14. Tariff No. *No. tarifaire*	15. Net Weight *Poids net*		16. Value *Valeur*
			lbs.	ozs.	

Dd. 434324 4/68 MFP

CUSTOMS/DOUANE C1

(May be opened officially)   *(Peut être ouvert d'office)*

Detach this part if the packet is accompanied by a Customs declaration **Otherwise it must be completed**

See instructions on the back

Detailed Description of Contents

(Désignation détaillée du contenu)

. . . .

. . . .

. . . .

. . . .

. . . .

Insert 'x' if the contents are:
(Faire 'x' s'il s'agit:)
a gift (*d'un cadeau*). . . . . ☐
a sample of merchandise
(*d'un échantillon de marchandises*). . . . . ☐

Value (Valeur) *(Specify the currency)*	*Net Weight* *(Poids-net)*

Customs declaration labels:
White label (above) for goods valued at *more* than £50, green label (left) for packets containing goods valued at *less* than £50

LETTERS

To countries outside Europe, the cheapest way to send a letter is by using an Aerogramme, obtainable at all post offices. The only disadvantage to these is that no enclosures are possible.

Other letters for countries outside Europe should normally be sent by airmail and to be typed on thin (airmail) paper and placed in a special airmail envelope (with a blue airmail label). Cost is calculated by weight — the rates are given in the *Postal Rates Overseas Leaflet* or *Compendium*. If there is no urgency, letters can be sent by surface mail.

For letters to Europe there is only one class of mail known as 'All-up'. Airmail envelopes and labels should not be used. The *Postal Rates Overseas Leaflet* and *Compendium* both contain a list of those countries classed as Europe.

CHRISTMAS CARDS AND PRINTED MATTER

Firms with many overseas customers may send them Christmas cards and by using the printed paper rates, are able to save postage. The printed paper rates are available for both airmail and surface mail outside Europe and there is a surface mail printed paper service for Europe. For surface mail the full rate must be paid. The cards must not contain more than five words of greeting, besides the printed message and a signature, and they must be in unsealed envelopes.

Details of the rates are given in the *Postal Rates Overseas Leaflet* or *Compendium*.

The printed paper services can also be used for catalogues, price-lists, direct mail and other publicity material or books and magazines.

SWIFTAIR

Swiftair is an international express service for letters and printed papers and is available to all countries.

Mail by Swiftair receives priority treatment in the UK, and in many countries overseas the letters are delivered by special messenger. The list of countries where special messenger delivery is given is contained in the Swiftair leaflet on display at post offices.

Letters for Swiftair must be handed over a post office counter or included in the firm's collection (but kept separate from other letters). They must bear a red Swiftair label at the top left-hand corner on the

A Swiftair label

address side of the envelope — below the blue airmail label, in the case of countries outside Europe. An *extra fee* is payable in addition to normal postage. A Certificate of Posting will be supplied free of charge on request at the time of posting.

ACCELERATED SURFACE POST (ASP)

ASP is cheaper than airmail and quicker than ordinary surface mail. It is a service for printed papers and combines air and surface (train, ship, road) transport.

The table below gives a comparison of times taken by various services.

	AIRMAIL	SURFACE MAIL	ASP
Australia	4–5 days	6–8 weeks	12–18 days
East Africa	3–4 days	8–12 weeks	11–15 days
Japan	3–4 days	6–7 weeks	8–12 days
USA	3–4 days	4–6 weeks	10–18 days
India	4–5 days	6–12 weeks	11–15 days

ASP is available to Europe and 80 countries outside Europe.

Items to be posted by ASP should be put in separate bags, labelled ASP and the Post Office will collect them.

BULK AIRMAIL

Bulk Airmail is another airmail service for printed papers sent overseas and the cost is based on the weight 'pence per kilo'. Bulk Airmail also has to be kept in separate bags labelled ready for collection by the Post Office.

INTERNATIONAL REPLY COUPONS

These are sold at the larger post offices in Great Britain and Northern Ireland, and are exchangeable in virtually all countries of the world for a stamp or stamps. The person to whom an International Reply Coupon

An international reply coupon

is sent takes it to his nearest post office and exchanges it for a stamp issued by his own country — British stamps are not accepted in any foreign country. An International Reply Coupon is a convenient means of 'prepaying' the cost of a reply from abroad.

Services for Sending Mail Quickly

DATAPOST

Datapost is a Post Office service which is for urgent letters, packets and parcels (up to $27\frac{1}{2}$ kg). It guarantees overnight delivery within the United Kingdom and very speedy delivery to many countries overseas. Datapost is now available on demand at post offices (previously it had to be arranged on a contractual basis only). Datapost mail travels separately from ordinary mail and is accompanied throughout by Post Office staff (except when in transit on flights overseas). Items sent by Datapost overseas get fast Customs clearance, which is another advantage of the service.

Datapost is especially suitable for sending computer material, from firm to firm, who use hired computer time, but it can be used for any items where a guaranteed delivery is important — laboratory specimens from hospitals or samples to prospective customers.

A receipt is given for all Datapost items, so that firms using the service have proof of delivery.

Datapost is also available for the COD service (p. 221).

EXPRESSPOST

Expresspost is the Royal Mail 'same-day' door-to-door courier service. An urgent letter or package will be collected following a 'phone call to the local Expresspost centre.

A COMPARISON OF INLAND AND OVERSEAS MAIL SERVICES

Name of service	Suitable for letters and parcels?	Suitable for letters/packets only (up to 1000g)?	Suitable for parcels (over 1000g)?	Delivery overseas?	Delivery inland?	Delivery same day?	Delivery first post next day?	Suitable for money/valuables?	Suitable for important documents?	Provides proof of posting and delivery?
Expresspost	Yes	Yes	Yes	No	Yes	Yes (inland)		Yes—combined with registration (see below)	No	Yes
Special Delivery	No	Yes	No	No	Yes	No	Yes	Yes—see above	No	Yes
Datapost	Yes			Yes to some areas	Yes	No	Yes	Yes—see above	Yes	Yes
Recorded Delivery	No	Yes	No	No	Yes	No	Yes if sent first-class	No	Yes	Yes
Registered Post	Yes	Yes	No	No	Yes	No	Yes	Yes	No	Yes
Swiftair	No	Yes	No	Yes	No	No	Yes	No	No	Yes
ASP (accelerated surface post)	No	No	Printed papers only	Yes	No	No	May be—depends on distance	No	No	No

For packages that have to travel across country, a combination of despatch riders and railway services is used to provide a same-day service.

Expresspost is useful for banks, hospitals and government departments because they know that valuable parcels will be taken care of and delivered without delay. All deliveries have to be signed for.

Payments can be made direct to the collecting (or delivering) messenger by franking machine, postage stamps, or cash.

Payment is based on distance.

The weight limit is usually 10kg but heavier packages may be accepted, depending on local resources.

Exercise 49

COMPARING POSTAL SERVICES

From the chart opposite, answer the following questions:

1) Which is the only mail service which will deliver *the same day*?

2) Which mail service is suitable for important documents?

3) Which mail services are suitable for valuables (if combined with registration)?

4) Which is the service to use for urgent airmail deliveries of letters?

5) Which is the service to use for sending printed papers overseas?

ROYAL MAIL SPECIAL DELIVERY

Royal Mail Special Delivery ensures that a first-class packet or letter will be delivered by first post the following morning (except Sunday) after posting *without fail*. If the letter arrives at the sorting office too late for the normal delivery service, a postman will go out specially to deliver it.

To send a letter (or packet — anything acceptable by normal first-class letter service) write your name and address *on the back* and ask for the service as you hand it in at the Post Office counter. You will be given a Certificate of Posting (see p.228). You pay the Royal Mail Special Delivery fee in addition to first-class postage. If, for any reason, the letter is *not* delivered by first post on the next working day, the special delivery fee is returned.

Royal Mail Special Delivery can be used in conjunction with Recorded Delivery and Registered Post (see pp. 229-30).

MARKING FOR SPECIAL DELIVERY

The words 'Special Delivery' must be marked above the address on the left-hand side of the letter or parcel. A broad blue or black perpendicular line must also be drawn from top to bottom on both the front and the back of a letter and completely round a parcel.

Comparison of Postage Rates

(A)   Letter Post and Parcel Post (at 1 January 1984)

	Letter Post		Parcel Post	
Weight	Second-class	First-class	National rate	Area rate
60g	12½p	16p	Not available	Not available
250g	33p	43p	Not available	Not available
500g	82p	63p	Not available	Not available
1000g	Not available	£1.62	£1.30	£1.10
3kg	Not available	£4.82	£2.00	£1.80

(B)   Recorded Delivery and Registered Post

	Recorded Delivery		Registered Post
Weight	Second-class	First-class	
60g	22½p	36p	£1.16 (minimum) must be sent first-class
250g	53p	63p	£1.43 (minimum) must be sent first-class
500g	83p	£1.02	£1.82 (minimum) must be sent first-class
1000g	Not available	£1.82	£2.62 (minimum) must be sent first-class

Parcel Post

Weight	Area rate	National rate
1000g	£1.10	£1.30
3kg	£1.80	£2.00
6kg	£2.30	£2.50
10kg	£2.90	£3.10
22½kg	£3.75	£3.95 (maximum weight for parcel post)

INTELPOST

Intelpost is the Post Office facsimile service (not to be confused with Bureaufax (see p. 107) for black and white copies of documents up to A4 size (297 mm x 210 mm). Colour originals may be used, but the copies will be black and white.

Copies will be sent by any Post Office which has the Intelpost sign, or a document for copying will be collected by messenger, on payment of an additional fee.

There are over 70 Intelpost centres in the UK linking the service with London. Major cities overseas, in the USA, Canada, France, West Germany, Sweden and the Netherlands, also accept and transmit Intelpost messages.

When handing the document over to be copied the counter clerk will want to know:

- Name, address, postcode and telephone number
- Number of sides to be transmitted
- Method of delivery (special messenger, personal collection or ordinary first-class post).

There is no service on Saturdays, Sundays, or public holidays either in the UK or in other countries which operate the service.

After transmission, the Post Office at the other end will either:

- Deliver by special messenger
- Deliver by first post the following day

Alternatively, the copy can be collected from the Post Office.

For immediate delivery by special messenger, there is an additional charge. It is slightly dearer than Bureaufax, but as many words as you like can be written on the sheet as long as they are readable.

When documents are handed in for transmission by Intelpost, they should have a margin of at least 10 mm all round. They should not be folded, as the crease affects the facsimile quality.

Special short message forms (cheaper than the A4 size) are available for messages, especially birthday or congratulatory messages. Greetings cards are available at a small extra charge.

Intelpost can be linked to facsimile transmission equipment in the firms' own offices.

Miscellaneous Post Office Services

These include:

- Providing British visitors' passports or application forms for standard passports

- Providing application forms for various licences (such as driving, television, dog, motor vehicle and franking machine)

- Providing application forms for the driving test

- Selling National Insurance stamps to the self-employed

- Paying various pensions and benefits

Exercise 50

INTELPOST

1) What are the three ways in which an Intelpost message may be sent?

2) Would it be possible to arrange for one to be delivered on a Saturday, Sunday, or Bank Holiday?

3) A document for sending by Intelpost will be collected by special messenger (instead of being handed in at a post office). Is there an extra fee for this?

4) What greetings messages are available?

5) Describe how a document should be prepared for transmission by Intelpost.

6) What is the maximum size of a document which can be sent by Intelpost?

7) Will colour originals be transmitted in colour?

8) Is it possible to use the Intelpost service to send documents overseas?

9) What details will the Post Office counter clerk want to know when a document is handed over for transmission by Intelpost?

Exercise 51

POST OFFICE MAIL SERVICES

What Post Office services would you use for the following?

1) A parcel containing a valuable piece of china, weighing 3½ kg?

2) A packet containing gold earrings valued at £50?

3) An envelope containing birth and marriage certificates?

4) Regular daily, weekly or monthly deliveries of computer or other urgent material?

5) The equivalent of a stamp to a pen-friend in Holland?

Answer the following questions.

6) What must you ask for at the Post Office if the firm you are working for requires proof that an unregistered or unrecorded letter has been posted?

7) Paying the postman for goods ordered from a mail order firm is called what?

8) Name one Post Office service for speedy delivery of letters and packets.

9) A green adhesive customs label has to go on a packet being sent abroad if the value is how much?

10) A white non-adhesive label is necessary for a parcel going abroad if the value is how much?

11) Compare the Business Reply Service with Freepost. Explain the reasons for using them (a) by firms (b) by customers.

12) If you moved house just before Christmas, how would you make quite sure that any Christmas parcels were sent on to you?

13) Compare the ordinary airmail service with accelerated surface post (ASP).

14) What are the advantages of using the Datapost service?

15) Explain the differences between Expresspost and Royal Mail Special Delivery.

Exercise 52

MORE ON MAIL SERVICES

1) You want to send a parcel weighing 1kg overseas by airmail to Wellington, New Zealand.
   a What will this cost?
   b How frequent is the service?
   c How long will it take from London to New Zealand?
   d What, if any, are the Customs requirements?
   (Use the *Post Office Guide*.)

2) Under what conditions are letters and postcards sent to Europe by airmail as the means of transmission without extra charge?
   (Use the *Post Office Guide*.)

   Under what conditions does this service include printed papers, samples etc.?

3) Mr Wood wants several extra 13-amp sockets fitted throughout the office. He asks you to obtain the names and addresses of three nearby electricians in order to obtain estimates. Provide these from your local *Yellow Pages*.

4) Mr Wood is considering the installation of a franking machine and asks you to provide information in answer to the following questions:
   a Is a licence necessary? If so, where can it be obtained?
   b When are payments for postage made?
   c How is franked correspondence posted?
   d What record, if any, has to be kept of the use made of the franking machine?

246

e How often, and by whom, must the machine be inspected? Why is this necessary?

f Which companies are licensed by the Postmaster General to supply franking machines?

5) Complete the blanks from the alternatives listed:

The Recorded Delivery Service provides a record of _____
- posting only;
- delivery only;
- posting and delivery as well as compensation if the packet is lost or damaged in the post.

A fee per packet is charged for this service _____
- in addition to postage;
- in place of postage;
- in lieu of postage.

Recorded Delivery packets must be _____
- put in a letter-box;
- handed in at a post office;
- retained by the sender after completion of a special receipt form.

6) What service does the Post Office offer enabling a firm to collect mail early in the morning before normal delivery by the postman?

7) State the overnight service available for sending computer material through the mail.

8) What Post Office service enables me to cover the value of a parcel against loss?

9) If I am in doubt about a postal service where can I find details of it?

Exercise 53

POSTAL ASSIGNMENTS

Obtain the current Postal Rates leaflet issued by the Post Office and calculate the cost of each of the following:

(i) a second-class letter, weight 40 g to Glasgow,
(ii) a first-class letter, weight 310 g to Jersey,
(iii) a first-class letter, weight 200 g to Dublin,
(iv) a registered letter, £450 value, weight 45 g to London,
(v) a second-class Recorded Delivery letter, weight 70 g to Leeds (advice of delivery requested at time of posting),
(vi) a parcel weighting 6 kg addressed to Bradford,
(vii) a compensation fee parcel to Birmingham weighing 8 kg, value £70.

Exercise 54

CALCULATING POSTAGE

By referring to the *Post Office Guide* calculate the amount of postage due on the following items, state the total expenditure and list the documents or labels which would have to be completed for despatch from a post office:

1)	Catalogue by second-class mail	84 g
2)	Letter by second-class mail	112 g
3)	Letter by Recorded Delivery first-class	28 g
4)	Second-class letter by Recorded Delivery	14 g
5)	Letter to Belgium	42 g
6)	Airmail letter to New Zealand	56 g
7)	Parcel (surface mail) to India	908 g
8)	Parcel — local	1½ kg
9)	Reply coupon for USA	
10)	Redirection of a parcel to another address in the same postal district	3 kg

Exercise 55

USE OF THE *POST OFFICE GUIDE*

1) If a number of tiles had to be sent by post, how should they be packed?

2) What is the cost of an envelope pre-printed with a first-class stamp?

3) What is the weight limit for second-class letters?

4) What is the special postage rate for the blind?

5) What is Selectapost?

6) How would a parcel containing a salmon posted in Scotland be marked?

7) What are the names and addresses of the three firms manufacturing franking machines?

8) How should fresh flowers be packed for posting?

9) How should live bees be packed?

10) How should umbrellas be packed for posting?

11) Is it possible to send *boxes* of matches by post?

12) Is red a colour approved by the Post Office for packets or envelopes?

13) What is an aperture envelope?

14) Can you send a parcel by Recorded Delivery?

15) What does the Post Office charge for redirecting letters after moving house?

16) How is an envelope marked when being despatched by Special Delivery?

17) What is Datapost?

18) What is Freepost?

19) Is the Compensation Fee service suitable for sending banknotes and coins?

20) How must a registered packet be packed?

21) What is the maximum weight for letter post?

22) Do printed papers posted abroad require customs declaration labels?

23) Where is the blue airmail label affixed on a parcel being despatched abroad by airmail?

24) Is it possible to send silkworms abroad?

25) Is it possible to send chewing gum to Moscow?

26) Is it possible to send a pigskin handbag to Saudi Arabia?

27) Is it possible to send cigarettes to the Vatican?

28) Is it possible to send raffle tickets to Israel?

29) Is it possible to send imitation pearls to Qatar?

FOR YOUR FOLDER

36. A SUMMARY OF POST OFFICE SERVICES

Write these notes in your folder, filling in the missing words and phrases.

1) A way of obtaining proof of posting of an important letter is by _____.

2) If proof of delivery as well as proof of posting is required for a package containing important papers, a _____ is the correct service.

3) Registered Post is the Post Office service to use for anything _____ (up to a certain weight) which is being posted *inland*.

4) Compensation is paid for lost articles according to the amount of _____.

5) Consequential Loss Insurance is a form of _____ insurance cover.

6) The Post Office service for parcels containing valuables (inland only) is _____.

7) A Post Office service which enables people on holiday or businessmen travelling around to collect their letters even when they are not sure where they will be staying is _____.

8) Two Post Office services which allow replies to be posted without paying for stamps are _____ and _____.

9) If you move to a new address, and want to be sure you will receive your letters, the Post Office service to use is the _____.

10) Two Royal Mail services for urgent letters or packets are _____ and _____.

11) The service of the above two which delivers *on the same day* is _____.

12) The service of the two in Question 10 which guarantees delivery by first post *next day* is _____.

13) The cheaper rate for parcels which have only to be delivered a few miles is _____.

14) An international express service for letters is _____.

15) ASP is the abbreviation for _____.

16) Full details of parcels to be sent overseas are in the _____.

17) The cheapest way to send an airmail letter abroad is by _____.

18) All letters go to _____ by airmail, so there is no need to affix an airmail label. This service is known as _____.

19) Letters and parcels sent by surface mail are cheaper but _____.

20) Surface mail is transported by ship, van or _____.

21) All packets and parcels posted abroad require a _____.

22) Where the value of the contents is under £50 a _____ label is required.

23) Where the value of the contents is over £50 a _____ label is required.

24) Parcels which may be allowed in duty free are _____ parcels.

25) Duty is imposed on some goods entering a foreign country to _____.

26) For sending the equivalent of a stamp abroad, an _____ is necessary.

27) The service offered by the Post Office which has replaced the telegram is _____.

Electronic Post

The Post Office offers a service called Electronic Post whereby the customer sends a computer tape to the appropriate Electronic Post Centre. The Post Office then prints the text and sends it to the address using first-class post. This service is particularly useful for bulk mailing, e.g. advertising leaflets.

Electronic 'Mail'

Electronic Mail is a term used to describe the transmission of messages along telephone lines between computers. It is not really mail in the normal sense of the word (i.e. letters) but it can offer an attractive service in certain circumstances.

All that a computer owner (or operator) needs is an attachment known as a *modem* which connects the computer to an outside telephone line, and a program — a set of electronic instructions specially written for this purpose. With this equipment the rest is easy. A letter of any desired length is 'typed' on the screen and given the command SEND. Within a few seconds, the text has passed along the telephone lines and is now in the memory of the computer in the home of a friend who may be hundreds or even thousands of miles away.

The task of the friend at the other end is equally simple. If his computer is switched on and in 'mail mode', all he has to do is to type the command READ on his keyboard and the text of the letter at once appears on his screen in the form in which it was transmitted a few seconds before.

If he is away from home, or busy with something else, the letter just waits until he is ready to switch on his computer, and read it. The whole procedure has taken a fraction of the time and price of ordinary letter writing.

The name of the service, currently being launched by British Telecom and a private company, is Micromail. At present, the equipment is expensive, but the price is likely to fall and will then be within the reach of thousands of ordinary people, in the way home computers are now.

CHAPTER 11

The Stationery Store

What 'Stationery' is

Stationery forms only a small part of the stock held in a firm, but it is becoming more and more expensive, and issues of stationery should be carefully controlled, for economy reasons.

Items which come into the category of 'stationery' include not only paper but such accessories as:

- staplers and staples
- hole punches
- adhesive tape
- paper clips and pins
- rubber bands
- bulldog clips
- treasury tags
- folders — all types (see p. 306)
- labels
- scissors
- rubber thimbles
- string and brown paper
- rubber stamps and pads
- wire baskets.

There are, of course, lots of different types of paper such as:

- typing paper – bond and bank, A4 and A5, white and coloured
- letterheading, A4 and A5 sizes
- memoranda, A4 and A5 sizes
- envelopes – all sizes
- carbon paper.

And there are also:

- typewriter ribbons
- duplicating paper – ink and spirit (see Chapter 12)
- duplicating ink
- ink stencils

In a small firm, the secretary (or her assistant) may be responsible for issuing stationery. As stock costs money and storage space in cupboards is always valuable in an office, it is important that no unnecessary 'stockpiling' of paper etc. takes place. A method of avoiding 'stockpiling'

Stationery Stock Card

Item Treasury Tags (boxes of 50) mixed colours

Maximum Stock 40 boxes
Minimum Stock: 10 boxes

Date	Receipts			Issues			Balance in Stock
198-	Quantity Received	Invoice No.	Supplier	Quantity Issued	Requisition No.	Department	
January 1							30 boxes
" 8				1 box	153	Reception	29 "
" 11				10 boxes	401	Filing dept.	19 "
March 1				8 boxes	477	Personnel dept.	11 "
" 3	25 boxes	450	Office Equipment Supplies Ltd				36 "

A filled-in stationery stock card

is to keep a careful record of everything in the stationery store on a stationery stock card, as illustrated above.

The stationery stock card shows the minimum amount below which the stock should not fall, and the maximum amount likely to be required. This should not be exceeded, otherwise money is tied up and storage space is being used unnecessarily. Maximum/minimum levels enable the secretary or clerk in charge of stationery stock to see at a glance from the stock card whether issues of certain items are increasing and to whom. Stock cards also enable the reordering to be done well before stock falls too low. In the card illustrated the person in charge should never allow the number of boxes of treasury tags to fall below 10, but she should never stock up to give a total of more than 40. The right-hand column keeps a record of the number in stock and when these fell to 11, she decided to reorder.

Reordering Stationery

Reordering of stationery stock is often done by the buying department and an order from the stationery supervisor is sent to this department at regular intervals – perhaps once a month – or when shortage causes an emergency.

Issuing Stationery to Staff

Stationery is ordered by staff on a stores requisition form (see overleaf). It is useful to have a checklist of all the items in the stationery store attached to the outside of the door, and circulated round to all staff likely

Stationery Requisition Job No. _____.	
From_____	
To _____	
QUANTITY	DESCRIPTION
Signed _____ Date _____	

Stationery Requisition Job No. _____	
From__ Department entered here	
To ____ Stationery store	
QUANTITY	DESCRIPTION
Amount required	Item required
Signature of person collecting stationery Signed_____ Date _Today's___	

to be ordering the stationery, so that the requisition forms for ordering stationery can be completed from it.

Shelves in cupboards containing stationery should be labelled. The cupboards must be kept locked, with keys in the possession of at least two people in case one is absent for any reason. Unlocked cupboards encourage the indiscriminate and haphazard issuing of stationery and also enable people to help themselves, with no records of who has taken which item.

Stationery store cupboard

Issuing of stationery must be carried out at certain times on pre-arranged days. No busy office worker can afford to be interrupted constantly and unexpectedly during a working day by requests for ballpoint pens or a typewriter ribbon. A notice stating times of issuing stationery should be clearly displayed on the door of the stationery cupboard and could also be circulated with the list of stationery available:

STATIONERY will be issued ONLY on Mondays, Wednesdays and Fridays between 0930 and 1030.

REQUISITIONS may be left in the basket marked "Stationery Requisitions" on the desk in my office; please state requirements clearly, to avoid any misunderstandings.

Stationery will be left ready for collection (if ordered in advance) in Room 601 which will be unlocked on Mondays, Wednesdays and Fridays between 0930 and 1030.

It is important for the clerk in charge to be very firm about not making exceptions to the rules about when stationery is issued – or very soon *everyone* will expect to be treated as special cases!

Stocktaking

Checking of stock in the stationery store must be done at regular intervals – about twice a year is normal – to make sure that the stock card balances are accurate and agree with the quantity on the cupboard shelves. It also gives a good opportunity for the stationery stock to be tidied and shelves relabelled if necessary. Counting sheets of paper one by one takes far too long, and a quick way to check is to make a two-inch notch in a piece of cardboard and measure the piles of paper, allowing approximately 400 sheets for every two inches. Most paper for duplicating and typing is delivered from the manufacturers in boxes containing one ream, and there are 500 sheets in each ream.

Empty boxes are worth keeping for placing 'orders' in readiness for collection.

Requisitions can be placed on top so that it is clear whose orders they are.

FOR YOUR FOLDER

37. STATIONERY STOCK CONTROL

Write these notes in your folder, filling in the missing words and phrases.

1) Issues of stationery in a firm must be carefully controlled because it is becoming more and more _____.

2) It is important that no unnecessary stocking of stationery takes place in a firm because _____ is always valuable in offices.

3) Maximum/minimum levels of stock enable the clerk or secretary in charge of stationery to _____ whether issues of stationery are _____ or _____ and to whom they have been issued.

4) It is useful to have a checklist of _____ so that people in a firm know what is kept in the stationery store.

255

5) Stationery required *for* the stationery store is ordered by the _____ department.

6) Cupboards containing stationery should have _____ shelves and be kept _____.

7) Issuing of stationery should be done at times and on days _____.

8) _____ should be carried out regularly to make sure that the balance on each stock card agrees with the quantity on the shelves.

9) A ream of paper contains _____ sheets.

10) It takes a long time to count individual sheets of paper (e.g. letterheading) and a quick way to check the number of sheets is to measure with a 2" notch in a piece of cardboard. Two inches = _____ sheets.

Exercise 56

STATIONERY STOCK CONTROL

1) Why is it important to keep accurate records of all stationery issued in a firm?

2) What is meant by 'minimum' stock?

3) What is meant by 'maximum' stock?

4) What are the two documents used in the issuing of stock?

5) What does the figure in the 'balance' column mean?

6) What is 'stocktaking' and why is it necessary?

7) Why is it important to issue stock only on certain days and at certain times?

8) Why is the locking of the stationery cupboard so important?

9) Which department reorders stock *for* the stationery cupboard?

10) What is 'stockpiling' and why is it important to avoid it?

Exercise 57

ASSIGNMENTS ON STOCK CARDS

1) *Stock card no 1 and requisition no 389* (see p. 257)

   a Stationery stock card no 1 is for wallet folders. What are these shaped like?

Stationery Stock Card   No. 1

Item Folders - wallet
A4

Maximum Stock 1000
Minimum Stock: 100

Date	Receipts			Issues			Balance in Stock
198-	Quantity Received	Invoice No.	Supplier	Quantity Issued	Requisition No.	Department	
Jan. 5							900
" 8				200	389	Filing	700
" 14				50	398	Reception	650
Feb. 1				100	453	Sales	550
" 10				400	468	Filing	150
" 15	800	130	H W Smug & Co.				950

Stationery Requisition   Job No. 389

From Filing Dept.
To Stationery Store

QUANTITY	DESCRIPTION
200	A4 Wallet Folders

Signed W. Walker   Date 8 January 198-

Stationery Requisition   Job No. 471

From Sales Dept.
To Stationery Store

QUANTITY	DESCRIPTION
2 reams	Typing paper, A4 Bank, yellow

Signed B. Barnes   Date 10 February 198-

Stationery Stock Card   No. 2

Item Typing paper A4
Bank, yellow

Maximum Stock 25 reams
Minimum Stock: 5 reams

Date	Receipts			Issues			Balance in Stock
198-	Quantity Received	Invoice No.	Supplier	Quantity Issued	Requisition No.	Department	
							15
Jan. 31	10	8310	Potts paper Co.				25
Feb. 10				2	471	Sales	23
" 15				15	490	Typing pool	8
" 24				3	511	Buying	5
" 25	20	10014	Potts paper Co.				25
March 1				5	529	Typing pool	20

b Which department used most of these folders?

c On which date was the stock of wallet folders lowest?

d On which date was the stock of wallet folders highest?

e Requisition no 389 gives quantity, description and size – what else *might* be important to the filing department?

2) *Stock card no 2 (see p. 257)*

Make out the other three requisitions which are shown on the stock card and number them 490, 511 and 529. Sign them yourself for the typing pool and exchange with someone else in your class for the buying department.

3) *Requisition nos 910, 923, 970 and 980 (see below)*

Make out a stationery stock card for these requisitions. Details of stock are as follows:

- maximum stock is 200 reams
- minimum stock is 50 reams
- supplier: Perfecta Printing Co
- balance in stock is 70 reams on 8 May 198—
- 50 reams are received on 31 May against Invoice 09439.

Complete by entering the balance in stock on 31 May 198—.

Stationery Requisition   Job No. _910_

From _Personnel Dept._

To _Stationery Store_

QUANTITY	DESCRIPTION
2 reams	Letterheading A4

Signed _F·Simms_   Date _9 May 198—_

Stationery Requisition   Job No. _923_

From _Sales Dept_

To _Stationery store_

QUANTITY	DESCRIPTION
5 reams	Letterheading A4

Signed _T·Tonks_   Date _11 May 198—_

Requisition   Job No. _970_

From _Buying Dept._

To _Stationery Store_

QUANTITY	DESCRIPTION
10 reams	Letterheading A4

Signed _L· Martin_   Date _23 May 198—_

Requisition   Job No. _980_

From _General Manager's Office_

To _Stationery Store_

QUANTITY	DESCRIPTION
3 reams	Letterheading A4

Signed _Jean Page_   Date _28 May 198—_

4) Below is an unfinished stock card. Copy the details on to another stock card and fill in the missing details.

Stationery Stock Card

Item: Ink Duplicating Paper - green

Maximum Stock 500 reams
Minimum Stock: 150 reams

Date 198-	Receipts			Issues			Balance in Stock
	Quantity Received	Invoice No.	Supplier	Quantity Issued	Requisition No.	Department	
Jan 31							300
Feb 17					471	Typing pool	150
" 27				10	519	Production	
March 4					531	Sales	100
" 12				75	588	Reprography	
" 15	250	3201	Potts Paper Co.				

5) The stock card below is wrong. Can you find the mistakes? Copy out the details on another stock card and correct the mistakes.

Stationery Stock Card

Item: Wire basket 3" x 11" x 15"

Maximum Stock 50
Minimum Stock: 10

Date 198-	Receipts			Issues			Balance in Stock
	Quantity Received	Invoice No.	Supplier	Quantity Issued	Requisition No.	Department	
1 Sept							40
21 "				3	1521	Reception	36
1 Oct				1	1602	Accounts	35
7 "				5	1621	Wages	20
3 Nov				10	1778	Filing	10
8 "	40	0553	Office Equipment Supplies Ltd.				50
15 "				5	1810	Personnel	55
3 Dec				6	2001	Sales	47

6) **a** Make out a stationery stock card for ball-point pens, black. Maximum stock is 120, minimum stock is 50. Balance in stock on 31 May 198— is 70. Then make out requisitions for each person overleaf who orders ball-point pens and get different people in your class to sign them. Enter each of them on your stock card. Number the requisitions 200 to 206. New stock arrives on 3 June 198—. If your stock card is correct, the balance in stock on 5 June 198— should be *103*.

b Enter the following on the stock card:

Betty Bloggs of reception rushes into the stationery store on Monday 1 June 198— at 0925 with a requisition for 6 black ball-point pens. (She is only just in time!) On Wednesday 3 June there is a delivery of stationery from H W Smug & Co, Barnsley, which includes 60 ball-point pens. The invoice number is 677891. Mrs L Timms from the typing pool brings a requisition for 3 black ball-point pens on 3 June as also does Fred Finch from the advertising department. On Friday 5 June there is a real rush for black ball-point pens — Sally Smart from the sales department wants 4; Ian Johnson from the personnel office wants 2; Martin Sparrow from the purchasing officer wants 3; and Tracey Twitter from 'wages' wants 6.

7) Make out requisitions for the following (in each exercise) and then enter them up on a stationery stock card, first adding maximum and minimum stock and 'Item' at the top of the stock card:

a Item: HB Pencils Max Stock: 300
                        Min Stock: 100
Supplier: H W Smug & Co, Barnsley

1 April 198—   Balance in stock was 110
2 April 198—   against Requisition No 745, 10 were issued to the sales dept.
4 April 198—   against Requisition No 777, 30 were issued to the drawing office
7 April 198—   against Requisition No 824, 10 were issued to the buying dept.
8 April 198—   against Invoice No 99926, 100 were received.

---

b Item: Boxes of staples No 19 ⅜"   Max Stock: 100 boxes
                                      Min Stock: 10 boxes
Supplier: H W Smug & Co, Barnsley

6 May 198—   Balance in stock was 100 boxes
7 May 198—   against Requisition No 901, 5 boxes were issued to personnel dept.
15 May 198—   against Requisition No 947, 10 boxes were issued to advertising dept.
22 May 198—   against Requisition No 961, 35 boxes were issued to typing pool
29 May 198—   against Invoice No 7361, 50 boxes were received.

---

c Item: Staplers F 19 Max Stock: 100
                         Min Stock: 25
Supplier; H W Smug & Co, Barnsley

1 June 198—   Balance in stock 30

4 June 198—	against Requisition No 1007, 2 were issued to the mail room
4 June 198—	against Invoice No 7441, 70 were received
10 June 198—	against Requisition No 1117, 3 were issued to the production dept.
17 June 198—	against Requisition No 1138, 3 were issued to the sales dept.

d Item: Typewriter ribbons, all black, for Adler/Olympia machines

Max Stock: 250

Min Stock: 10

Supplier: Office Equipment Supplies Ltd, Manchester

1 July 198—	against Invoice No 2472, 100 were received (balance: 150)
3 July 198—	against Requisition No 1243, 5 were issued to the general manager's office
10 July 198—	against Requisition No 1276, 3 were issued to the typing pool
17 July 198—	against Requisition No 1305, 10 were issued to personnel dept.
18 July 198—	against Requisition No 1309, 12 were issued to the buying dept.
20 July 198—	against Invoice No 2779, 30 were received.

CHAPTER 12

Copying and Duplicating

Carbon Copies

There are two main types of carbon paper – 'single' is coated on one side and double on both sides. Single carbon paper is the one most widely used and is available in various 'weights', i.e. thicknesses. 'Heavyweight' produces one or two clear copies but lasts a long time; 'medium-weight' produces up to five copies at a time; and 'lightweight' gives more than five copies but can be used only a few times before the copies are no longer clear.

Most firms today use what is known as 'long-life' carbon paper which is plastic-coated and is clean, easy to handle and less likely to curl or crease. It is this type of carbon paper which will be referred to from now on. Carbon paper is available in a variety of strong colours – red, black, blue, purple and green. It is often useful for identification purposes to send a certain colour to a particular department, or person.

Each sheet of medium-weight or heavyweight carbon paper can be used about 200 times. When the centre of A4 sized carbon paper is no longer producing good, clear copies, it should be cut in half (to give two sheets of A5). This will redistribute the wear.

CARE OF CARBON PAPER

Carbon paper should be stored flat, preferably in a box, away from radiators in a cool place.

Creased carbon paper produces 'trees' on the carbon copies. A 'treed' carbon copy is the sign of a careless typist.

A carbon copy with trees

Careful erasing prolongs the life of carbon paper. Rubber dust should be brushed off the carbon paper after erasing, away from the type basket on to the desk. The typewriter carriage should be moved as far as possible to left or right before rubbing out (see p. 163).

HANDLING CARBON PAPER

Some typists use carbon paper with the top left- or right-hand corner cut away. This enables the carbon paper to be shaken out while the carbon copies are held between thumb and first finger.

A carbon paper with the corner cut away

ONE-TIME CARBONS

These are a thin, inexpensive type of carbon paper, often used for interleaving documents supplied in sets – teleprinter rolls, computer stationery, invoices, statements, etc. and after removal from the documents are scrapped. One-time carbon saves the typist inserting carbons, although she still has to take them out. Another use for 'one-time' carbons is with ink stencils (see pp. 272 – 7).

CONTINUOUS STATIONERY

This consists of sets of documents which are fed in from a continuous roll attached to a typewriter by a special attachment (see p. 161). After each document has been typed, it can be torn off the roll by means of perforations, and the next document is brought into the machine, ready for typing. Continuous stationery increases the speed with which the typist produces the documents – inserting carbons, placing the 'set' in the typewriter and removing the carbons often takes far more time than actually typing the information on the documents.

Continuous stationery may be interleaved with 'one-time' carbons or NCR paper (see p. 264).

A backing sheet with folded end helps to keep carbon and typewriting paper straight and level (see also p. 163).

NUMBERS OF COPIES OBTAINABLE BY CARBON PAPER

The maximum number of copies is obtainable by using lightweight carbon paper and thin ('flimsy') typing paper – this will be about 8 or 9 readable copies on a manual typewriter.

Using the same lightweight carbon paper and 'flimsy' typing paper, an electric typewriter may possibly produce about 12 copies, with pressure control set at maximum.

Using medium-weight carbon paper (which is the most generally used weight in offices) and 'bank' typing paper ('bank' is slightly thicker than 'flimsy') a manual typewriter will produce about 6 readable copies.

Several copies produced by carbon paper from one typing are often referred to as 'manifolds', and typing a document with several carbon copies is known as 'manifolding'.

NCR

NCR when used in connection with making copies means 'no carbon required'. NCR paper produces copies by the use of chemicals, either on the back of the paper, or on the back and the front. NCR paper is supplied in sets, lightly attached at the top and thus saves the typist inserting and removing carbons. NCR paper will produce about five clear, readable copies. It is used for invoices, orders, statements, Telex messages, computer print-outs.

NCR paper is clean to handle, quicker for the typist, and less storage space is required in the stationery store cupboard for boxes of carbon paper. NCR is, however, more expensive than ordinary paper plus carbon paper. It is also difficult to make corrections on the copies – erasing is almost impossible, and it is necessary to use a special corrective which has to be painted on. The final disadvantage is that it is very easy to mark NCR copies accidentally as people often do not realise that documents are NCR-coated. Even franking envelopes in the post can mark NCR copies occasionally.

FOR YOUR FOLDER

38. CARBONS AND CARBON COPYING

Write these notes in your folder, filling in the missing words and phrases.

1) The thickness of carbon paper is referred to as its _____.

2) Different coloured carbon copies may be sent to _____.

3) To make the maximum use of carbon, A4 size should be cut in _____ and reused as _____. This will _____ _____.

4) 'Trees' on carbon copies are caused by _____ in carbon paper.

5) Carbon paper should be stored _____ away from _____.

6) Careful _____ prolongs the life of carbon paper.

7) Cutting away the _____ or _____ of carbon paper enables the typist to shake out the carbons without handling them.

8) A _____ with folded end helps to keep carbon and typing paper _____.

9) A manual typewriter will produce about _____ copies, using 'bank' typing paper and _____ carbon paper.

10) To produce the maximum number of carbon copies it is necessary to use _____ paper and _____ carbon paper on a manual typewriter.

11) NCR means _____.

12) NCR paper produces copies by means of _____.

13) NCR saves the typist's _____ is _____ to handle and less _____ is required in the stationery store cupboard.

14) It is, however, difficult to make _____ on NCR copies.

15) NCR copies can also be _____ marked.

16) NCR paper is more _____ than ordinary typing paper and carbons.

17) Inexpensive, thin carbon which is used once and then scrapped is called _____.

18) Sets of documents which are fed into a typewriter from a roll at the back of a typewriter on a special attachment are called _____.

19) Carbon used in this type of stationery may be _____ or _____.

Exercise 58

CARBON AND CARBON COPYING

1) Explain the term 'manifolding'.

2) Compare NCR with 'one-time' carbons, and give the disadvantages and advantages of each.

3) How does continuous stationery save a typist's time?

4) Explain the term 'weight' when used in connection with carbon paper.

5) Paper is available in different thicknesses. 'Flimsy' is known in the papermaking trade as airmail. 'Bond' is good quality paper used for top copies, letterheading, etc. Explain how 'bank' paper is used and what its quality is.

Office Copiers

Using carbon paper means that copies are made at the same time that the original is typed. Systems which exactly copy an original *after* it has been typed (or written) are:

- photocopiers
- heat transfer machines
- dual spectrum copiers
- dyeline (diazo) copiers
- electrostatic photocopiers.

PHOTOCOPYING

'Wet' photocopying is a photographic process which uses light and chemicals. The copy produced is slightly damp — this method is used infrequently for this reason.

The word 'photocopying' is now generally used to describe 'electrostatic copying' which is 'dry' photocopying (see p. 267).

HEAT TRANSFER COPYING

Heat transfer copying (also known as 'thermography') will not copy ball-point ink – only inks which have a carbon content (fibre-tipped pens, typewriter ribbon, indian ink) or lead pencil. Copies tend to fade after a time and are, therefore, useful for internal work only. A heat (thermal) copier will also make a master for a spirit duplicator or dyeline copier, an ink stencil for an ink duplicator and transparency for an overhead projector. Special paper is needed for heat transfer copies, which is expensive. A thermal copier will also 'laminate', that is, coat sheets with a thin film of plastic to protect from dust.

DYELINE (DIAZO)

This is a system mainly used in drawing offices. It involves the use of light and chemicals plus special paper. It is the cheapest form of photocopying but the copy is likely to fade.

DUAL SPECTRUM

This system uses light and heat and produces a 'dry' copy on specially treated paper, from a negative of the original which is then processed through heat to produce a dry copy. Paper for the copies is expensive and because each one has to go through two processes, it is slow. 'Dual' means 'two'.

The 'dry' process of copying is very popular in offices today because of the delay caused by waiting for damp copies to dry. Where only a few, exact copies (facsimiles) are required, the dual spectrum or heat transfer (thermal) copier are the most convenient.

ELECTROSTATIC COPYING (MODERN 'DRY' PHOTOCOPYING)

When hundreds, or perhaps thousands, of exact copies are needed urgently, the electrostatic system of copying is the most efficient. It produces a dry copy every half-second at the touch of a button on plain (bond) paper without the use of chemicals. Instead it operates by using static electricity. (You can demonstrate static electricity by combing your hair and then using the comb to pick up a small piece of paper.) Electrostatic photocopiers use a special powdered ink combined with this force to produce copies. Because no specially treated paper is used, the copies are cheaper than those produced by other types of photocopier. Plates for offset-litho duplicators (see p. 280) can also be made on an electrostatic photocopier.

Some electrostatic photocopiers will reduce the copies in size thus saving paper. The name Xerox is widely used for dry-copying and means (in Greek) dry. It is, however, a trade mark, and there are other electrostatic photocopiers available (e.g. Mitsubishi, Canon).

Photocopiers which require special paper produce more expensive copies than those which use plain paper, but the latter are much more expensive to buy and do not justify this extra cost unless large numbers of copies are needed frequently.

There is a type of photocopier that can reproduce coloured copies, but it is still very expensive and unlikely to become widely used in offices except for specialised uses.

A modern plain-paper photocopier

Guidelines on Making Photocopies

Modern photocopiers are simple to use, provided a little care is taken over positioning the 'master' copy — the one from which all the copies are to be made. Make sure that it is within the frame indicated on the photocopier, and placed square inside this, otherwise the copies will not be centrally placed on the paper, and even, in some cases, will have tops, bottoms or one side cut off completely, making the copy useless.

SAFETY

If a photocopier is not working (check that it is plugged in and switched on first, of course), phone for a mechanic from the firm who supplied it. *Do not attempt to put it right yourself!*

Don't use equipment marked 'Out of order'!

FOR YOUR FOLDER

39. OFFICE COPIERS

Write these notes in your folder, filling in the missing words and phrases.

1) Exact (facsimile) copies produced by all office copiers have the advantage of being completely _____.

2) These copies are therefore especially suitable when speed is vital, and when the original document being copied contains diagrams, technical

data or is in a foreign language, and the typist could easily make a _____.

3) The copying system widely used in drawing offices is _____.

4) Special paper required for the dual spectrum system is _____ to buy.

5) The dual spectrum system produces a _____ copy but is slow because the process involves both light and heat.

6) A thermal copier (heat transfer copier) uses _____ to produce copies.

7) A thermal copier also produces overhead projector transparencies and _____ in addition to masters for dyeline copiers.

8) Some thermal copiers also produce _____ stencils.

9) Thermal copiers will not reproduce _____.

10) When large numbers of copies are required, the most efficient, cheapest and quickest method of dry copying on to plain paper is _____.

11) Copiers which copy on to plain paper are expensive to buy (or lease) and are only necessary if _____ of copies are to be made regularly.

12) There are copiers available which will reproduce _____ but they are very expensive.

Duplicating

The word 'duplicating' refers to the production of a large number of copies whereas 'copying' refers to a small number (about six) or a single copy.

Electrostatic photocopiers both duplicate and copy, because they produce, very quickly, as many or as few copies as required.

SPIRIT DUPLICATING

A method which produces many copies from a master sheet, cheaply and quickly, is spirit duplicating. It gets its name from the spirit which is fed into the duplicator and which washes off a little of the carbon at the back of the master sheet to print each copy. It is not suitable for documents which are intended to be sent out of a firm (external use) because the copies are not 'crisp' and of sufficiently high quality. In fact, they are 'carbon' copies, although the carbon which produces them is of a different type to that used in typewriters. It is called *hectograph* carbon.

269

A spirit duplicator

Spirit duplicating has the great advantage of being the only method where colour can be introduced easily and effectively in one 'run'.

The master sheet for spirit duplicating can be written on by (ball-point, pencil or any sharp-pointed instrument) or a mixture of all three and typed on or drawn on; one side of the master sheet is coated with china clay, and it is this side which is placed downwards on the carbon paper, with the carbonised surface upwards. Thus when writing or typing on the master sheet, a 'mirror' image is transferred to the china clay side by the carbon.

Typing is carried out in the normal way, but with a slightly firmer touch. A backing sheet is essential so that the maximum amount of carbon is transferred to the master sheet. There is no necessity to switch the typewriter ribbon off by means of the 'stencil' switch. After use, the special carbon is scrapped, although small, unused pieces can be kept for the purpose of correcting errors. Any errors should either be scraped off the back of the master sheet (it is this side which does the printing) or erased with a special eraser, or painted over with correcting fluid and allowed to dry. If scraped off with a penknife or razor blade, care should be taken not to make a hole in the master sheet. After the mistake has been removed, by whatever method, a small piece of unused carbon (from the small unused pieces rescued from larger sheets) should be placed behind the error, and the correction typed very firmly over the top, or written over, as the case may be.

270

Colour is changed easily by changing the sheet of carbon behind the master sheet. There are seven different coloured carbons available: green, red, blue, yellow, brown, black and purple.

Each master sheet will produce about 300 copies. If more are required, a second master sheet is needed.

Spirit-duplicated copies fade if left in daylight for any length of time. Spirit masters can be stored and re-used, if kept flat, in protective paper folders, away from daylight. It is essential to label and date them clearly so that they can be identified when required.

Masters for a spirit duplicator can also be made very quickly by a thermal copier (see p. 266).

Paper used for spirit duplicating is non-absorbent and is suitable for writing on with ball-point pen. It is therefore useful for duplicating forms with blanks to be completed for internal use in a firm.

Spirit duplicating is particularly suitable for diagrams, maps and job cards where colour is essential. It is cheaper than other forms of duplicating when about 200 copies are required, but the quality of the work is not good enough to be used for external work.

FOR YOUR FOLDER

40. SPIRIT DUPLICATING

Write these notes in your folder, filling in the missing words and phrases.

1) A spirit 'master' will produce approximately _____ copies.

2) Spirit masters can be typed on, written on or drawn on. When you are typing, the typewriter is not switched to _____.

3) The special carbon is placed carbonised side upwards behind the _____.

4) Errors on a spirit master can be removed by a special eraser, penknife or razor blade or _____.

5) Retyping after removing an error must be done over _____.

6) Colour is quickly and easily changed by _____.

7) Spirit duplicating is the only method of duplicating where colour can be produced effectively and easily in one _____.

8) Spirit masters can be reused if stored _____ and interleaved to prevent the carbonised surface from coming into contact with other spirit masters.

9) Copies made by a spirit duplicator _____ if left in daylight.

10) Spirit duplicating is especially suitable for maps, diagrams, forms for internal use and _____.

Ink Duplicating

This is sometimes referred to as 'stencil' duplicating, because the ink in the duplicator goes through the spaces made on the 'stencil' by the typewriter keys.

An ink duplicator

Stencils are thin, tough, fibrous sheets, coated with a wax-like composition. They can be typed on, written on, or drawn on, although writing and drawing needs a special tool called a stylus, with a special steel tip. A steel plate under the stencil gives a firm surface to write or draw on.

Stylus pens

A stencil 'set' supplied by the manufacturers consists of a backing sheet, and a stencil, in between which is a piece of carbon, usually 'one-time' carbon coated on both sides. This gives a copy on the backing sheet which is easier to read for checking than the typing on the stencil, and also an impression on the back of the stencil which enables the typist to see her work as she types it. Also, the carbon paper checks the 'chopping out' of o's, p's, b's if her touch is too heavy.

While a stencil is being typed, the ribbon on the typewriter is switched off by using the stencil switch and the typeface strikes the stencil direct, over the ribbon, making the impressions through which the ink in the duplicator will pass.

272

Capital letters, figures, and fractions should be typed a little more heavily than normal, o's, c's, e's, b's, p's, full stops, commas and hyphens, as well as the underscore more gently, otherwise holes will be made in the stencil which will then print blobs of ink instead of letters.

If a mistake is made, liquid corrective (it is usually pink or white in colour) is painted over the error, a pencil inserted behind the stencil and over the backing sheet and carbon. When dry (after about 45 seconds) the correction can be typed with a firm (but not too hard) touch.

A liquid stencil corrective applied to a stencil

It is most important to remember to type in the corrections after painting on corrective, because if it has been applied and forgotten, the copies duplicated will contain blank spaces which will then have to be filled in on each sheet, separately – very time-consuming especially if thousands of sheets have been run off!

The completed stencil should be read through *before* it is taken out of the typewriter, as it is easier to make corrections then. Replacing it into the typewriter and realigning is always more difficult.

The copy on the backing sheet should be used for the final check and the safest method is for the typist to read to a colleague – it is always difficult for someone to spot their own errors.

The typeface should always be cleaned after typing a stencil, because the stencil tissue will clog letters such as a's, o's, p's and b's especially. Cleaning the typeface before typing a stencil is good practice too, to ensure a good clear stencil.

A thin sheet of clear plastic film placed over a stencil before starting to type helps to avoid clogging the typeface and also prevents cutting out o's, p's, b's, etc. if the typist has a heavy touch.

There are now special stencils for use with 'daisy wheels' on electronic typewriters.

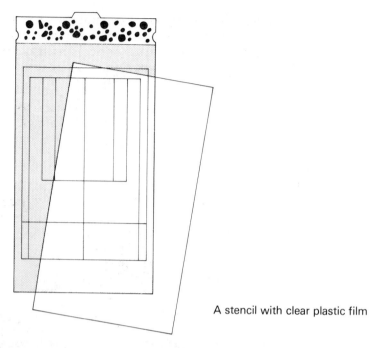

A stencil with clear plastic film

If a signature is needed on the duplicated copies, this should be done after the final checking of the stencil, with a stylus. Remember, if this is overlooked someone may be faced with the prospect of signing his or her name 5000 times!

I should have signed the stencil!

After typing, checking and signing (if required) the 'one-time' carbon is discarded, but the backing sheet remains on – it is used to smooth the stencil on to the drum of the duplicator and also to help to store the stencil if it is to be reused.

The paper used for ink-duplicating is semi-absorbent (so that the ink does not smudge) and is available in many pastel colours as well as white. Because it is slightly absorbent, it is not as suitable for writing on as spirit duplicating paper, which has a smooth surface.

Ink-duplicated copies are of good quality and suitable for external use as well as internal. About 5000 good clear copies can be obtained from one stencil if it is handled carefully and expertly.

When more than about a dozen good-quality copies of a document are required, ink duplicating is the cheapest way of producing them.

Colour can be introduced by changing the tube of ink on the duplicator, and by typing a stencil for each colour change. The duplicator drum has to be changed too, and the work on each stencil carefully aligned so that the various colours fit where required.

Ink stencils can be stored and reused; suspending in a cabinet or placing flat in an absorbent folder are the best methods. It is important to label stencils if they are to be reused, otherwise it will be difficult to identify them. One copy of the stencilled sheet should be attached, for reference.

Stencils suspended in storage cabinet

Some work to be typed on a stencil is complicated and involves columns and careful layout. In this case, it is better to type it out on plain paper first, to check spacing across and lines down, before starting a stencil. Stencils are not cheap and it is wasteful to scrap them unnecessarily.

'Grafting' on a stencil consists of cutting out the word, phrase or even a complete paragraph and replacing it with a fresh piece of correctly-typed stencil – this replacement piece is called the 'graft'.

It requires a lot of patience and practice, and spoiled stencils should be kept for this purpose. The 'graft' should be slightly larger than the piece which has been removed and is affixed to the stencil with corrective, which must be allowed to dry thoroughly before the stencil is placed on the duplicator. If the graft is a fairly large one, turn the stencil over and reinforce the corrective from the back, all around the edge of the join.

Grafting consists of cutting out a word phrase or even a whole paragraph, and replacing with a fresh piece of stencil, correctly typed.

Grafting

An electronic scanner will make stencils for an ink duplicator speedily and accurately, as also will a thermal copier (see p. 266).

An electronic scanner for making ink duplicator stencils

It is frequently said that 'anyone who can type can type a stencil'. So they can, after a fashion, but there is rather more to it than that. The finest quality stencil work depends upon the skill used in typing and operating the duplicator. Here is a checklist for typing an ink stencil:

Before starting to type have you:

- Cleaned the typeface on your machine thoroughly? One clogged character will, by its repetition ruin the appearance of the whole page.
- Switched the typewriter to stencil? (*Most important.*)
- Put correction fluid close at hand?
- Placed plastic film over stencil?
- Made sure the stencil is absolutely flat and smooth on the typewriter roller? (Any bulging will cause creases and cracks.)
- Typed a draft of any complicated work?

While typing have you:

- Remembered about typing capitals etc. more firmly and o's, p's etc. more lightly?
- Started to type well below printed 'safety-line' on stencil at top? (If too near it will smudge on the copies.)
- Retyped over all 'blanked-out' errors? (Hold up to light to make sure.)
- Checked *again* for errors?

After typing have you:

- Had someone else to check from the backing sheet while you read to them?
- Had the stencil signed? (If required.)
- Found out how many copies required and on what colour paper?
- Found out whether the stencil is to be stored for reuse?

FOR YOUR FOLDER

41. INK DUPLICATING

Write these notes in your folder, filling in the missing words and phrases.

1) An ink stencil will produce several _____ copies if handled with care.

2) An ink stencil can be stored and reused by _____ or _____.

3) Paper used for ink duplicating is _____ and not suitable for writing on with ball-point.

4) Before starting to type on ink stencil, the typeface of a typewriter should be cleaned and the typewriter ribbon switched _____.

5) Complicated stencils should be _____ first on plain paper.

6) The special tool for writing on an ink stencil is called a _____.

7) While writing or drawing on an ink stencil, it is necessary to place a _____ underneath the stencil to give a firm surface.

8) Capital letters, figures and fractions should be typed _____ than normal.

9) Full stops, underscore, hyphen, comma, o's, p's, b's, c's should be typed more _____ than normal.

10) If a mistake is made, _____ is painted over the error, allowed to dry and the correction _____.

11) If stencils are to be stored for reuse, it is important to _____.

12) Colour can be introduced on an ink stencil by changing the tube of ink, changing the drum on the duplicator and _____.

13) Ink-duplicated copies are of sufficiently high standard to be used for _____ work.

14) Plastic film placed over stencil before typing prevents _____ and also _____.

15) Ink stencils can be produced by a thermal copier and an _____.

Exercise 59

INK AND SPIRIT DUPLICATING

1) What would be the better method of duplicating to use in the following circumstances (assuming that your office had both a spirit and an ink duplicator):
   a sending 100 memos around to branch managers?
   b sending 1500 circular letters to customers?
   c duplicating 500 programmes for the firm's annual pantomime?
   d producing diagrams of a new process to be used in a workshop for 30 employees?
   e producing about 250 forms to be completed by employees in connection with a pension fund?
   f producing about 3500 price-lists to send out to other firms?
   g producing 50 copies of a sales chart with several colours?
   h producing 30 copies of the minutes of a meeting held by the sales manager?
   i producing 30 copies of an agenda for the next sales meeting?
   j producing 500 copies of the works magazine?

2) You have been asked by your employer to help to decide whether to purchase a spirit or an ink duplicator. Set out the various advantages and disadvantages of each.

3) Spirit duplicating is the system which enables colour to be changed easily. How is this done?

4) If you make a mistake on a spirit master, how do you put it right?

5) How many copies would a spirit master give (maximum)?

6) Could you store a spirit master and reuse it?

7) Name three different documents which a spirit master would be especially useful for.

8) What happens to spirit master copies if they are left in daylight?

9) Do you switch your typewriter to 'stencil' when typing a spirit master?

10) Is it possible to write on a spirit master?

11) When typing an *ink* stencil, what do you type twice (or harder than normal)?

12) What do you type more *lightly* on an ink stencil?

13) How do you correct an error on an ink stencil?

14) Can you reuse an ink stencil after it has been on the duplicator?

15) What do you write with on an ink stencil?

16) How many copies would you hope to get from an ink stencil (maximum)?

17) What do you use if your typewriter cuts letters out of an ink stencil?

18) What is *grafting*?

19) What special attention does a typewriter need before and after typing an ink stencil?

20) Which produces the best typed copies, ink or spirit?

One use of spirit duplicating

Exercise 60

DUPLICATING ASSIGNMENTS

(If you are unable to type your teacher could type these for you, ready for you to run off.)

Spirit

1) Draw a simple sketch map of the area around your school/college showing the railway stations and bus stations and any landmarks which would be helpful to a visitor who is a stranger to the area. Indicate the scale. The top of the sketch map must be north.

2) Draft a notice giving the date, time and place of a meeting to be held in your firm for the sales representatives of five areas – Midlands, West, North, South, East. Each area will have a meeting on each of five different dates – vary the colour for each meeting on the same sheet.

3) Draw up a programme for a works outing to London to go to the theatre by coach at Christmas. There will be a meal on the way to the theatre.

Ink

4) Type an ink stencil for the minutes of the meeting of the works social club at which the outing to a London theatre was agreed. Run off 12 specimen copies (or, alternatively, one for each member of your class). An ink stencil would in fact be needed for these minutes because there are 500 members of your works social club!

5) Type an ink stencil for a circular letter to customers of your firm telling them about an exhibition of your products which will be held in a large hotel in your area in about a month's time. Include a tear-off slip which can be returned to your firm, indicating whether they are likely to attend or not. Run off 12 specimen copies.

6) Type an ink stencil of a programme for a school play – run off sufficient copies for one copy each for your class.

Offset-litho Duplicating

Offset duplicating (or simply 'offset') involves taking an impression first on a rubber cylinder and from the rubber cylinder printing on to paper. This gives a clearer, smudge-free impression and produces high-quality work which is like printing. 'Litho' is the abbreviated form of 'lithography' which means literally 'printing by stone'. Printing by stone is a process using grease and water that was discovered about 200 years ago This principle of oil and water not mixing is still used in offset-lithography, but today thin metal or paper plates are used instead of stone for the master copy.

The old-fashioned way of lithographic printing

If you mop up some spilt liquid with a tissue and then press the tissue against a piece of paper, the resultant damp patch is 'offset'.

Different colours can be introduced into offset-litho duplicating, but a separate master and 'run' through the duplicator is needed for each colour.

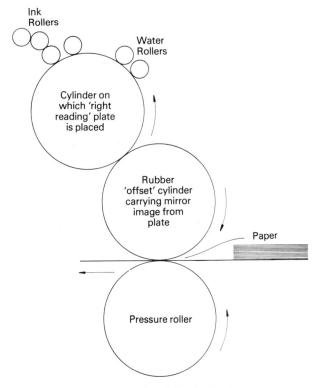

The principle of offset-litho duplicating

There are many different kinds of plates, and it is important to choose the appropriate plate for the number of copies required.

Metal plates can produce tens of thousands of copies. If only several hundred are needed, a paper plate is more economical. Both paper and metal plates can be reused if stored carefully in labelled and dated folders. Plates must be handled only at each end, as any finger prints will cause smudges on the copies.

Erasing on a paper plate can be done with a special offset-litho eraser. Erasing on a metal plate can be done with a glass brush or pumice block.

Paper used for the copies produced by an offset-litho duplicator is often of very high quality, and the copies are therefore not cheap; but the work is suitable for any printing work needed by a firm – letter headings, catalogues, price-lists, order forms and invoices.

Offset-litho duplicators are expensive to buy (or lease) and the outlay is only justified if very large numbers (hundreds of thousands) of documents are to be run off regularly. Otherwise the cost will not be recovered – forms, letter headings, etc. are more economically produced by an outside printer.

The modern, desk-top offset-litho duplicator is clean and easy to use, after initial instruction by a skilled operator.

An offset-litho duplicator

Master plates can be written on with ball-point or pencil, and typed on.

Typing requires a special offset-litho typewriter ribbon.

Master plates can also be produced by an electrostatic copier (see p. 267) or an electronic scanner (see p. 276).

REPROGRAPHY COMPARISONS

Process	Approximate No. of Copies	Speed	Cost	Quality	Colour	Master Storage	Disadvantages	Advantages
Offset-litho	Dependent upon type of plate used – metal: tens of thousands; paper several hundred	Excellent	Paper is often more expensive than that used for ink or spirit duplicating	Excellent	Yes	Yes	Operation of equipment needs special training	Plates for offset-litho can be made by electrostatic photocopier from any copy
Office copiers (excluding heat transfer copiers) (see pp. 266 – 7)	Unlimited	Excellent	High – paper is expensive	Excellent	Is possible but copies and equipment are expensive	Yes	Cost of paper and, sometimes, cost of equipment	Ease of operation
Facsimile-transceiver	One at a time	Excellent	Paper and equipment expensive	Excellent	No – see above	Yes	Only possible to send copies to recipients who have transceivers	Speed and accuracy
Word processing(see pp. 156 – 7)	Unlimited	Excellent	High cost of equipment, although silicon chips are reducing the cost rapidly	Excellent	No	Yes, in a 'memory'	Operation of equipment needs special training. VDU may cause eye-strain	Corrects errors, inserts para-graphs, re-arranges material auto-matically. Stores material in a 'memory' and re-types if required

REPROGRAPHY COMPARISONS

Process	Approximate No. of Copies	Speed	Cost	Quality	Colour	Master Storage	Disadvantages	Advantages
Carbon copies	10/12 max (6 on a manual type-writer)	Erasing slows down production speed	Low in material, high in time	Top copy only is good quality. Carbon copies suitable for internal distribution	Yes, with different coloured carbons or paper	—	Time is wasted by handling carbons	Any competent typist can produce carbon copies
NCR		Regulated by speed of typist	Special chemically treated paper is expensive	As above	No	—	Easily marked accidentally. Erasing is not possible	Clean—no carbons to handle
Spirit duplicating	200/300	Good – on an electric duplicator	Low – paper and master sheets inexpensive	Suitable for internal distribution only	Yes – very effectively and easily	Yes, with care. Can be reused	Copies fade in daylight	Master sheets can be written on or typed on. Master sheets can also be made by a thermal copier
Ink (stencil duplicating)	Several thousand	Excellent	Low – paper and stencil inexpensive	Excellent, suitable for external distribution	Is possible only by typing a separate stencil for each	Yes – in an absor-bent folder or susp-ended	The best results are achieved by typing, but it is possible to draw or write on an ink stencil with a special stylus	Stencils for ink duplicating can be made by a thermal copier or an electronic stencil cutter (scanner)

284

FOR YOUR FOLDER

42. OFFSET-LITHO DUPLICATING

Write these notes in your folder, filling in the missing words and phrases.

1) Colour can be introduced in offset-litho duplicating, but each colour requires a _____ plate and a _____ run.

2) Tens of thousands of copies can be produced by _____ plates.

3) Several hundred copies can be produced by _____ plates.

4) Offset-litho master plates can be reused if _____.

5) They must be held at the ends as finger-prints cause _____.

6) The work produced by an offset-litho duplicator is of a very high standard, suitable for catalogues, letter headings and _____.

7) The copies are not cheap and not economical unless _____ quantities are required regularly.

8) Master plates for an offset-litho duplicator can be produced by an electronic scanner and _____.

9) They can also be written on with _____ or _____.

10) Typing on an offset-duplicator plate requires a special _____.

CHAPTER 13

Filing, Indexing and Storing

A filing spike

What is wrong with this way of filing papers?

Write down all the disadvantages you can think of, and then read the next page and check your answers.

Why filing on a 'spike' is not very efficient

1) All the papers have holes in them.

2) The papers will get dusty.

3) If the bottom papers are wanted, all the others have to be taken off first.

4) The papers will get very creased around the edges.

Even so, a spike *may* be useful for keeping some papers which are unlikely to be referred to again — e.g. stores requisitions (see p.253).

Why File?

Filing means putting away papers so that they can be found when they are wanted. Everyone has papers of some sort — a birth certificate, a school report, examination certificates. These papers have to be kept because of the information on them, which may be needed at a later date.

Firms keep papers for the same reason, and they have large quantities of papers, because all their records are stored on them.

We have seen that a spike is not a very good way of filing but it is better than leaving papers in heaps, in no particular order.

It takes a long time to find one particular document if it is in a large stack of filing waiting to be put away.

Filing should be done several times a day if possible, so that the files are up-to-date.

The reason for filing!

There are several different systems of filing, but whichever system is used in a firm, dealing with filing should be done in the same way.

Trays for collecting filing

The first step to be taken when preparing to file is to collect all the papers together.

Some offices have labelled trays or wire baskets into which all the papers ready for filing are placed during the day.

These trays should be emptied frequently by the filing clerk.

While she is sorting, it is important for her to check that the papers have been attended to and may be filed. How does she know this?

Special marks or 'release symbols' are used in firms to indicate that a document has been dealt with, and may be filed. There are some examples of 'release symbols' below. These are:

- a line across the paper
- a large 'F' for 'File'
- an instruction (stamped on the paper with a rubber stamp) to file the paper.

Examples of 'release symbols'

Any documents which do not have the firm's release symbol on them should be put on one side into a tray labelled 'queries' so that the filing clerk can return them to the department they came from for confirmation that they can be filed, and for the release symbols to be added.

A filing clerk circling 'filing point' while pre-sorting the filing

While looking for release symbols, the filing clerk would be able to check the 'filing point' at the same time. The 'filing point' is the name under which the paper will be filed. It is a help if the filing point is circled or underlined on the paper with a coloured felt pen while pre-sorting.

Papers are often fastened together with paper clips or pins. These should be taken out before filing, and replaced by staples. Paper clips catch on to other papers accidentally, and pins can cause painful pricks.

After pre-sorting, checking for release symbols and marking the filing points, the next step when dealing with filing is:

PLACING THE PAPERS IN THE RIGHT FILE

This is the most important part of the whole of the filing process. A paper placed in the wrong file will be very difficult to find and could well be lost for ever.

The most recent paper is always placed on top of all the other papers in a file. These papers will have been filed in date order, too, so that the oldest paper is at the bottom, or back of the file.

Papers should be flat and square in the file so that they remain uncreased.

The other reason for placing papers carefully in a file is to keep them clean and free from dust, but mainly:

Filing is done in order to find documents when needed.

More annoyance, frustration and waste of time is caused in firms by not being able to find a paper that is needed quickly than almost anything else.

A trolley with wire trays is useful for the collection of filing

After collecting the filing, the next step is to sort it into the order in which it will be filed. This is called 'pre-sorting'.

Pre-sorting saves time, as the papers are in the right order before they are taken to the filing cabinet, and there is no need to make frequent journeys to and from the filing cabinet.

A desk-top sorter is divided into sections each labelled with a letter of the alphabet, and papers are placed behind the flaps in their right section.

A desk-top sorter

What Sort of Papers are Filed?

Much filing consists of letters which have come into a firm.

These incoming letters have the name of the firm printed in large type at the top of the paper, with the address, telephone number, possibly an international telegraphic address and Telex number — if they have one — printed underneath. Incoming business letters from firms are easily recognisable by a filing clerk. They are filed under the names of the firms who have sent them — this would be the 'filing point' which the filing clerk would circle or underline while pre-sorting.

HEATWELLS LTD

Received
13 Feb 198-
0900

Filing point

Pilgrim Street
WOLVERHAMPTON
WH33 5BQ

Tel: 532 666

Telex: 356774

Our Ref JK/DC

12 February 198–

Messrs Grant and Binns
Fairfield Works
Lincroft Trading Estate
MARSTON   M85 4TB

Dear Sirs

Our engineer, Mr G K Adams, will be calling at your works on Monday, 20 February, to discuss with your Chief Engineer the possibility of installing a new heating system in your canteen.

This has already been discussed with Mr Stephens, your Canteen Manager. Perhaps he could be present when Mr Adams calls. He hopes to be at your firm by 10 am on 20 February.

Yours faithfully
HEATWELLS LTD

Release symbol

John Kemp
Sales Manager

A business letter, with release symbol, ready for filing

Replies to Letters

When replies to letters are typed, a carbon copy is typed at the same time, and this is sent, with the letter which has been answered, to the filing clerk. They are filed in the same file.

Carbon copies do not need release symbols, as they are copies of outgoing letters.

A filing clerk would soon learn to recognise carbon copies because they are often on coloured paper, but also there is no printed name of the firm at the top of the letter.

CS/KP

12 February 198–

Heatwells Ltd ⟶ *Filing point*
Pilgrim Street
WOLVERHAMPTON
WH33 5BQ

For the attention of Mr J Kemp Sales Manager

Dear Sirs

Your letter dated 12 February has been passed on to me, and I look forward to meeting your engineer, Mr G K Adams, when he calls on the 20 February at 10 am, to discuss the proposed new heating system in the canteen here.

Yours faithfully
MESSRS GRANT & BINNS

C Stephens
Canteen Manager

A carbon copy of the reply sent to Heatwells Ltd. Note that there is no firm's name at the top of the letter.

There is another type of business letter, besides business letters from firms. This is a personal business letter – one sent from a private individual to a firm.

There would be no printed name at the top of a personal business letter. Instead, there would be a private address, either typed or written. Some people do have their own printed notepaper, but this would still consist of address and telephone number, if they had one. There would be no name at the top of the paper.

25 Avoncroft Avenue
St Andrews
MARSTON
M96 6TB

Received
14 Feb 198-
0915

13 February 198-

Messrs Grant and Binns
Fairfield Works
Lincroft Trading Estate
MARSTON
M85 4TB

FILE

For the attention of the Personnel Manager

Release symbol

Dear Sirs

Junior Shorthand-Typist

I am interested in your advertisement for a junior shorthand-typist, which I saw in last night's "Evening News", and give below details of my experience and qualifications:

Date of birth:	5 May 196-
Nationality:	British
Shorthand qualifications:	LCC certificate for 80 wpm
Typewriting qualifications:	RSA certificate Stage 3 (speed 50 wpm)
Other qualifications:	English CSE Grade 1
	Mathematics CSE Grade 2
	Office Practice RSA Elementary

Since leaving college in July 198- I have been employed as a typist in the Typing Pool at Griggs & Howe's Mail Order Company and would now like to move to a firm where I have an opportunity to use shorthand.

I am attending evening classes in shorthand at the college.

If you would like me to attend for an interview, I will be pleased to do so at any time to suit your convenience.

Yours faithfully

Elaine Knowles (Miss)

Filing point

A personal business letter

293

Personal business letters would still need release symbols to show that they had been dealt with.

In addition to letters, copies of outgoing letters, and other documents, there would be memos for the filing clerk to deal with. Many memos are not important enough to be filed, but occasionally there will be one which has to be kept for future reference.

Ref HH/OM

Filing point

15 February 198–

Miss Elaine Knowles
25 Avoncroft Avenue
St Andrews
MARSTON
M96 6TB

Dear Miss Knowles

Junior Shorthand-typist

Thank you for your letter dated 13 February in connection with the above vacancy.

Would you please call at this office on Tuesday, 21 February at 11 am? If you report just before that time at the Gate-keeper's Lodge, he will arrange for you to be shown to the Personnel Dept.

If this date and time is not convenient, would you please let me know and I will arrange an alternative appointment.

Yours sincerely

H Hancox
Personnel Manager

The carbon copy of a letter sent to Elaine Knowles in reply to her application for the post of junior shorthand typist

As well as letters, memos and carbon copies of letters, filing would include invoices, quotations, orders, credit and debit notes coming into a firm. The 'filing point' on invoices, credit notes, debit notes and orders is usually a number, and these documents would be filed in order of the number (numerical filing). Letters are usually filed alphabetically, in order of the name of the sender, or the person receiving the letter.

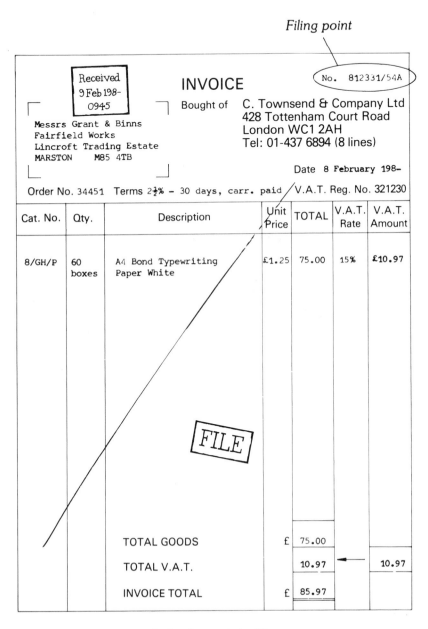

An invoice ready for filing

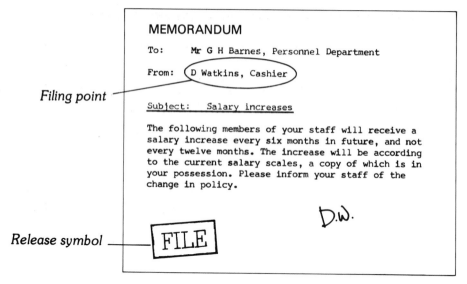

Filing point

Release symbol

MEMORANDUM

To: Mr G H Barnes, Personnel Department

From: D Watkins, Cashier

Subject: Salary increases

The following members of your staff will receive a
salary increase every six months in future, and not
every twelve months. The increase will be according
to the current salary scales, a copy of which is in
your possession. Please inform your staff of the
change in policy.

D.W.

FILE

A memorandum ready for filing

Copies of all these documents would be amongst a collection of filing, too.

A complete file borrowed should be replaced by an empty folder, ruled up and headed, known as an 'absent wallet'.

The wallet folder can then be used by the filing clerk for filing papers while the borrowed file is out.

The file for Dee Bros. has been borrowed and is marked 'Out'

Miscellaneous Files in a Filing Cabinet Drawer

A miscellaneous file is used for storing papers when there is no file for them.

When four or five papers have been received from the same firm, the filing clerk should then make out an individual folder for them.

A convenient place for a miscellaneous file is at the front of each division of the alphabet.

Papers are placed in alphabetical order in a miscellaneous file.

Placing papers in the right files is only one part of a filing clerk's job. It is the most important part, but she will also have other duties to carry out.

One of these is the lending of files and papers.

"THE NEXT THING, OF COURSE, IS TO UPDATE OUR FILING SYSTEM"

An efficient filing clerk will not let her files, or papers, be taken away without first making a note of:

- name of borrower and his or her department
- title of file or paper
- date on which it was borrowed
- date on which it was returned.

One single paper taken out of a file should be replaced by an 'out' card, similar to the one below:

			OUT	
Name of file	Borrower	Department	Date borrowed	Date returned

An 'out' card

Exercise 61

'OUT' CARDS IN FILING

Make a copy of an 'out' card and fill it in from the following details:

1) On 10 January 1978 Mrs K Lowndes of the personnel department borrowed the file of Mr H K Phillips. The file was returned on 12 January.

2) On 18 January 1978 Miss G Quinton, sales manager's secretary, sales department, borrowed the file of Shield Business Systems Ltd. The file was returned two days later.

3) On 21 January Mr B Simms, of the purchasing department, borrowed the file of Smallwood & Prince. He returned it on 24 January.

4) On 25 January Mr F Young, accounts department, borrowed the file of Stokes & Dalton Ltd. He returned it on 28 January.

5) On 30 January Mrs O Smithson, filing department, borrowed the file of Mr G Bailey and returned it the same day.

Cross out each name as the file is returned and before entering the next.

Cross-referencing

Firms may change their names, due to mergers or take-overs. People change their names, especially women when they get married, so a filing clerk has to organise a system in her files whereby anyone looking under an out-of-date name will be directed to the new name. This is done by means of a 'cross-reference'. A sheet is made out like the one opposite, and placed in the files under the *old* name.

Cross-referencing can also be used for goods and suppliers, e.g. for suppliers of typewriter ribbons, look under 'stationery'; for suppliers of carpets look under 'floorcoverings'.

Cross-referencing can also be used for letters dealing with two topics (a customer pays for an item and makes a complaint — file under Payments and Complaints, having taken a photocopy).

CROSS-REFERENCE SHEET
FOR CORRESPONDENCE FOR:
Waring and Simpson Ltd
SEE:
Swift Engineering Company Ltd

Exercise 62

ASSIGNMENT ON CROSS-REFERENCE SHEETS

Rule up 6 cross-reference sheets as under:

CROSS-REFERENCE SHEET
FOR CORRESPONDENCE FOR:
SEE:

Then fill in each cross-reference sheet with the following details (number each sheet):

1) The British United Airways file is often asked for under BUA.

2) For 'Upholstery firm' see 'Cattell & Guest, 1 Bromsgrove Road, Birmingham'.

3) The firm of Parker & Downs are now known as the Downs Export Co.

4) Correspondence from Feckenham of Barmouth is to be filed in future under 'Camping equipment: awnings' in a subject filing system.

5) For supplies of garden top soil see 'Greenfield Turf Supplies, 26 Driftwood Close, Southcrest, Deal'.

6) Miss Jane Heward is now married. Her married name is Slater, and correspondence will be filed under 'Mrs John Slater'.

Pending Papers

It is not always possible to deal with documents as soon as they are received. Some papers have to be kept while waiting for further information. These papers are known as 'pending' papers. 'Pending' means 'waiting for a decision'. A box file or lever arch file is useful for keeping 'pending' papers in, until they have been dealt with and can be filed in the main filing system.

A lever arch file

A box file A ring binder Another type of box file

Ring binders are useful for 'pending' papers, too, as they have special cards in them called guide cards. These guide cards are used to divide the papers into different sections.

An expanding file with sections, sometimes called a 'concertina' file,

An expanding folder A bulky file

could be used for 'pending' papers, and could also be used for pre-sorting papers, instead of a desk-top sorter with flaps. Another use for an expanding file would be for personal or confidential papers, which have to be taken around but still need to be arranged so that individual papers can be found quickly.

Bulky Items

Box files and ring binders may also be useful for very bulky papers, which would take up too much room in a filing cabinet and make it very heavy to open. For example the typescript of an author's book may consist of 300 pages of A4, and it could easily be kept in a box file or even put away in a cupboard.

Many offices collect A4 reports and various magazines. These can be kept tidy in magazine files which can then be placed neatly on a shelf. Books can of course be kept on bookshelves.

Front and side views of a magazine file

Storing Large Documents

Maps, photographs, drawings, and charts are too large to be stored in the standard filing cabinets. They must, however, be kept flat. If they are folded, they will crack along the folds and if they are rolled up they are difficult to keep flat when they are taken out to be used.

A horizontal plan chest with wide, shallow drawers is one way to store large documents satisfactorily.

A horizontal plan chest

301

A vertical suspension plan chest is another way, where the documents are suspended from rods in a chest deep enough to hold them.

A vertical suspension plan chest

Old Files

Eventually, some files become so packed with papers that they have to be 'thinned' out. This is done by taking out the oldest papers from the back of the file and transferring them to files which are stored out of the current filing system; they may still be needed for reference, so they should be labelled clearly, and dated, and a note of which papers have been removed placed in the current file.

These out-of-date files are called 'dead' files or 'transfer files'.

As papers cannot be kept for ever, they are eventually destroyed and the most efficient way of destroying papers is to 'shred' them in a special

A paper shredder

NOT THIS . . . BUT THIS!

The end of the filing system – but only after official instructions! No papers should ever be destroyed without authority to do so by a responsible person in a firm machine called a paper shredder. The shredded paper can then be used by the packing department – a very practical piece of recycling.

As well as making useful packing, shredded papers cannot be read by anyone who may be looking for confidential information.

The Filing Clerk's Job

- Collection of papers.
- Pre-sorting – checking for release symbols – noting filing point. Queries placed on one side for checking later.
- Placing papers in correct file, latest paper on top.
- Lending files or papers only when record of borrower has been correctly completed.
- Completing cross-reference sheets for any files where names have been changed.
- Organising miscellaneous files for single papers which have to be filed until four or five have been received from the same firm.
- Filing as frequently as possible – preferably several times a day.

The Supervisor's Job

- Arranging for 'dead' files to be made, so that bulky files are thinned out.
- Obtaining instructions from a responsible member of the firm for papers no longer required to be shredded.

FOR YOUR FOLDER

43. FILING

Write these notes in your folder, filling in the missing words and phrases.

1) Filing means _____ so that they can be found when they are needed.

2) Filing should be done _____ times a day so that files are _____.

3) The first step to be taken when preparing to file is to _____.

4) The filing clerk will know that documents have been dealt with and may be filed by special marks known as _____ on the papers.

5) Examples of these special marks are: line across the page
large 'F' for 'file'
_____.

6) The name under which a paper is to be filed is called the
_____.

7) Papers should be fastened together with _____ as pins can be dangerous and paper clips gather up other documents.

8) Papers are placed in folders with the _____ on top.

9) The main reason for filing is to _____.

10) Equipment for collecting filing from different departments may be _____ or _____.

11) Pre-sorting filing saves frequent journeys to and from the filing cabinets and a _____ is useful for pre-sorting.

12) A great deal of filing consists of letters which have come into a firm and _____ of letters which have been sent out of a firm.

13) As well as letters, filing may also include invoices, quotations, orders and _____.

14) An OUT card is used for _____.

15) If a complete file is borrowed, it should be replaced by _____.

16) A miscellaneous file is used for _____.

17) If firms change their names due to mergers or take-overs, a _____ sheet is necessary, placed in the files under the *old* name.

18) A pending file is used for _____.

19) Suitable containers for pending papers are: lever arch file
box file
ring binder
_____.

20) When papers are no longer needed, they should be _____ (but only after official instructions!).

21) Files which have become bulky should have the excess papers removed from the back of the file and stored (dated and labelled) away from the current files in a _____ file.

Exercise 63

FILING

Copy the following passage, filling in the blank spaces with one of the words in the following lists. Each word or group of words is used once only:

dead	note	cross-reference
several	filing point	sheet
name of firm	collecting papers	up-to-date
recent	uncreased	placing papers in
find	release symbols	correct files
pending	miscellaneous	desk-top sorter
	expanding	absent wallet

It is important that files are _____, so filing should be done _____ times a day. Dealing with a pile of filing is divided into three steps:

1) _____.
2) pre-sorting.
3) _____.

A _____ helps with pre-sorting, as it saves unnecessary trips to and from filing cabinets. A filing clerk can tell that papers have been dealt with and can be filed by _____ which should be on all papers which have come into a firm. Carbon copies of documents which have been sent out of a firm will not have them. Carbon copies have no _____ printed at the top. While pre-sorting, the filing clerk may find it helpful to underline the _____ which is the name or title under which the paper will be filed. The most _____ paper is always placed on top of a file. Papers should be flat and square in a folder so that they remain _____. Filing is carried out in order to be able to _____ documents quickly. A record of borrowed files should be kept by placing an _____ with the file's details on it, together with the name of the borrower and the date borrowed. Papers for which there is no file should be placed in a _____ file. Out-of-date files are eventually taken out of the current files, dated, labelled and transferred to _____ files. A _____ of these out-of-date files must be made in the current filing system, so that anyone looking for them knows where to find them. A _____ should be made out and placed in the files when a firm, or person, changes its name. Sometimes documents cannot be dealt with at once and have to be put on one side for a short time, away from the main filing system. These are known as _____ files. An _____ file, sometimes known as a concertina file, would be suitable for filing these papers.

Exercise 64

MORE ON FILING

1) What is filing?

2) Why do firms file papers?

3) Why should filing be done as many times a day as possible?

4) What are release symbols?

5) Not all papers have release symbols on them, but can still be filed. What sort of papers could be filed without release symbols?

6) What equipment would be useful for the collecting of filing?

7) What equipment could be used for sorting filing?

8) Besides release symbols, what else does a filing clerk look for while sorting filing?

9) Besides letters, many other documents have to be filed. Amongst them would be memoranda – short notes sent from office to office in the same firm. Why has the example of a memo been headed 'memorandum'?

10) Explain the differences between an 'out card' and an 'absent wallet'.

11) What would be filed in a miscellaneous file?

12) What would be filed in a 'dead' file?

13) What would be filed in a 'pending' file?

14) What is a cross-reference sheet?

15) How are papers filed in a miscellaneous file?

16) Shredding papers is a very efficient way to make use of old files. Why is this a good way to destroy old files from a security point of view?

17) Who gives instructions in a firm to destroy old files?

18) A simple but not very efficient way of filing papers is on a 'spike'. What is wrong with this method?

Folders

Papers are usually kept in folders. One type is the wallet folder which has flaps and gussets so that it can expand.

Alternatively papers may be kept in a simple folded piece of cardboard, with the back slightly longer than the front. This has no flap or gussets. It has the disadvantage of having no means of fastening papers in, so that they easily drop out. The name or title of the file is written on the longer, back portion of the folder. The thin cardboard used for folders is called 'manilla' and varies in thickness and colour.

A wallet folder

A manilla folder

Some folders have a spring, or metal clasp, which fastens the papers safely into the folder and allows them to be turned over like the pages of a book. This method ensures that papers cannot drop out of a folder accidentally, but slows down the process of filing, because the papers have to be perforated before they are placed in the folder.

A folder with a metal clasp

A folder with a spring clasp

Labelling Files

Labels for files can be flat, on the top edges of the pockets:

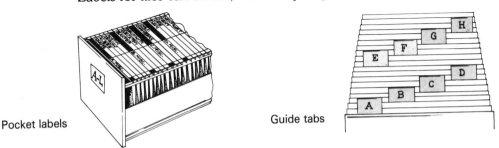

Pocket labels

Guide tabs

Also, labels for files can be on projecting tabs, which are not directly behind each other, but are 'staggered' so that they can all be seen easily. These are known as 'guide' tabs.

Colour is useful to help the filing clerk to find files quickly.

Different types of document, for example, could be in different coloured clear plastic folders.

Each section of an alphabetical filing system could have different coloured folders for easy identification of files.

Coloured guide tabs help the filing clerk to find files quickly, too.

Useful Filing Accessories

- Perforator – or paper punch – for perforating papers which are to be held in folders or ring binders.
- Staplers – standard size and long-arm.
- Embossing labeller – for labelling filing cabinet drawers.
- Guillotine or paper trimmer.
- Clear adhesive tape – for repairing torn documents or folders.

Bulldog clips

Treasury tags

Hole punches

Paper trimmer

Guillotine

- Labels – for labelling files.
- Cards – in various sizes – for card indexes.
- Reinforcing washers – for strengthening perforations.
- Treasury tags – for holding papers together loosely so that they can be turned over for reading easily.
- Bulldog clips – springs for holding papers firmly.

Vertical Suspension Filing Cabinets

Files are conveniently stored in deep drawers in filing cabinets. The filing cabinets may have two, three, or four drawers.

Vertical suspension filing cabinets. They need three times their actual floor space so that a clerk has room to stand in front of one when open. Note that filing cabinet drawers must be clearly labelled so that it is easy to find files quickly

Files stand upright – vertically – in the drawers and should be supported and held by pockets linked together. These pockets 'suspend' the files and prevent them from slipping to the bottom of the filing cabinet drawer. The correct name for this type of filing is vertical suspension filing. The weight of the files is taken by the rails, so keeping the files in perfect shape.

Vertical suspension filing

Files in a filing cabinet drawer without pockets

Lateral Filing Cabinets

These take up less floor space than vertical suspension filing cabinets, as there are no drawers to be opened – the files are arranged side by side, like books on a shelf. The word 'lateral' means 'from the sides'. Lateral filing cupboards can also be extended upwards towards the ceiling, but it will be essential to have a safe means of reaching the top shelves. Pockets in lateral filing cupboards are suspended in a similar manner to those in vertical suspension filing cabinets.

A sophisticated lateral filing system with horizontally sliding modules

FOR YOUR FOLDER

44. FILING EQUIPMENT

Write these notes in your folder, filling in the missing words and phrases.

1) Thin cardboard used for folders is called _____.

2) Labels for files can be flat, on top edges of pockets, or on projecting tabs which are 'staggered'. Staggered tabs are known as _____ tabs.

3) Filing accessories include perforator, stapler, embossing labeller, labels, reinforcing washers, bulldog clips and _____.

4) Filing cabinets containing files in vertical pockets, one behind the other, are vertical _____.

5) The weight of the files is taken by rails, so keeping the files in _____.

6) Files suspended in pockets arranged side by side is _____ filing.

7) The system of filing in No 6 is the one which saves _____.

8) Large maps, plans, photographs and charts should not be rolled or folded but filed in _____ chests either horizontal or _____.

Exercise 65

FILING EQUIPMENT

1) Describe the different types of folder used for filing.

2) What are 'guide' tabs?

3) Explain how colour could be used effectively in filing.

4) Vertical suspension filing cabinets need more space than lateral filing cabinets. Explain why this is so.

Safety

The top shelves in a lateral filing cupboard may be out of reach for some people, and a suitable step-ladder avoids accidents caused by standing on chairs or other makeshift objects.

Standing on a chair to reach the top shelf is dangerous!

A low stool on castors saves an aching back while filing in the bottom drawers of filing cabinets and is easy to move around.

Low filing stool

Vertical suspension filing cabinets usually have three or four drawers. These should always be closed after use. If the top drawer is left open while the bottom drawer is used, for instance, a nasty crack on the head could result, and if the top two or three drawers are all left open together, the filing cabinet could topple over on the unlucky filing clerk! Also, if the bottom drawer is left open, it may trip up an unwary passer-by.

Situations to avoid!

Filing cabinets should not be placed behind doors

Security of Filing Systems

Special fireproof filing cabinets are obtainable, guaranteed by their makers to protect papers from severe fire hazards. Many fireproof filing cabinets preserved their contents against enemy fire bombs in 1940.

All filing cabinets which contain confidential documents should be locked whenever the office is left unoccupied, and at the end of each day before the staff go home.

Filing cabinets usually have protruding locks, as part of the structure. These lock all the drawers in a cabinet at once, when the lock is pressed in. The idea of the protruding lock is to show when the filing cabinet is *unlocked* – it makes it obvious to the filing clerk not to forget to lock up before she goes home.

FOR YOUR FOLDER

45. SECURITY OF FILING SYSTEMS

Write these notes in your folder, filling in the missing words and phrases.

1) Filing cabinets can easily cause nasty accidents if the bottom drawer is left _____ or the filing cabinet is placed behind a _____.

2) Top shelves in a lateral filing cabinet may be out of reach, and a _____ should be used, not a chair or other makeshift object.

3) To ensure that important documents are safe in the event of a serious fire, special _____ are obtainable.

4) All filing cabinets containing confidential papers should be _____ whenever the office is unoccupied.

5) Filing cabinets usually have protruding locks, which make it obvious when the cabinets have been left _____.

6) Filing in the lower drawers of a filing cabinet can cause an aching back. This can be avoided by using a _____.

Microfilming

An alternative to plan chests for very large documents is to reduce them in size by a process known as microfilming.

Microfilming reduces documents to the size of a postage stamp. Eight thousand A4 sized documents will go on to a roll of microfilm 100 feet long. A single storage cabinet 4½ feet high will hold microfilms of one and a half million documents.

Microfilm is available in several forms. The following are convenient for filing:

- *Microfiche* – a sheet of film which holds 98 micro-images. A micro-image is an A4 sized document reduced in size 24 times.

Microfiche

- *Aperture cards* have pieces of microfilm inset into them. They are usually punched cards for use in computers or punched card installations.

ACID SOILS	3	12
GROUP	FOLIO	PAGE

BRITAIN

Wild flowering plants

Type Heather

Aperture cards

JACKETING

Microfilm can be stored in a special protective transparent wallet or envelope, but it is difficult to remove the microfilms from this protective covering. This way of storing microfilms is known as microfilm 'jackets'. It has the advantage of making it almost impossible to lose a microfilmed document.

Microfilm on spools or reels is not suitable for filing and has to be stored in specially designed microfilm cabinets.

A reel of microfilm

Microfilm cassettes or cartridges are easier to handle and less likely to be damaged than reel film but are more expensive. Reel, cassette and cartridge films all suffer from the same disadvantage – it is difficult to locate any one particular section which may be required quickly.

EQUIPMENT

The following equipment is required for microfilming:
- camera
- platform
- jacketing machine
- reader or reader/printer.

The equipment is not cheap. The total cost would be about £5,000. Film is about £2 for 100 feet, which is relatively inexpensive.

Viewing. Enlarging on to screen for reading off

Storing a reel of microfilm   Filing microfiche

Storage. Microfiling takes under two per cent of normal file space

A microfilm camera

Prints from microfilm. Any number of copies can be made. Negatives are stored for future use

Microfilm can be produced directly from computer output, without any intermediate paper copy. This is known as COM, computer output on microfilm.

Firms use microfilming in many ways, including:

- for ordinary documents, to save filing space
- for large documents – maps, plans, photographs – to save space taken up by plan chests.

Libraries also use microfilming for back numbers of magazines and newspapers and to microfilm copies of thick, heavy books, so that they do not have the problem of carrying them from room to room.

Telephone and Postcode directories for the whole of the UK are available on microfiche.

Museums microfilm very old and valuable papers so that the originals need not be handled.

The other advantages of microfilming are, in addition to space saving:

- postage is cheaper than postage for originals, especially airmail
- duplicate copies of documents can be filed so that they are available in case of damage to originals by fire.

Apart from the cost of the equipment, the disadvantages are:

- a reader is needed to be able to see the documents
- any particular section on reel or cassette is not easy to locate quickly when needed.

FOR YOUR FOLDER

46. MICROFILMING

Write these notes in your folder, filling in the missing words and phrases.

1) Microfilming reduces documents to the size of a _____.

2) The most suitable forms of microfilms for filing are _____ and _____.

3) Microfilm on spools or reels has to be stored in specially designed microfilm cabinets. There is another disadvantage to this type of microfilm – it is difficult _____.

4) Equipment required for microfilms includes a camera, platform, jacketing machine and _____.

5) The reader/printer not only magnifies the microfilm so that it can be read easily, it also _____.

6) COM means _____.

7) As well as saving the space taken up by ordinary files, firms use microfilming to save _____.

8) Microfilms are also useful as duplicate copies of documents in case of _____.

9) The disadvantages of microfilming are the cost of the equipment, the necessity for a reader to be able to see the documents properly and _____.

Exercise 66

MICROFILMING

1) What is microfiche?

2) Explain jacketing microfilms.

319

3) What are aperture cards, and how are they used?

4) Microfilming is used by other organisations besides firms. Name two of them, and explain how they use microfilming.

Classifying Filing

Filing can be 'classified' in several ways. Classifying filing means the system by which it is stored. Most filing is in alphabetical order, because this is a simple system to follow. People's names are filed in alphabetical order of their surnames. Firms, societies, organisations and clubs are filed in alphabetical order of their registered names.

Alphabetical filing has one disadvantage – some letters will hardly be used at all (X and Z for instance) and so parts of an alphabetical filing cabinet may be half-empty. Also, a thorough knowledge of the alphabetical filing rules is necessary to use an alphabetical filing system.

The top drawer in a filing cabinet, with the files arranged in alphabetical order of surnames or firms' names

General Rules for Alphabetical Filing

PEOPLE

Use surnames as filing points:

DOBSON	Michael
EVANS	Thomas
GRAYSON	Kate
HAYNES	Anne
MARTIN	Jane
OLIVER	William
QUENTIN	Carole
SIMMS	Margaret
WATKINS	Sarah
YEOVIL	Simon

Sometimes there are people with the same surname, in which case place the first names in alphabetical order:

HARRISON   Elizabeth
HARRISON   John
HARRISON   Peter
HARRISON   Theresa
HARRISON   William

Occasionally, there may be identical first names and surnames. When this happens, file by second name, or initial, if full second name is not known:

BROWN   Carole F
BROWN   Carole Joanne
BROWN   Carole W
BROWN   Carole Yvonne
BROWN   Carole Z

If there are identical first names and surnames, filing has to be done in alphabetical order of the towns in which the people live:

MARCH   Roy   Birmingham
MARCH   Roy   Coventry
MARCH   Roy   Huddersfield
MARCH   Roy   London
MARCH   Roy   Worcester

File names with prefixes such as: van, de la, O' under the prefix: (i.e. the prefix and the word is treated as part of one word name)

DE BRAY   Martha
DE LA PARKE   Laurence
O'TOURKE   Patrick
VAN DE VEMEER   Vera

'MAC' NAMES

File all Scottish names beginning with Mc, Mac or M' as if they were all spelt Mac:

McBETH   Thomas
M'BRIDE   Martha
McHENRY   Ian
MACKENZIE   Henry
MACMASTERS   Janet
McPHERSON   Martin

Some Irish names begin with M', Mac or Mc, too.

McNEIL   Sean
MACMAHON   Siobhan

St Genesius
patron saint
of secretaries

St Matthew
patron saint of
book-keepers
accountants
and tax-
collectors

St Gabriel
patron saint
of telephonists
and postal
workers

File all 'saint' surnames beginning with ST as if this were *spelt* Saint:

ST Gabriel
ST Genesius
ST John Ervine
ST Martin's Finance Co Ltd
ST Matthew
ST Philip's Benefit Building Society

Ignore titles altogether from the point of view of filing:

BROWN   Lady Jane
BROWN   Margaret
BROWN   Mrs Tina
GREY   Mrs Sally
GREY   Sir William
REDD   Alan
REDD   Lord George
SILVER Dr Mark
SILVER Noreen
WHITE   Lady Elizabeth
WHITE   Sir Harold
WHITE   Rev. Vincent

File a shorter surname before a longer one, when you have names like these.

MARCH   Andrew
MARCHE   Andrew
MARCHWARD   Andrew

Short before long!

File hyphenated names by the first part of the name (i.e. ignore the hyphen and treat whole name as one word):

CARTER-BROWN   James
SIMSON-ELLIS   Mary
TAYLOR-JACKSON   Richard
WILLIAMS-KING   Helen

FIRMS

Some registered names of firms include a first name. If so, file under the surname:

Ernest G Williams & Co Ltd
File as   Williams   Ernest G & Co Ltd

When the registered name of a firm includes two surnames, file under the first surname:

Hickson and Garrett Ltd
File as   Hickson and Garrett Ltd

File any firm's name which includes a number as if the number were spelt in full:

The 45 Club
File as   *Forty-Five*   Club (The)

Ignore the words 'The' and 'A' in names of firms:

The O'Brien Steel Works Limited
A Modern Printing Company
File as   *Modern* Printing Company (A)
                   O'Brien Steelworks (The)

Firms whose names consist of initials should be filed before firms whose names are written in full:

LKJ Engineering Co Ltd
Lamb's Furniture Co Ltd

unless it is known what the initials stand for, in which case the filing is done normally:

ICI Ltd   file under: Imperial Chemical Industries Ltd
AA   file under: Automobile Association
RAC   file under: Royal Automobile Club

FOR YOUR FOLDER

47. FILING ALPHABETICALLY

Write these notes in your folder, filling in the missing words and phrases, and putting the names in the right order.

1) If there are two surnames which are identical, then the _____ names should be used as a filing point:

   Elizabeth Jones
   Robert Jones
   Deborah Jones
   Linda Jones.

2) If there are two names with the same surname and the same first name, then filing should be under _____.

   Peter Jackson, Coventry
   Peter Jackson, Hull
   Peter Jackson, Cardiff
   Peter Jackson, Sunderland
   Peter Jackson, Birmingham.

3) File hyphenated names by the _____ part:

   Martin Allan-Jenkins
   Donald Efans-Jones
   Peter Forbes-Robertson
   Claire Carter-Dobson
   Susan Simms-Anderson.

4) File names such as:

   de la Porte
   van Hagen
   O'Connor   under the _____ part.

5) Titles such as Mr, Mrs, Dr, Sir, should be _____
   Mr F K L Dixon
   Dr M Jenkinson
   Lady Sylvia Barker
   Mrs F J Dawson.

6) 'A' and 'The' in the title of a firm or organisation should be _____.

   The Kleenwyte Detergent Co Ltd
   The Midlands Duplicating Co Ltd
   A Superior Office Cleaning Agency.

7) Scottish names, whether starting with 'Mc', 'Mac' or 'M' should be filed as if all spelt _____.

   McLellan
   McVitie

MacMillan
McMaster
M'Bride.

8) Numbers in the names of firms or organisations should be filed as if the numbers were _____.

The 2001 Publishing Co Ltd
The 15th Century History Society
The 45 Club.

9) When it is not known what initials in the name of a firm stand for, file _____.

A & A Builders Ltd
LCP Fuels Ltd
GPR Developments Ltd
CK Sports Ltd
W & E Printing Ltd.

10) Names which begin with St are always filed as if spelt _____.

St Clair-Jones
Saint Clair-Johnson
St John's Antiques
St Paul's Printing & Label Co Ltd
Saint Simeon's Society.

11) When it is known what groups of initials stand for file _____.

TUC
MEB
BBC
ITV
NCB.

12) Names which have the same letters at the beginning such as:

Johnson
Johnston
Johns
John
should follow the rule _____ before long.

Exercise 67

FILING ALPHABETICALLY

1) Write the following names in the correct alphabetical order:

David Jones
D Jones
D A Jones
Dr D Montgomery-Jones.

2) Write the following firms' names in the correct alphabetical order:

Messrs Carter and Francis, Solicitors
The Midland Secretarial Agency
A L Carter and Company Limited
Middleton and Langdale, Sons and Co Ltd.

3) Write the following names of hotels in the correct alphabetical order:

The White Lion Hotel, Basingstoke
The White Lion Hotel, Alcester
The Angel Inn, Ipswich
The Angel Inn, Keswick
The Star Hotel, Ledbury
The Feathers, Ledbury.

4) Write the following names in the correct alphabetical order:

Jan van Meeren
William de la Pole
Peter O'Connor
Mary Mackintosh
Roberto di Lorenzo
Sarah O'Malley.

5) Write the following hairdressers' names in the correct alphabetical order:

The 20th Century Salon
Betty's Hairstyling Salon
Scissors
The Unisex Salon
11th Hour Shampoo and Set
A First-Class Hairdressing Salon.

6) Write the following names in the correct alphabetical order:

James St John
Mary Saint Claire
Michael Sinclair
Robert St John Ervine
Marie Sainte
Deborah St Nicholas.

Exercise 68

FILING POINTS

Make a list of all the above names in Exercise 67 in the correct alphabetical order and under each filing point. (Example: Littlewoods Organisation Limited (The).)

Exercise 69

FILING THE RIGHT WAY AROUND

Which name would be filed first in the following pairs of names:

1) G MacKnight
   L McKnight.

2) Thomas Jones
   T P Jones.

3) Sir Walter Appleby
   Andrew Appleby & Co Ltd.

4) Arnold & Co Ltd
   G T Arnold.

5) Mary Machin
   Martin Machin.

6) John Manning, Cardiff
   John Manning, Taunton.

7) Jean Hilton-Johns
   Jean Johns.

8) Donal Mackintosh, Glasgow
   Donal McKintosh, Edinburgh.

9) Michael O'Shea
   Michael Oliphant.

10) John Parsons & Co Ltd
    Johnson & Nesbit Ltd.

11) Lieut Col James Edmunds
    Right Hon Earl of Essex.

12) Dame Margaret Shaftesbury
    Mrs Margaret Shafto.

13) William Smith
    William Smithe.

14) Robert Smithers
    Robert Smithson.

15) W T C Transport Co Ltd
    Watson Transport Co Ltd.

16) BBC
    NBC.

17) F I O Craig
    Fiona Craig.

18) The 21st Century Supply Agency
    The Twisted Chimney Antique Shop.

19) Sainsbury & Co
    K P St Albans.

20) Dirk van Olesen
    Dick Vardon.

Numerical Filing

Numerical filing

This uses numbers instead of letters to divide the filing pockets of a filing cabinet. It is easy to use because each new file is given the next number and added to the end of the existing files. Numerical filing is especially useful in insurance companies, building societies and hospitals, where policy-holders, members or patients are each given a number. Numbers are difficult to remember, however, and an alphabetical index of all the names has to be kept, with the numbers of the files against each name. This is another example of 'cross-referencing'.

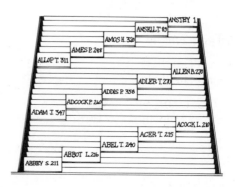

An alphabetical card index for a numerical filing system

Chronological Order

This is filing in order of the date. Most papers are placed in files in date order, with the latest paper on top, and the oldest at the back of the file.

Geographical Order

This is filing in alphabetical order of areas – either towns, countries, or continents. A travel agent would find geographical filing useful. Gas and electricity boards make use of geographical filing systems. Export departments and sales departments in firms file documents in this way.

A geographical filing system

Subject Filing

This is a useful method of filing papers under topics. Each topic or 'subject' is filed in alphabetical order. It is especially useful for filing personal papers.

Subject filing systems

With subject filing, cross-referencing would be useful. For example: 'For salaries, see wages' and 'For PAYE, see income tax'.

FOR YOUR FOLDER

48. CLASSIFYING FILING

Write these notes in your folder, filling in the missing words and phrases.

1) 'Classifying' filing means the system by which it is _____.

2) Most filing is done in alphabetical order of _____ or _____.

3) Numerical filing uses _____ instead of letters to divide the filing pockets of a filing cabinet.

4) Numerical filing is especially useful in insurance companies, building societies and _____.

5) Because numbers are difficult to remember an _____ index has to be kept with the numbers typed or written against each name. This is an example of _____.

6) Filing in order of the date is _____ filing.

7) Geographical filing is filing in alphabetical order of _____.

8) Filing in alphabetical order of topics is _____ filing.

Exercise 70

CLASSIFYING FILING

1) Explain why the bottom drawer of a filing cabinet might be half empty.

2) Numerical filing is sometimes called 'open-ended'. What does this mean?

3) Geographical filing is still done in alphabetical order of areas. What would be the main sub-division and how would the filing be organised?

4) Explain how cross-referencing could be used in connection with subject filing.

Indexing

Textbooks, reference books, any books containing facts, have indexes at the back, arranged in alphabetical order. Newspapers and magazines have indexes, too, similarly arranged. Indexes are added to books, newspapers and magazines so that readers are able to find the information they want, quickly and simply, without wading through the entire book or magazine. Indexes are needed in offices for many reasons:

- Frequently used telephone numbers
- Internal telephone numbers – extension numbers
- Callers' business visiting cards
- Alphabetical index for a numerical filing system.

All the above indexes could be typed out, or written in a book with indexed pages. These methods are quite satisfactory until new numbers have to be added, or old ones taken out, which makes the list untidy and difficult to read.

An indexed book

Exercise 71

INDEXING NUMERICALLY

On the left, overleaf, is a newspaper index. It is arranged in alphabetical order of topics. Rearrange it in numerical order of pages, putting the page number first, as below:

Page Number	Topic
20	Motors
21	Motors
22	Motors
23	Motors
24	Supermart
25	Supermart

Which would be the easiest, and quickest, method of classification to enable you to find the topic you wanted?

Exercise 72

INDEXING ALPHABETICALLY

On the right, overleaf, is an index to the small advertisements in a newspaper.

Rewrite it so that the advertisements are all in alphabetical order, as below:

Description of Advertisement	Number
Accommodation available	19
Accommodation wanted	20
Business & Commercial Premises for sale	16

THE DAILY NEWS CLASSIFIED INDEX

Appointments	26, 27, 29, 58, 59, 60, 61, 62, 64, 65, 66, 67, 68, 69
Posts in Education & Research	26
Accountancy & Finance	69
Overseas	58, 59, 60
Engineers	52, 64, 65
Sales & Marketing	66, 67, 68
Business to Business	54
Courses and Seminars	26
Entertainments	34, 35, 36, 37
Holidays & Travel	44, 45, 46, 50
Travel U.K.	50
Travel Overseas	44, 45, 46
Self Catering	45, 46
House & Garden	46
Motors	19, 20, 21, 22, 23
Personal	50-51
Collectors	50-51
Sale & Wanted	50-51
Swimming Pools	50-51
Tuition	50-51
Property	46, 47, 48, 49
Abroad	49
Country	46, 47
London & GLC area	47, 48, 49
Mortgages	47
Supermart	24, 25

GUIDE TO THE CLASSIFIEDS

(1) Situations Vacant (Professional & Trade)
(2) Situations Vacant (Office)
(3) Situations Vacant (Sales Representatives)
(4) Situations Vacant (Domestic)
(5) Situations Vacant (Agricultural)
(6) Situations Vacant (Part-time)
(7) Situations Wanted
(8) Business Opportunities
(9) Properties For Sale
(10) Properties To Let
(11) Properties Wanted
(12) Properties (Exchange)
(13) Financial/Money To Lend
(14) Land For Sale/To Let
(15) Land Wanted
(16) Business & Commercial Premises For Sale
(17) Business & Commercial Premises To Let
(18) Business & Commercial Premises Wanted
(19) Accommodation Available
(20) Accommodation Wanted
(21) Flats Available
(22) Flats Wanted
(23) Nursing Homes
(24) Travel & Holidays
(25) Caravans & Boats For Sale
(26) Caravans & Boats Wanted
(27) Caravans & Boats To Hire
(28) Motor Cycles & Cycles For Sale
(29) Motor Cycles & Cycles Wanted
(30) Cars & Commercial Vehicles For Sale
(31) Cars & Commercial Vehicles Wanted
(32) Car & Van Hire
(33) Trailers
(34) Driving Tuition
(35) Motor Spares & Accessories
(36) Motor Services & Repairs
(37) Motor Insurances
(38) Plant & Machinery For Sale
(39) Plant & Machinery Wanted
(40) Plant & Machinery For Hire
(41) Radio TV & Musical For Sale
(42) Radio TV & Musical Wanted
(43) Radio & TV Rental
(44) Radio & TV Repairs & Service
(45) Home Appliances For Sale
(46) Swap Shop
(47) Expert Services Offered
(48) Expert Services Wanted
(49) Home Improvements
(50) Photography
(51) Education & Tuition
(52) Personal
(53) Lost & Found
(54) Furniture, Furnishings & Carpets For Sale
(55) Furniture, Furnishings & Carpets Wanted

Indexing Minutes

Minutes (after being signed by the chairman) must be kept in a Minute Book, where they provide a record of decisions taken at the meetings of the association. A useful method is to paste each page of the Minutes into the book, and number each page — this avoids pages being removed at a later date.

Each topic mentioned in the Minutes can then be indexed in alphabetical order, at the back of the Minute Book, and the page number referred to (i.e. cross-referenced — see p. 298 – 9).

Card Indexes

A better method than a list or an indexed book is a card index. Separate cards are easy to add to, or to remove cards from, and the cards can be stored in boxes with lids or in small drawers.

Index cards can be typed on, or written on, and are large enough to contain several lines of information (e.g. name and address as well as a telephone number).

ROTARY CARD INDEX

Another desk-top method of storing card indexes is on a wheel which revolves. This is called a rotary card index. It stores more cards in a smaller space than that taken up by boxes or drawers and all the cards are within easy reach of the filing clerk.

A large rotary card index

Exercise 73

ASSIGNMENT ON CARD INDEXES

Below is an example of a card which is to be filed in a card index used in connection with a numerical file:

```
┌─────────────────────────────────────────────────────────────┐
│  BAXTER        Mrs Linda Katherine          File No 4551     │
│                                                              │
│                13 Hill Top Road                              │
│                GREENFIELD                                    │
│                Sussex                                        │
│                                                              │
│                Tel: 0864 778 437                             │
│                                                              │
│                                                              │
│                Account opened 5 March 1984                   │
│                                                              │
│                                                              │
│                                                              │
└─────────────────────────────────────────────────────────────┘
```

Rule up five similar rectangles, and then make out index cards as the above example for the following:

1) Mr John Edwards opened an account on 31 January 1983. His address was then 27 Temple Street, Birmingham. He moved to 28 Freeth Street, Walsall on 6 June 1984. His telephone number is now 0922 765 211. His file number is 4001.

2) On 12 February 1984 Miss Lorraine Austin opened an account. Her file No is 4325. She is not on the telephone. Her address is 22 The Square, Wilmslow, Cheshire.

3) File No 4440 was opened on 28 February 1984 for Mr Arthur West. His address is 65 Stanley Road, Wigton, Cumbria. His telephone number is 09654 334 865.

4) Mrs Jacqueline Saunders opened an account on 1 March 1984. Her file No is 4501. Her address is 10 High Street, Newark, Notts. Her telephone number is 0636 115 778.

5) Mr Frank Moreland opened an account on 3 March 1984. His address is 248 Grange Road, Weedon, Northants. His telephone number is 0327 668 343. His file number is 4548.

Exercise 74

ADDITIONAL QUESTIONS ON CARD INDEXES

1) Why is an alphabetical card index necessary for a numerical filing system?

2) What is the advantage of a card index over a written or typed list?

3) What other information, apart from an index for a numerical filing system, is often kept in the form of a card index?

4) Would an index card be typed, or written?

5) Card indexes are usually in boxes, or drawers, or on a wheel which revolves. This is called a rotary card index. What is the advantage of a rotary card index over an ordinary card index?

Exercise 75

ADDITIONAL ASSIGNMENTS ON CARD INDEXES

Make a card index of the surnames of your classmates.

Find an index to a newspaper or magazine, and make a card index from it.

Make a card index of all your singles or LPs.

Make a card index of all the hairdressers, or all the florists, in the *Classified Trade Directory*.

Make a card index of all the schools and colleges in your area.

Visible Edge Cards

Another method of storing cards is in a visible edge card index. Here the cards overlap, leaving the bottom edge of the card 'visible'. The bottom edge is used for the title, name of number of the card. Coloured markers or 'signals' are useful to draw immediate attention to any card which may need to be used frequently.

Visible edge cards in shallow drawers   Visible edge cards in a tray

Exercise 76

ASSIGNMENT ON A VISIBLE EDGE CARD

Below is a price-list for a special sale of camping equipment.

TERRIFIC PRE-SEASON SAVINGS ON CAMPING EQUIPMENT!!

CABANON FRAME TENTS	Sleeps	Rec. Price or Estimated Value	SALE PRICE
Elvire	3	£113	£89
Emelia	4	£146	£115
Emmanuelle	5	£165	£129
Pervenche	5	£300	£235
Vis-a-Vis	6	£139	£99
CROWN FRAME TENTS			
Royal	4	£125	£99
Regent	5/6	£177	£129
Majestic	4	£197	£139
Imperial	4	£194	£149
BLACKS FRAME TENTS			
Manitoba	5	£320	£185
Columbia	4	£375	£245
GOODALL FRAME TENTS			
Chalet	4	£150	£85
Quantock 4	4	£178	£109
Quantock 6	6	£244	£149
Continental 4	4	£244	£165
Continental 6	6	£310	£195
WALKER FRAME TENTS			
Texas	6	£239	£175
Arbi Madrid	5	£295	£199
El Patio Luxe	6	£376	£269
Chalet Suisse Luxe	6	£390	£279
Chalet Grande Luxe	6	£440	£299
RINCO FRAME TENTS			
Costa Del Sol	6	£250	£199

TRAILER TENTS			
Rover Super	Everyman's	£659	£399
Rapide	Everyman's	£749	£599
Popular	Conway	£645	£550
Campa Deluxe	Conway	£745	£625
Corsica	Conway	£845	£725
CONTINENTAL STYLE RIDGE TENTS			
Ariel I	Octopus	£25	£17.50
Ariel II	Octopus	£31	£22.50
Panther	Selrig	£30	£22.50
Tradition III	Cabanon	£53	£39.50
Isabelle Sport	Cabanon	£109	£69.50
Sirocco I	Lichfield	£34	£22.50
ULTRA LIGHTWEIGHT BACKPACKING TENTS			
Solite	Blacks	£56	£39.50
Parklite	Blacks	£63	£42.50
Kamplite	Blacks	£69	£49.50
Monark	Blacks	£73	£55.50
CARAVAN AWNINGS			
Popular 10'	Raleigh	£83	£49.50
Popular 12'	Raleigh	£90	£55.50
Popular 14'	Raleigh	£94	£59.50
Deluxe 11'	Raleigh	£96	£67.50
Deluxe 14'	Raleigh	£104	£75.50
Deluxe 16'	Raleigh	£110	£85.50

Later in the year, after the sale, the firm selling this camping equipment finds it useful to have a record on a visible edge card of the different price ranges of the tents. The edge of each card shows the price range, and the remainder of the card has on it the rest of the information about the tents, as below.

Type of tent	Grade	Name	Price
Continental Ridge style			
	Ariel I	Octopus	£25
	Panther	Selrig	£30
	Ariel II	Octopus	£31
	Sirocco I	Lichfield	£34
	Tradition III	Cabanon	£53
Ultra Lightweight backpacking tents			
	Solite	Blacks	£56
	Paklite	Blacks	£63
	Kamplite	Blacks	£69
	Monark	Blacks	£73
TENTS	Price range	£25 – £100	

A visible edge card

Make out visible edge cards for tents from £100 to £200, and from those between £200 and £300. Then make out a separate visible edge card for the really large tents over £600 in price.

How could you mark the card giving details about the tents priced at between £200 and £300 so that you could find it quickly?

What is the main advantage of visible edge cards, which are held in frames, and a card index, where the cards are loose, in a box or drawer?

STRIP INDEXES

Strip indexing is a method of making an indexing list on narrow strips of thin cardboard. These strips are then mounted in a frame, and the frame can be placed in a holder on the desk top or mounted on the wall. So that it is possible to type on these narrow strips, they are attached to a backing sheet and can be peeled off when they have been typed on, and placed in a panel in the correct order. The strips can be moved easily up and down the frame or panel, or taken out and replaced by new strips, and are therefore especially useful for information which is constantly changing, such as prices, telephone

A strip index held in
a loose-leaf ring binder

numbers or addresses. As the strips are so narrow, only one line of information can be typed on them.

The strips are available in about six different colours, and effective use can be made of the different colours for easy identification of various groups of prices, or different sections of the alphabet.

It is also possible to obtain strips which are in a perforated sheet, and can be torn off, after typing. These may then be held in panels in a ring binder.

Typing a strip index

A strip index held in a frame

Organisation of Filing

CENTRALISED FILING

With centralised filing all the firm's filing is stored in one large area under the supervision of trained experts in filing. The advantages of centralised filing are:

- Staff are engaged on filing and nothing else, and so are able to organise a smooth-running system.
- Junior staff are trained by the supervisor and so become efficient at filing.
- Equipment is used to the full.

There are two main disadvantages of centralised filing:
- Files may be out when needed.
- The centralised filing area may be a long way from some offices, causing inconvenience and waste of time when files are required.

Departmental Filing

Departmental filing means that each department carries out its own filing. It has the advantage of keeping all files near at hand and convenient for quick reference, but it means that many more filing cabinets are in use around a firm than are really necessary, thus wasting money as well as space. Also staff trained to carry out more specialised work (such as shorthand-typists) may be spending some of their time filing, when this could be done in a centralised filing office by filing clerks.

FOR YOUR FOLDER

49. ORGANISATION OF FILING

Write these notes in your folder, filling in the missing words and phrases.

1) Centralised filing is where all the firm's filing is stored in one large area and is looked after by _____.

2) Organisation of filing in this way is _____ because staff are engaged on filing and nothing else.

3) One of the disadvantages of centralised filing is that the files may be _____ when needed.

4) Another disadvantage is that the filing department may be a long way from some offices, causing _____ and _____ when files are needed.

5) Filing which is done by typists, shorthand-typists and secretaries in their own departments is called _____ filing. This is convenient for the office staff because papers are _____.

6) Departmental filing adds _____ to the jobs of shorthand-typists, secretaries or typists.

7) A disadvantage of departmental filing is that some of the filing cabinets may be _____.

Exercise 77

ORGANISATION OF FILING

1) Compare departmental with centralised filing and explain the advantages and disadvantages of each.

2) Why would the job of a filing clerk in charge of a centralised filing area be a very important one?

3) Filing is sometimes described as a boring job. Explain why this is a totally wrong description.

4) Filing is one of the most important clerical jobs in a firm. Explain why this is.

Exercise 78

CROSSWORD ON FILING

Copy (or photocopy) this grid before filling it in.

Across

1 When filing, it is very important to place papers in the _____ files (5)

3 When a file becomes too bulky, the correct procedure is to make a _____ file (4)

5 Besides answering the telephone, _____ of the most important office jobs is filing (3)

7 _____ filming reduces papers to a very small size (5)

11 This type of indexing is very useful for telephone numbers and price-lists (5)

Down

2 Filing and answering the telephone are _____ of the most important office jobs (3)

3 Chronological filing is filing in order of _____ (5)

4 A filing clerk will be permanently _____ a state of chaos unless she files frequently (6)

6 Numerical filing is filing in order of _____ (7)

7 Loud _____ will be caused by lost files! (5)

340

Across

13 Which is filed *last* – ONAT or ONAY? (4)
14 A special mark on a document showing it has been dealt with and may be filed, is called a _____ _____ (7, 6)
16 Which would be filed *first* – NOD, NED or NID? (3)
17 This should be clearly written on a file (5)
19 Before filing papers, pre_____ them (4)
21 Visible _____ cards are held in books or frames (4)
23 To file well is _____ efficient (2)
24 The most _____ paper is placed at the front of the file (6)
28 Which would be filed *first* – AUK, ANK, ASK, ART or AWK? (3)
29 Which would be filed *last* – ROOK, ROOD, ROCK or ROOB? (4)
32 A paper wrongly filed could well be _____ for ever (4)
34 Large maps, drawings or photographs are filed in _____ chests (4)
36 The efficient filing clerk should be able to _____ to the right file when a document is wanted (3)
37 File _____ soon as you can (2)
39 File papers _____ the correct files (2)
40 Which would be filed *last* – SEAT, SLAG, SNAG or SCAR? (4)
42 When sorting papers before filing, it is important to note the filing _____ (5)
43 Is De La Bere filed under De or La? (2)
44 One way to deal with papers no longer required is to _____ them (5)
45 _____ and Electricity Boards use geographical filing (3)
46 Which would be filed *last* – REES, REAS, REED or REEL? (4)
47 Do filing several times a _____ (3)

Down

8 Filing means storing papers _____ the right order so that they can be found quickly (2)
9 An out _____ should be placed in the files when a paper is borrowed (4)
10 Which would be filed *last* – ROE, RYE, RUE or RAE? (3)
12 It is necessary to _____ papers in order to find them (4)
15 The name of the filing system where the files are arranged like books on a shelf is _____ filing (7)
18 These could be 14 across (5)
20 _____ be an efficient filing clerk is to do a very important job (2)
22 Papers which are allowed to pile up instead of being filed at once will cause _____ if they are wanted urgently (6)
25 Filing just once a day may not be often _____ to keep it from piling up (6)
26 A desk _____ sorter is useful for pre-sorting filing (3)
27 Which would be filed *last* – GRANT, GRAIN, GRALL, GRANE or GRANO? (5)
30 Labels for files can be flat _____ the top edge of the suspension pocket (2)
31 Which would be filed *first* – KNIELY, KNEELY, KNELLY or KNOLLY? (6)
33 Which would be filed *first* – TYPER, TYLER, TAPER or TOPER? (5)
35 _____ across a document could be 18 down (5)
36 Filing papers keeps them _____, clean and uncreased (4)
38 Which would be filed *last* – SODE, SODA, SADE or SADO? (4)
41 You feel you are a complete _____ if you cannot find a paper you have been asked for! (3)

SECTION D MONEY MATTERS

CHAPTER 14

Petty Cash

What is Petty Cash?

The word 'petty' means 'small'. Petty cash means, therefore, small amounts of money paid out, or received.

Every firm finds it necessary to have cash available for payment of small items, for which the services of a bank would not be convenient. Examples of payments by petty cash are:

- Tea, coffee, milk, sugar for the office staff
- Bus or taxi fares
- Parking meter fees
- Coins for charity-collecting boxes
- Postage stamps
- Magazines for reception
- Flowers
- Cleaner's wages
- Cleaning materials – polish, soap, dusters
- Small items of office stationery – labels, shorthand notebooks, envelopes.

Looking after Petty Cash

Money used for petty cash must be kept in a lockable cash box with a removable tray, so that bank notes can be stored safely under the tray. The box must be locked in a cupboard, out of sight, when not being used.

A lockable cash box

The person in charge of petty cash is sometimes a secretary, sometimes a senior clerk. He or she saves the chief cashier's time by paying out ('disbursing') money for small items.

The petty cash book is usually kept on a system called the imprest system. The word 'imprest' means 'advance' or 'loan'. Under the imprest system a sum of money to equal the amount which has been spent is disbursed by the chief cashier to the petty cashier at the end of a regular period – usually a week or a month.

Thus, if the clerk in charge of petty cash has started the week with £20, and spent £18.30 by Friday, she will ask the chief cashier for £18.30. This amount (the 'imprest') will bring the total in her cash box back to the original £20. The amount left in her cash box before going to the chief cashier for an 'imprest' is £1.70. This £1.70 is known as the 'balance' – that is, the amount *not* spent or paid out to other people to spend, out of the £20 imprest.

Petty cash vouchers authorise the payments made from petty cash

Petty cash vouchers must be signed by the person *receiving* the money, and also by the person authorising the payment – e.g. a manager, supervisor or senior secretary. The clerk in charge of the petty cash must not pay out any money, however small the sum, without a petty cash voucher. In addition, a receipt should be produced for anything bought out of petty cash, when it is possible to obtain one. Bus and train tickets should be kept and handed to the petty cash clerk. VAT is reclaimable only when receipts can be produced.

The postage book (p. 209) is kept as a record of stamps bought and used, and acts as a receipt – the Post Office does not normally give a receipt for stamps sold by them, although they will do so if it is required specially. A voucher would have to be signed for stamps bought for an office, of course.

At any time, the petty cash clerk can make a quick check of the petty cash by totalling the amount on the vouchers and adding to it the cash in her box. The final amount should equal the amount started with originally.

Filling in a Petty Cash Form

In petty cash account sheet No. 1 (p. 348) each item on the petty cash sheet has been entered twice – once under 'Total Paid' and once under its own special heading – one of the analysis columns.

'Stamps' under 'Postage'
'Tea, coffee, sugar' under 'Office expenses'
'Cleaner's wages' under 'Cleaning'.

Analysis columns enable the office manager, petty cash clerk and chief cashier to see at a glance whether too much is being spent on a certain item. Analysis column headings vary from office to office, which is why they are left blank for the petty cash clerk to fill in. It is useful to head one column 'Miscellaneous'. This can be used to enter any item which does not normally have to be paid for out of petty cash, i.e. does not fit under other headings.

A column headed 'Stationery' would be used for all items normally bought at a stationers – string, ball-point pens, shorthand notebooks, pencils, rubber bands, staples, adhesive tape, envelopes, A4 and A5 bond and bank, blotting paper, postcards, typewriter ribbons, typewriter erasers, liquid typewriter corrective, carbon paper, paper clips, rubber stamps and pads, glue, scissors, ink, bulldog clips, treasury tags, rulers, folders, index cards, and so on. Only occasional items should be bought with petty cash – most stationery is bought by the buying office and issued under stationery stock control in a large firm (see Chapter 11).

A column headed 'Travel' would be used for bus fares, train fares and taxi fares. Larger amounts would have to be authorised by the

Cash received in this column.

Year over top of column.

Voucher number.

Analysis columns totalled separately.

Date cash received.

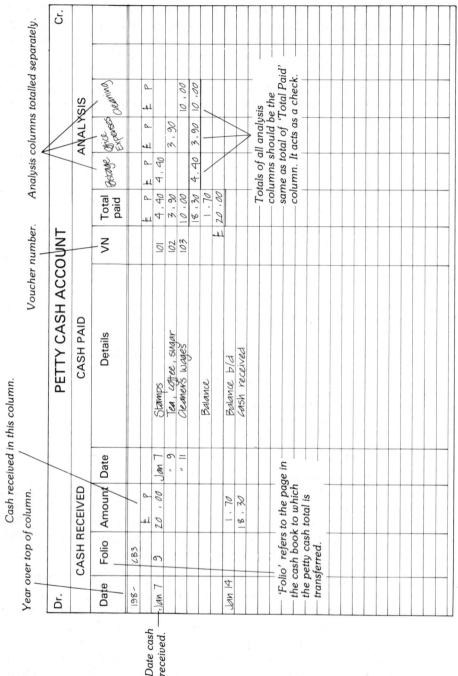

PETTY CASH ACCOUNT

Dr.								ANALYSIS		Cr.
CASH RECEIVED			CASH PAID							
Date	Folio	Amount	Date	Details	VN	Total paid	Postage	Office Expenses	Cleaning	
		£ P				£ P	£ P	£ P	£ P	
198–										
Jan 7	CB3		Jan 7	Stamps	101	4.40	4.40			
	9	20.00	" 9	Tea, coffee, sugar	102	3.90		3.90		
			" 11	Cleaner's wages	103	10.00			10.00	
						16.30	4.40	3.90	10.00	
				Balance		1.70				
						£20.00				
Jan 14		1.70		Balance b/d						
		18.30		Cash received						

'Folio' refers to the page in the cash book to which the petty cash total is transferred.

Totals of all analysis columns should be the same as total of 'Total Paid' column. It acts as a check.

department dealing with travel and would not come out of petty cash (air fares, for example).

'Office Expenses' can be used for small items – tea, coffee, sugar, milk, flowers.

Any item which occurs fairly regularly would need its own analysis column heading – i.e. meter fees for parking or flowers for reception.

'Cleaning' would include soap, polish, dusters, window cleaning as well as the cleaner's wages.

'Postage' would include any surcharge paid on letters arriving understamped (see p. 205) and purchase of international reply coupons, registered envelopes and stamped envelopes, as well as stamps.

Each analysis column is totalled separately, and the combined totals should agree with the 'total paid'. If they do not agree, a mistake has been made. This 'cross-checking' ensures that any mistakes can be spotted and corrected.

The difference between the 'total paid' and the amount of cash received is the 'balance' – i.e. the amount remaining in the petty cash box.

The 'balance' is brought down first on the petty cash sheet, and the amount of imprest (i.e. cash to restore the balance to its original amount) is written underneath. The petty cash sheet is then ready for the next entries.

The folio number of the petty cash sheet refers to the page number in the cash book in which petty cash is entered – e.g. 'CB3' means 'cash book, page 3'.

FOR YOUR FOLDER

50. PETTY CASH

Write these notes in your folder, filling in the missing words and phrases.

1) The word 'petty' means _____.

2) Money used for payments out of petty cash must be kept in a lockable cash box with a _____ tray, so that _____ can be safely stored underneath.

3) The cash box must be _____ in a cupboard when not being used.

4) Petty cash book is usually kept on the _____ system.

5) Under this system a sum of money to equal the amount which has been spent is disbursed by the chief cashier to the petty cash clerk at the end of a _____ period – usually a week or a _____.

6) Petty cash is not paid out unless a voucher is produced, signed twice – once by the person _____ the money and once by the person _____ the payment.

7) In addition a _____ should be produced whenever possible.

8) At any time, the petty cash clerk can make a quick check of her petty cash by totalling the amount on the _____ and adding it to the _____ in her box. The final amount should equal the _____.

9) Each item on a petty cash sheet has to be entered twice – once under 'total paid' and once under its own special heading – one of the _____ columns.

10) Petty cash is used in offices for the payment of _____.

Exercise 79

ASSIGNMENTS ON PETTY CASH

1) Rule up your own petty cash sheet and call it no 2.

Make out five petty cash vouchers and number them 103, 104, 105, 106 and 107.

Date them for 1, 2, 3, 4 and 5 February respectively, 198—. The folio is CB3. *(continued on p. 352)*

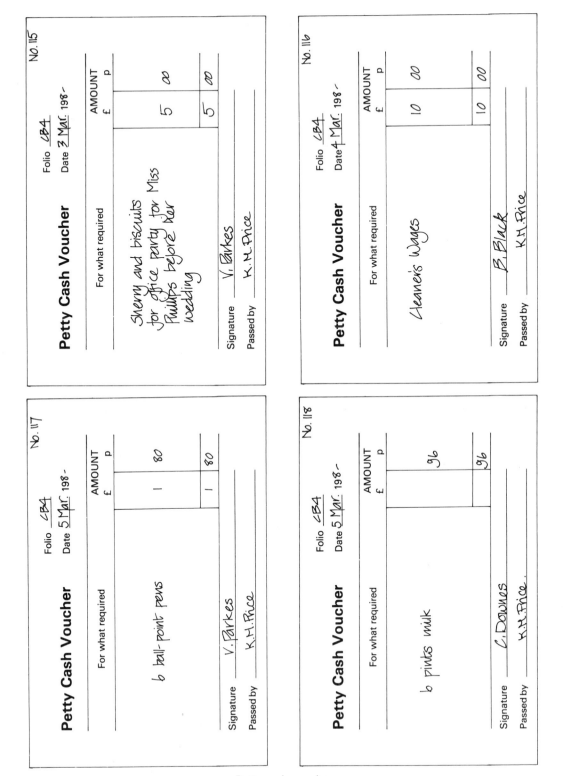

Petty Cash Voucher

No. 115

Folio CB4
Date 3 Mar. 198-

For what required	AMOUNT	
	£	p
Sherry and biscuits for office party for Miss Phillips before her wedding	5	00
	5	00

Signature _____ V. Parkes

Passed by _____ K. M. Price

Petty Cash Voucher

No. 116

Folio CB4
Date 4 Mar. 198-

For what required	AMOUNT	
	£	p
Cleaner's Wages	10	00
	10	00

Signature _____ B. Black

Passed by _____ K. M. Price

Petty Cash Voucher

No. 117

Folio CB4
Date 5 Mar. 198-

For what required	AMOUNT	
	£	p
6 ball-point pens	1	80
	1	80

Signature _____ V. Parkes

Passed by _____ K. M. Price

Petty Cash Voucher

No. 118

Folio CB4
Date 5 Mar. 198-

For what required	AMOUNT	
	£	p
6 pints milk		96
		96

Signature _____ C. Downes

Passed by _____ K. M. Price

Petty cash vouchers

351

Petty cash voucher no 103	Stamps	£10.00	Analysis column – Postage
Petty cash voucher no 104	Tea-towels	£2.50	Analysis column – Cleaning
Petty cash voucher no 105	Milk	64p	Analysis column – Office supplies
Petty cash voucher no 106	Bus fare	90p	Analysis column – Travel
Petty cash voucher no 107	Surcharge on letter	10p	Analysis column – Postage

Sign the vouchers yourself as the person receiving the money. Exchange with your neighbour for her to sign as person authorising the payment.

Enter the vouchers on a petty cash sheet and number the sheet 2. Your total amount of petty cash can be carried from petty cash sheet no 1 (p. 348).

The balance on petty cash sheet no 2 should be either £5.68 or £6.86 or £5.86.

Your petty cash sheet no 2 should show the correct figure.

2) Petty cash sheet no 3 (p. 353)

This petty cash sheet is unfinished.

Add up the analysis columns, check with 'total paid' and enter the balance.

Bring balance down on 15 February 198—and restore the imprest to £20.

3) Petty cash sheet no 4 (ruled by you).

Enter vouchers nos 113–118 (pp. 350 – 1) on petty cash sheet no 4, carrying down balance and cash received from petty cash sheet no 3, after you have completed it.

Finish off the petty cash sheet in the usual way, ready for the next week's entries.

4) Petty cash sheet no 5 (incorrect) (p. 354)

Two of the analysis columns have been totalled incorrectly.

The 'total paid' is wrong; therefore the balance is incorrect, too.

Copy out petty cash sheet no 5 and put the mistakes right.

5) Petty cash sheet no 6 (ruled by you).

Enter the following on petty cash sheet no 6:

Analysis column headings: postage, stationery, travel, office expenses, miscellaneous, cleaning

Balance brought down:	£9.52	
Cash received	£20.48	
June 8	Window cleaning	£5.00
June 9	Adhesive tape	£1.30
	Stamps	£10.00
June 10	Coffee and tea	£1.55

(continued on p. 355)

PETTY CASH ACCOUNT

Dr.   Cr.

| CASH RECEIVED | | | CASH PAID | | | | ANALYSIS | | | |
Date	Folio	Amount	Date	Details	VN	Total paid	Postage	Stationery	Travel	Misc.
198–	CB3	£ P	198–			£ P	£ P	£ P	£ P	£ P
		5 . 86		Balance b/d						
Feb 8		14 . 14		Cash received						
			Feb 8	Charity collection box	108	0 . 50				0 . 50
			9	Stamps	109	5 . 50				
			10	International Reply coupon	110	0 . 25				
			11	Envelopes	111	1 . 20		1 . 20		
			12	Train fare C.Downes	112	3 . 35				
						10 . 80				

Petty cash sheet no 3

353

PETTY CASH ACCOUNT

Dr.   Cr.

CASH RECEIVED				CASH PAID				ANALYSIS				
Date	Folio	Amount	Date	Details	VN	Total paid	Postage	Travel	Stationery	Office Expenses	Misc.	
		£ p				£ p	£ p	£ p	£ p	£ p	£ p	
198-	CB4											
June 1		5.80		Bal. b/d								
		24.20		Cash received								
			June 1	Stamps	121	15.00	15.00					
			" 2	Taxi fare	122	2.50		2.50				
			" 3	Flag seller	123	0.50					0.50	
			" 3	Parking meter	124	0.40					0.40	
			" 4	String	125	0.35			0.35			
			" 5	Tea and sugar	126	0.83				0.83		
			" 5	2 new cups	127	0.90				0.90		
						20.58	15.00	2.50	0.35	2.63	0.50	
						9.42						
		9.42		Bal. b/d		£30.00						
		20.58		Cash received								

Petty cash sheet no 5

June 11	Soap	90p
June 12	Cleaner's wages	£10.00
	Bus fare	40p
12	Flagseller	50p

Total, enter balance, bring down in usual way, restoring the imprest to £30 for 15 June 198—.

Exercise 80

BALANCING THE PETTY CASH

1) On 31 March 198—your balance of petty cash in hand was £5.25 and cash received was £24.75. Enter up the following, and bring down the balance on 14 April 198—.

April	1	Stamps	£5.50
April	1	Polish and dusters	£1.65
April	2	Taxi fare	£1.45
April	3	Envelopes	45p
April	6	Soap	70p
April	6	Stamps	£4.50
April	7	Train fare	£2.30
April	7	Pencils	£1.20
		String	35p
April	9	Surcharge on letter	24p
April	10	Coffee, tea	£1.75
April	11	Window cleaning	£2.00
April	12	Milk	32p
April	13	Bus fare	20p

2) Date for one week ago.

Cash received is £20

Travelling expenses	£1.60
Stamps	£2.00
Electric light bulbs	£1.05
Typing paper	£1.50
Tea, sugar and coffee	£1.75
Stamps	£1.00
Airmail letter forms	55p
Milk	45p
Fares	60p
Shorthand notebooks	£1.10

Balance the petty cash, show amount of cash received from cashier and take balance down to start again for the next day.

CHAPTER 15

Buying and Selling

Buying

An example of an ordinary, everyday 'business transaction' is when a customer goes into a shop, chooses what he or she wants to buy, pays for it (perhaps receives a receipt) and is given change. The exchange of goods for money forms part of everyone's lives — the shopkeeper makes a small profit on each transaction, which helps to pay the rent of the shop, lighting, heating, and the wages of any assistants he may have.

Similarly, all firms, large and small, make their profit by selling goods or providing services for which people are prepared to pay.

Employees of firms do not go 'shopping' for anything they want to buy on behalf of the firm. Instead, they write to the suppliers of these goods asking for details — price, delivery date, catalogues or leaflets giving any other information necessary. This is known as an 'enquiry' and it may be a short letter as below.

```
                    SHAW & SHORT LTD
                        Wholesaler

                       Whitaker Street
                        MANCHESTER
                         M96 8TB
  Tel: 432 888                              Telex: 990 111

  Our Ref: PM/JK                            15 November 198-

  The Sales Manager
  Office Equipment Supply Co Ltd
  Knightley Road
  BROMSWOOD    Lancs
  T45 7BC

  Dear Sir

  I am interested in buying an addressing machine and noticed
  in your recent advertisement in Office Equipment News that
  you manufacture several models. Could you please send me details
  of prices and delivery dates, together with descriptive leaflets
  or catalogues?

  Yours faithfully
  SHAW & SHORT LTD
     Peter Mason

  Peter Mason
  Purchasing Officer
```

A short letter of enquiry

Alternatively, an enquiry may be on a specially printed form, which asks for the same information, as below:

SHAW & SHORT LTD
Wholesaler

Whitaker Street
MANCHESTER
M96 8TB

Tel: 432 888   Telex: 990 111

ENQUIRY FORM

To: ....   Date: ....
....
....
....

Dear Sir

I am interested in buying ....

Could you please send me details - prices, delivery dates, leaflets and/or catalogues as soon as possible?

Yours faithfully
SHAW & SHORT LTD

Peter Mason
Purchasing Officer

An enquiry form

The enquiry form, with its printed paragraph, saves the typist's time or can, when necessary, be filled in in handwriting, if no typist is available.

Peter Mason, the purchasing officer of the firm of Shaw & Short Ltd, made the first step in his 'shopping' for his firm — his intended purchase being an addressing machine.

A few days later Mr Mason received a reply from the suppliers he had written to, enclosing some leaflets illustrating several addressing machines, a price-list and delivery dates.

Mr Mason, before making up his mind which one to buy, would probably want to see a demonstration of one or two machines, and even ask for one to be left with his firm for a week so that it could be tried out.

Then, the sales manager of Office Equipment Supply Co Ltd would be asked to send a quotation for the machine decided upon, to Shaw & Short Ltd.

```
QUOTATION

OFFICE EQUIPMENT SUPPLY CO LTD
Knightley Road
Bromswood
Lancs
T45 7BC                        Tel 859 333              Telex: 674231

To: Shaw & Short Ltd                       Date: 1 December 198–

    Whitaker Street

    Manchester                             No: BAM 16

    M96 8TB


    For the attention Mr Peter Mason, Purchasing Officer

    Dear Sirs

                                    15 November
    In reply to your enquiry dated .............. we have
    pleasure in quoting you as follows:
```

Quantity	Description	Catalogue No	Price	VAT	Total
1	Addressing machine	HG 732–89	£190	£27.79	£217.79

```
    Delivery: ex stock          Terms: 2½%  30 days

    P Benson
    Sales Manager
```

A quotation

The quotation from Office Equipment Supply Co Ltd would be one of several from different firms; the purchasing officer will then be able to choose which addressing machine would be the most suitable, basing his choice upon:

- Price.
- Delivery – whether it would be available immediately, or whether he would have to wait, possibly several weeks.
- Suitability for the work it would have to do. There are some very large addressing machines which also fold and insert letters into the envelopes. Mr Mason was interested in one which automatically printed envelopes only – he did not want the folding and inserting attachments.
- Terms of payment. Some firms offer more than others – some offer none at all.

After taking the above factors into account, Mr Mason and the mail room supervisor decided to arrange a demonstration of the addressing machine manufactured by Office Equipment Supply Co Ltd. After the demonstration, it was left with them for a week, to try it out in the mail room, and the decision was then made to buy it.

```
                                        SHAW & SHORT LTD
                                        Whitaker Street
Date 12 December 198-                    MANCHESTER
                                        Tel: 859 333    Telex: 674231
To Office Equipment Supply Co Ltd

   Knightley Road

   BROMSWOOD  Lancs

   T45 7BC                              No. ____526____

Please supply & deliver

| Cat          | Qty | Description        | £    p  |
|--------------|-----|--------------------|--------|
| HG<br>732-89 | 1   | Addressing machine | 190    |
|              |     |        + VAT       | 27.79  |

Terms  2½%  30 days                    Total  £217.79

Delivery  Ex stock        Signed _____
                                    Purchasing Officer
```

An order form

The next step in this business transaction was to send an order. Orders have to be signed by the purchasing officer of a firm or one of his assistants with authority to sign. Orders are numbered, and dated, and copies are sent to:

- Accounts department
- Mail room supervisor (who will use the addressing machine)
- Purchasing department files.

Information on an order is based on the quotation.

Selling

When the order from Shaw and Short Ltd was received by Office Equipment Supply Co Ltd the details on it were checked by the sales department (price and delivery) before passing it to stock control. Delivery had been stated on the quotation as 'ex stock' which means that it could be taken out of stock and despatched at once.

Before sending the addressing machine, the sales department of Office Equipment Supply Co Ltd sent an 'advice note' to Shaw and Short Ltd, advising them that it would be sent that day. Packed into the box containing the addressing machine would then go a 'delivery note' which would have to be signed by the customer and given back to the driver of the van which brought the machine – any damage would be noted on the delivery note.

At the end of the month following the delivery of the addressing machine the 'invoice' would be sent by Office Equipment Supply Co Ltd to Shaw and Short Ltd. An invoice is a 'bill'. It is numbered, dated, quotes the customer's order number, and sets out the full price,

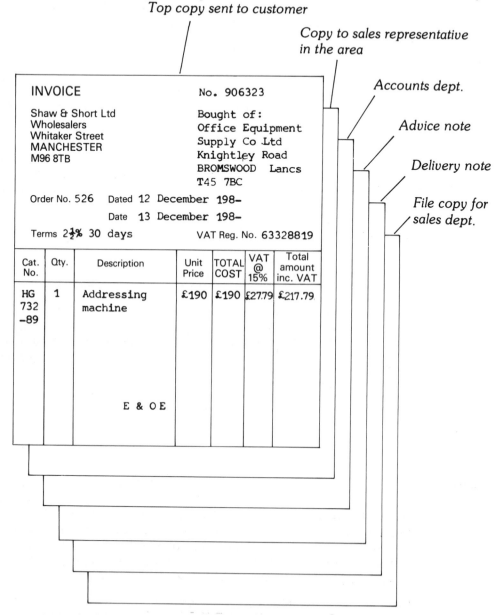

Top copy sent to customer

Copy to sales representative in the area

Accounts dept.

Advice note

Delivery note

File copy for sales dept.

INVOICE   No. 906323

Shaw & Short Ltd   Bought of:
Wholesalers   Office Equipment
Whitaker Street   Supply Co Ltd
MANCHESTER   Knightley Road
M96 8TB   BROMSWOOD   Lancs
                                    T45 7BC

Order No. 526   Dated 12 December 198–

              Date   13 December 198–

Terms 2½% 30 days   VAT Reg. No. 63328819

Cat. No.	Qty.	Description	Unit Price	TOTAL COST	VAT @ 15%	Total amount inc. VAT
HG 732 –89	1	Addressing machine	£190	£190	£27.79	£217.79

E & O E

Note that VAT is worked out on £190 less 2 ½ % cash discount (i.e. £185.25).

These copies are different colours for easy identification. They would be NCR or one-time carbon and possibly continuous stationery to save time (see p. 209)

E & O E means 'errors and omissions excepted'. If the typist makes a mistake when typing the price, it does not bind the seller (in this case, the typist could have typed £19.00 which would have made a great deal of difference).

360

plus VAT and terms of payment. In this case, if Shaw and Short Ltd pay for the addressing machine within 30 days of receipt of the invoice, they are entitled to deduct 2½ per cent from the cost – 2½ per cent of £190 is £4.75 making £185.25 to which £27.79 VAT is added totalling £213.04, and so the amount of the cheque sent to Office Equipment Supply Co Ltd is £213.04 if sent within 30 days of receipt of invoice. VAT is added after all discounts are deducted, including cash discount for prompt payment whether the customer pays promptly or not.

All firms pay for goods after the goods have been received – no money is sent with orders. The 'terms' mentioned on the quotation are an encouragement to a customer to pay promptly. The terms can vary from firm to firm. Some firms do not offer any, in which case the terms are described on the invoice as 'net'.

When a large quantity of goods is being purchased, a firm may offer a trade discount to the customer. This is deducted by the seller when he makes out the invoice and is not affected by *when* the customer pays – it is quite separate.

Other Printed Forms

In addition to the forms already mentioned there are three others frequently used in business transactions.

PRO FORMA INVOICE

This is a special type of invoice sent *before* the goods are delivered if:
- Credit standing of customer is in any doubt (i.e. he may be a new customer)
- Goods are sent on approval (on a sale or return basis)
- Goods are sent to an agent or sales representative, who has goods on a sale or return basis.

DEBIT AND CREDIT NOTES

These notes are sent after the invoice. A 'debit note' indicates to the customer that he was undercharged on the invoice and owes the supplier more than was stated on the invoice. A 'credit note' indicates to the customer that he was overcharged on the invoice and owes the supplier less than was stated on the invoice. A 'credit note' would also be sent for packing cases returned, goods returned as damaged, or not as ordered.

STATEMENT

A 'statement' is sent to a customer at the end of each month by most firms, and shows how much he has paid to the supplier during the month, how much he has bought and any credit or debit due to him. The last figure in the right-hand column shows how much the customer still owes when the statement is made up, or if his account is clear.

DEBIT NOTE

Shaw & Short Ltd
Wholesalers
Whitaker Street
MANCHESTER
M96 8TB

No 387
12 December 198–

Dr to:

Office Equipment Supply Co Ltd
Knightley Road
BROMSWOOD
Lancs
T45 7BC

Order No: 433   VAT Reg No 63328819

Date	Description	Amount
198–		
19 December	Undercharge on Invoice No. 906341	£ 12.00

CREDIT NOTE

Shaw & Short Ltd
Wholesalers
Whitaker Street
MANCHESTER
M96 8TB

No 423
21 December 198–

Dr to:

Office Equipment Supply Co Ltd
Knightley Road
BROMSWOOD
Lancs
T45 7BC

Order No: 487   VAT Reg No 63328819

Date	Description	Amount
198–		
21 December	Packing cases returned against Invoice no. 906353	£ 7.00

362

```
STATEMENT


Shaw & Short Ltd                    Office Equipment Supply Co Ltd
Wholesalers                         Knightley Road
Whitaker Street                     BROMSWOOD     Lancs
MANCHESTER                          T45 7BC
M96 8TB
                                              Payments
                                                 and
Date             Invoice No.        Purchases   Returns    Balance

198-                                   £                      £

13 December      906323             217.79      ----       217.79
19 December      906341              12.00      ----       229.79
21 December      906353             ----         7.00      222.79



                                                          The last
                                                          balance in
                                                          this column
                                                          is the
                                                          amount owing
```

FOR YOUR FOLDER

51. BUYING AND SELLING

Write these notes in your folder, filling in the missing words and phrases.

1) Usually the first step a firm makes in a business transaction is sending an enquiry to another firm. This may be a _____ or _____.

2) The department in a large firm which carries out the buying of goods for the whole firm is the _____ department.

3) The reply to an enquiry, sent from the _____ department of the firm supplying the goods, is a _____.

4) The choice of where to place an order depends upon price, suitability of goods and terms of payment, as well as _____.

5) Terms of payment vary from firm to firm. Some firms offer only net. Terms are an inducement to customers to pay _____.

6) After deciding which firm to buy goods from, the next step is to send an order. The information on the order is based on a _____.

7) An order has to be signed by _____ or his _____.

8) An invoice is sent after the goods have been delivered to the customer – usually at the end of the following month. *Before* goods are

despatched, a copy of the _____ as a goods advice note is sent to customer.

9) Another copy of the invoice is packed with the goods as a _____ note.

10) A detailed copy of the invoice is sent to customer after he has received the goods, usually at the end of the month following delivery. Other copies of the invoice go to _____ and _____.

11) An invoice gives details of the unit price (price each), total price, terms, and _____ is added.

12) E and OE on an invoice means _____.

13) Delivery 'ex stock' means _____.

14) The document sent to customer when he has been *undercharged* is a _____.

15) The document sent to customer when he has been *overcharged* is a _____.

16) At the end of each month, a customer receives a document setting out how much he has spent, how much he has paid, and how much he still owes. The name of this document is _____.

17) A *pro forma* invoice is sent before goods are delivered if credit standing of customer is unknown, for goods on approval (sale or return) or to a _____.

18) A trade discount is offered for _____.

Exercise 81

PRICE-LISTS

Refer to the price-list opposite.

1) What does 'delivery ex stock' mean?

2) What does 'trade discount on orders for 3 machines or over, 10 per cent' mean?

3) What does 'terms 2½ per cent 30 days' mean?

4) Why is the price-list dated?

5) Work out the VAT on a standard 12 inch carriage typewriter, manual.

6) Work out the VAT on a standard 12 inch carriage typewriter, electric.

7) What would be the cost (not including VAT) of two portable typewriters with pre-set tabulators?

8) Work out the invoice price (i.e. 10 per cent trade discount deducted and VAT added) for five portable typewriters with variable tabulators (electric).

OFFICE EQUIPMENT SUPPLY CO LTD
Knightley Road
BROMSWOOD
Lancs
T45 7BC   Tel: 859 333   Telex: 674231

PRICE-LIST

TYPEWRITERS

Catalogue No	Description	Price VAT not included
BG 78-21	Portable with pre-set tabulator Elite typeface. Manual.	£40.00
BG 79-22	Portable with variable tabulator Elite typeface. Manual.	£68.00
BG 80-23	Portable with variable tabulator Elite typeface. Electric.	£99.50
BG 81-24	Standard typewriter (12" carriage) Pica or Elite typeface. Manual.	£170.00
BG 82-25	Standard typewriter (12" carriage) Pica or Elite typeface. Electric.	£360.00
BG 83-26	Standard typewriter (15" carriage) Pica or Elite typeface. Manual.	£185.00
BG 84-27	Long carriage typewriter (20" carriage) Pica or Elite typeface. Manual*.	£200.00

All machines supplied with a set of cleaning tools, a cover, and
a felt mat.
Portable typewriters have a carrying case with handle in addition.

TRADE DISCOUNT on orders for 3 machines or over - 10%

DELIVERY ex stock

* DELIVERY for long carriage (non-standard) typewriters
approximately 6 weeks.

TYPEWRITER ACCESSORIES

AT 100-28	Ribbons- all black, plastic carbon	£15.00 for 20
AT 100-29	Ribbons- black and red " "	£15.20 for 20
AT 101-30	Ribbons- all black, fabric	£12.00 for 20
AT 101-31	Ribbons- black and red, fabric	£12.20 for 20
AT 102-32	Ribbon cassettes, all black	£1.10 each
AT 103-33	Ribbon cassettes, black and red	£1.20 each
AT 103-34	Correcting ribbons	£3.20 each
AT 104-35	Typewriter covers (for 12" and 15")	£1.75 each
AT 105-36	Typewriter mats, black felt	80 each

TRADE DISCOUNT on orders minimum value £15.00 - 15%

Terms: (on all orders) 2½% 30 days

1 August 198-   (This cancels all previous price-lists)

9) Then deduct 2½ per cent which customer would be entitled to subtract from the amount he pays if within 30 days of receipt of invoice.

10) Work out the price for 100 typewriter ribbons (black and red), fabric. Add VAT at 15 per cent and deduct trade discount of 15 per cent.

11) Work out the price for eight typewriter covers, adding VAT. Would this be of the minimum value for trade discount of 15 per cent?

12) What would be the VAT (15 per cent) on 250 ribbons, all black, plastic carbon?

13) What would be the trade discount on 250 ribbons, all black, plastic carbon?

14) Work out the VAT on one correcting ribbon.

15) What would be the trade discount on 20 typewriter ribbons, black and red, plastic carbon?

Office Routine for Purchasing Goods

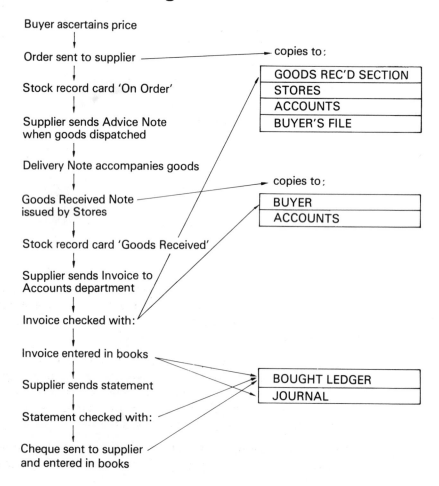

Buyer ascertains price
↓
Order sent to supplier ———————————→ copies to:

GOODS REC'D SECTION
STORES
ACCOUNTS
BUYER'S FILE

Stock record card 'On Order'
↓
Supplier sends Advice Note when goods dispatched
↓
Delivery Note accompanies goods
↓ ———————————→ copies to:

BUYER
ACCOUNTS

Goods Received Note issued by Stores
↓
Stock record card 'Goods Received'
↓
Supplier sends Invoice to Accounts department
↓
Invoice checked with:
↓
Invoice entered in books
↓

BOUGHT LEDGER
JOURNAL

Supplier sends statement
↓
Statement checked with:
↓
Cheque sent to supplier and entered in books

Credit Control

A sale is not complete until goods are paid for.

Credit (monthly account) is very convenient to businesses – payment is made at the end of each month.

Precaution must be taken to prevent bad debts.

Overdue accounts should be put on a stop list. Coloured flashes may be used to indicate a 'stopped' account. Flashes may also be used to indicate habitually slow payers. If shortages of goods occur, preference will be given to customers who pay promptly.

Persistent follow-up of overdue accounts is essential. First statement should be followed by a copy statement, then by a personal letter or telephone call. When everything has been tried, legal action may be taken – this may result in the debtor being bankrupted.

Dealing with overdue accounts

In the case of limited companies particular care is necessary in granting credit. The only safe way is to make preliminary examination of its affairs at Companies House in Cardiff. These will indicate size, profitability and rate of growth of company.

Firms must always take up references on new customers before granting credit. This may be a trader's reference (a supplier with whom the customer has been trading for some time) or a banker's reference. (The new supplier's bank will obtain this from the customer's bank.) A trade protection society may also be consulted.

When references have been obtained a strict control of credit levels must be exercised until customer is well known and well regarded (i.e. if £50 credit is allowed this should on no account be exceeded by the customer).

Delivery of goods may be withheld until enquiries are made.

If customer urgently needs goods, cash on delivery service may be used or a *pro forma* invoice (see p. 361).

Terms Used in Buying and Selling

Carriage fwd:	The buyer pays for carriage
Carriage paid:	The seller pays the carriage
Carrier's risk:	The carrier is responsible for loss or damage to goods in transit except under certain conditions
Cash discount:	An allowance, e.g. 2½ per cent, offered to a buyer to induce him to pay promptly. The rate and period are shown on the monthly statement of account
Ex stock:	From stock
Ex works:	The buyer pays carriage from the factory
F.o.b.:	The seller pays all expenses until the goods have been loaded on to the ship
Franco:	In addition to paying all carriage and insurance, the seller will pay customs duties
Loco:	The buyer takes the goods from their site and pays all subsequent charges
Owner's risk:	The owner can claim on the carrier only when misconduct by his servants can be proved
Pro forma invoice:	Used for goods sent on approval, or as a form of quotation
Terms net monthly:	The full amount shown on the statement of account is due
Trade discount:	An allowance, usually expressed as a percentage, given to enable the wholesaler or retailer to make a profit. It is also given to encourage bulk buying, special displays, or to customers of long standing

Customer's Record Cards

A customer's record card is kept in some firms so that a quick reference can be made by clerical workers in the sales department to information which may be needed, such as:

● name of purchasing officer
● name of his assistant
● how long the firm has been a customer

- whether the customer has any overseas branches
- the name and telephone number of the sales representative in the area
- credit-worthiness.

CONFIDENTIAL

CUSTOMER'S RECORD CARD

Name .... Shaw & Short Ltd., wholesalers .... Account No .... 60091 ....

Address .... Whitaker Street .... Telephone No......... 859 333 ....

.... MANCHESTER   M96 8TB .... Telex No ...... 674231 ......

....

Area .... North West ....

Representative in area .... Margaret Pratt .... Telephone No.. 576 311 ....

Name of firm's purchasing officer .... Peter Mason ....

Extension No ...... 79 ....

Purchasing officer's assistant .... Sandra Summers ....

Extension No ...... 78 ....

Average total value of goods purchased per month ... £300 ....

Average total amount credited per month .... £300 ....

Sales Representative seen with/~~without~~ appointment (delete whichever does not apply)

On Direct Mailing List   Yes/~~No~~ (delete whichever does not apply)

Other relevant information

First order placed .... 8 February 198– ....

Firm's overseas branches . None ....

A customer's record card

Exercise 82

ASSIGNMENT ON A CUSTOMER'S RECORD CARD

Rule up a blank customer's record card and write (or type) in the headings. Then fill in with details overleaf:

Customer: Grosvenor Manufacturing Co Ltd
Grosvenor Works, Thorne Trading Estate, Nottingham
NS4 3IB
Tel 221 884   Telex 998 753
Representative in area: Simon Newman Tel 931 222
Name of firm's purchasing officer: Elizabeth Smith (Mrs) Ext 47
No purchasing officer's assistant.

Average total value of goods purchased per month: £1,000
Average total amount credited per month: £1,000
Sales representative seen without appointment (if prepared to wait about 30 minutes).
Not on direct mailing list.
First order placed: 10 August 198—.
Overseas branches in Paris and Milan.

Exercise 83

ASSIGNMENT ON PRICE-LISTS (refer to price-list on page 365)

1) *An order*
   Make out an order for Grosvenor Manufacturing Co Ltd for:
   60 typewriter ribbons, black and red, fabric
    3 correcting ribbons

2) *Invoice*
   Make out one copy only for above. Supplier: Office Equipment Supply Co Ltd. Enter correcting ribbons at £5.20 ea.

3) *Credit note*
   Make out a credit note for overcharge for sending three correcting ribbons and charging for four.

4) *Statement*
   Construct a statement with the following information on:
   Opening balance owing £35.50
   Payment of £50
   Invoice as above
   Show final amount owing
   Put in appropriate dates and invoice no.

Exercise 84

BUYING AND SELLING

1) Name two sources of information available to a purchasing department.
2) Trade discount is given for prompt payment. True/False?
3) Who pays the delivery and transport costs on goods purchased 'ex works'? Purchaser/Supplier?

4) After a quotation has been accepted what document will a purchasing officer send to a supplier of goods as confirmation?
5) What is received by a purchaser in reply to a letter of enquiry?
6) Who normally signs an internal requisition?
7) Why do firms allow cash discounts?
8) Who receives the top copy of a purchase order?

Exercise 85

MULTIPLE-CHOICE QUESTIONS ON BUYING AND SELLING

1) In reply to enquiries, a purchasing department will expect to receive:

   a a quotation
   b a credit note
   c an invoice.

2) 'Carriage forward' means:

   a the seller pays carriage
   b the buyer pays carriage
   c the carriage is included in the price.

3) 'Ex stock' means:

   a no stock available
   b within two weeks
   c immediate from stock.

4) Most firms will give credit to prospective customers without making enquiries or asking for references:

   a true
   b possibly
   c false.

5) If goods are returned, chargeable 'empties' returned or an invoice has been overcharged, the seller issues:

   a a debit note
   b a credit note
   c a consignment note.

6) A statement of account is sent out:

   a after each transaction
   b at fixed intervals, usually monthly
   c only once a year.

7) Cash discount is offered to buyers:

   a to enable them to make a profit
   b to encourage them buy in bulk
   c to encourage them to pay promptly.

8) 'F.o.b.' means:

   a the buyer pays all expenses
   b the agent pays all expenses
   c the seller pays all expenses until the goods are loaded on the ship.

9) If invoices were typed in sets with copies to various departments, which would be the odd man out?

   a accounts
   b sales
   c purchasing.

Exercise 86

MORE ON BUSINESS TRANSACTIONS

1) From the following particulars, rule up and complete an invoice form:

   On 15 February 1977, James Lyon & Co Ltd, of Sizewell, Kent, sold to William Walters, 271 Main Drive, Coventry, West Midlands, the following goods:

   10 reams ruled paper A4 @ £1.20 a ream
   25 reams plain paper A5 @ £1.10 a ream
   Trade discount allowed was 25 per cent
   Cash discount allowed was 5 per cent 7 days or 2½ per cent 30 days.

   Mr Walter's order no was 6073 and delivery was carriage paid. VAT applies at 15 per cent.

2) Explain the meaning of 'cash discount 5 per cent 7 days or 2½ per cent 30 days'.

3) What is the meaning of the abbreviation VAT?

4) Why does Mr William Walters need to have this invoice?

5) Who pays the cost of carriage for the goods in this particular transaction?

6) Invoices are usually typed with several copies. The top copy is sent to the customer, and one is retained for filing. Suggest where two other copies might go.

7) Hallamshire Supplies Ltd, Norfolk Road, Sheffield, a firm of wholesalers, supplied P Wells & Co Ltd, with the following goods on 18 January 198—:

4 refrigerators	@	£60 each
10 electric mixers	@	£15 each
10 electric fires	@	£12 each
6 spin dryers	@	£35 each
Trade discount	20%	
Cash discount	2½%	one month

On 20 January P Wells & Co returned one refrigerator and two spin dryers which had been damaged in transit. They also drew the attention of the suppliers to the catalogue price of the fires which was £10 each.

8) What action would Hallamshire Supplies take when the goods were returned and they received the complaint about the overcharge on the fires?

9) Using the above information, rule up a statement of account which would be sent by Hallamshire Supplies to P Wells & Co at the end of January 198—. Fill in all the necessary details.

10) Explain the difference between a cash discount and a trade discount.

Exercise 87

ASSIGNMENTS ON INVOICES

INVOICE

WILTON, WATKINS AND IRVINE LIMITED,
93 BOWLING STREET,
SHEFFIELD SH3 4AD

Quote this number on all communications

DATE   YOUR ORDER NO.

QUANTITY	DESCRIPTION	RATE	£

---

1) On 1 May your company (Wilton, Watkins and Irvine Ltd) sold 20 tables to J Berry Ltd, 10 Lower Street, Sornborough at £15 each. You allow a trade discount of 15 per cent and 4 per cent cash discount within one month.

    a Complete the invoice on p. 373 for this sale.

    b Distinguish between trade discount and cash discount.

    c What sum would J Berry Ltd pay if the account were settled on 15 May?

    d What would have to be paid if the account were settled on 15 June?

INVOICE

BARRY FABRICATIONS LIMITED

WALSALL   W3P 8YY

Invoice Number

Tel: Walsall 236511
Telex: 646172

| Date | Your order | Terms |
| | Despatch date | Carr Paid |

Qty.	Description	Code Number	Unit Price	Price	VAT	TOTAL

TOTAL VALUE

Delivery address

---

2) Complete the above invoice from the following details: Porterhouse Printers Ltd, of Cantwell Road, Plymouth, Devon, ordered exactly one week ago (order no 92746) 24 three-drawer metal filing cabinets, 90 cm high, fitted with lock, colour ocean-blue, and six file cupboards with two folding doors 180 cm high and fitted with rails for five rows of lateral filing. For the first item the stock code is 12/07/0169, at £20.70 each totalling £496.80, and for the second item 12/06/0159, six off at

£25.40 each totalling £152.40. Porterhouse want these goods sent to their Exeter branch, which is at 27 Totnes Road. Barry's will despatch today by British Rail and will give 12½ per cent 14 days discount, invoice no being 73/822353. *Include the total of the goods, but ignore VAT calculations and entries.*

List other documents likely to be made out at the same time as this invoice.

Exercise 88

INTERPRETING A STATEMENT

Answer the following questions on the statement below:

1) What is the name of the supplier?
2) What is the reference number of the customer's account?
3) How much did the customer owe at the beginning of the period?
4) How much did the customer spend during the month of September?
5) How much did the customer pay during the period?
6) How much did the customer owe at the end of September?

STATEMENT

Williamson & Co. Ltd.
16 George Street
BATH

Mr P Freeman
295 Portland Avenue
LONDON W1D 9QX

A/c 6/F138

Date		Purchases	Payments and Returns	Balance
July 1	Balance forward			2.40
10	Cash		2.40	
Sept 18	Goods	17.32		
21	do.	5.91		
25	do.	29.18		
30	do.	51.77		
	Cash		20.50	
	Credit note		2.50	81.18

375

Exercise 89

ASSIGNMENTS ON WRITING ORDERS

1) Prepare an order for:

   10 reams no 64 Mill Bond Paper, A4 @ £1.20 per ream;
   10 reams no 50 Bank Paper, A4 @ 65p per ream;
   5000 Abermill Bond White Envelopes @ £4.50 per 1000.

   The supplier's terms are net, thirty days against statement and delivery is free of charge by their own delivery service.

2) You work for Stiggins and Bleach Ltd, of 49 High House, Chisleworth, London, W1, a firm with several branches, and are told to order six gross black lead HB pencils @ £1.57 per gross and two dozen quality hexagonal pencils @ £1.80 per gross from Cowerby Stationery Supplies Ltd, 29–31 The Rise, Hilchester, Anyshire. You usually receive five per cent discount for orders over £6.00 from this company. Delivery is required at the head office: the stationery department.

   Draft a letter, ordering the above goods.

CHAPTER 16

Wages and Salaries

Wages or Salaries

The two words 'wages' and 'salaries' have exactly the same meaning, but over the years a tradition has been established of describing wages paid weekly (or hourly) as 'wages' and wages paid to non-manual workers (usually monthly) as 'salaries'. The advantage of having wages paid every week is that it is easier for the wage-earner to 'budget' – that is, pay for travelling, food and clothes. If the employee is paid monthly, he or she may spend a lot for the first two weeks of the month and then be in debt for the last two weeks.

Many years ago, employers often paid workers in 'kind' – that is, not with money but with goods of various types. A farm worker, for example, might receive milk, eggs, or a free cottage; a clothing worker might receive a piece of cloth. Another system paid the workers with vouchers which could only be exchanged at shops owned by the employers. Many such practices are now banned under the Truck Acts of 1831 and 1870. Employees must be paid in notes and coins of the realm or cheques or credit transfer into a bank account (see p. 407) under the Payment of Wages Act 1960.

Rates of Pay

There are several ways of calculating wages.

PIECE WORK AND BONUS SCHEMES

Under a piece work system of payment, workers are only paid for each article produced or operation carried out. Workers employed where bonus schemes operate (either individual or group) receive a flat-rate wage per week, below which their earnings cannot fall for a standard week, and earn bonus for all production over the set target figures.

TIME RATES

Under this arrangement a rate is set for each hour worked. A higher rate is paid for overtime – that is, any time worked beyond what is a normal working day. This system boosts the pay of workers who are punctual and are willing to work long hours. Deductions for lateness are usually made.

Each worker, when he arrives at work, 'clocks in' – that is, he puts his card in the machine attached to a clock and the machine stamps the time on the card. When he leaves, he takes the card out and another time is stamped on the card.

DAY	IN	OUT	IN	OUT	Total
am MON pm					
am TUES pm					
am WED pm					
am TH pm					
am FRI pm					
am S pm					
am SU pm					

CLOCKED	OVERTIME
SHIFT ALLOWANCE	OVERTIME ALLOWANCE
SHIFT ADJUSTMENT	OVERTIME ADJUSTMENT
£	£

OTHER ADJUSTMENTS

EXPENSE CODE	AMOUNT
	£
	£
	£
ADJUSTMENT CODE	AMOUNT
	£
	£

The front and back of a clock card (also called a 'time' card)

The stamped time cards act as a record of attendance (many office workers who are not on 'time rates' have to 'clock in' for this reason). Also, the time cards are used to work out wages for those on time rates. Frequently, the worker is identified by a number which becomes his clock number.

COMMISSION

Many people engaged on selling the goods their firm makes receive a commission on sales and are paid a relatively small weekly or monthly salary because of this. A salesman who is good at selling is able to increase his salary far more than one who is less hard-working and this acts as an incentive to sell.

FOR YOUR FOLDER

52. WAGES AND SALARIES

Write these notes in your folder, filling in the missing words and phrases.

1) Wages paid to non-manual workers, usually monthly, are known as _____.

2) Weekly wages have the advantage of enabling the workers to _____ more easily.

3) Monthly salaries can encourage the worker to spend too much in the first fortnight of the month and then get into _____ towards the end of the month.

4) All employees – manual and non-manual – must be paid in notes and coins or cheque or _____.

5) Where workers are paid for each article they make, or each operation they carry out, this is known as a _____.

6) A time rate is where a rate is set for each _____.

7) Overtime is sometimes paid for at a higher rate. Overtime is any time worked beyond what is a _____ working day.

8) All manual workers on piece rates or time rates have to clock in and out. The stamped time cards act as a _____.

9) A salesman is able to increase his salary by selling large quantities of his firm's goods on which he is paid _____.

Gross and Net Pay, Deductions

The rate agreed with an employer (whether calculated on an hourly, weekly or an annual basis) is the *gross* wage or salary. Before any wages are paid to employees, certain deductions are required to be made by law – otherwise known as statutory deductions. Other deductions are agreed by the employee (i.e. they are voluntary) and when all deductions have been totalled and taken away from the gross pay, the remainder (known as net pay) is paid to the employee. The difference between gross and net pay can be quite large. It is often a shock to someone receiving their first pay packet.

STATUTORY DEDUCTIONS (REQUIRED BY LAW) FROM PAY

National Insurance contributions – scaled according to earnings (employers also pay National Insurance on behalf of each employee). National Insurance contributions are calculated on *gross* pay. The employer is responsible for forwarding both his contribution and his employee's to the Inland Revenue. Every person over 16 is liable to pay National Insurance contributions, whether still at school or not, if they earn over £27 a week. The percentage of gross salary to be paid is reviewed annually by the Department of Health and Social Security.

NATIONAL INSURANCE

There are three rates for National Insurance contributions:

- Standard – paid by most people.
- Reduced – paid by certain married women and widows.
- Nil – because a worker has reached pensionable age (*but* the employer still has to pay his contribution).

Self-employed people (those working for themselves, such as hairdressers, decorators, windowcleaners) pay less than standard contributions because the benefits to which they are entitled are less – no unemployment pay, for example.

National Insurance numbers are sent to all schools for school leavers by the Department of Health and Social Security, to whom application should be made if the number is lost.

PAYE (INCOME TAX)

The second statutory deduction from pay is income tax (known as PAYE – Pay As You Earn, because it is deducted weekly or monthly from everyone who earns a regular income).

The amount of income tax deducted from wages depends upon a code number which is allocated by the Inspector of Taxes, who works for the Inland Revenue Department. This code number is based upon the information contained in a form supplied by the Collector of Taxes (Form P1) to everyone earning money regularly. It is essential that this form be filled in and returned to the Collector of Taxes, otherwise the maximum amount of tax will be deducted under an Emergency Code Number allocated by the tax office. Form P1 is usually sent out each year to everyone who is a wage-earner.

Income for the purposes of Income Tax means:

- Wages (or salaries)
- Overtime
- Bonuses or Christmas gifts in money
- Interest from savings accounts
- Dividends from shares
- Pension
- Holiday pay
- Commission
- Rent from furnished lettings
- Profits from businesses and professions
- Social security benefits
- Tips received in connection with employment
- Perquisites (cars, houses, telephones), known as 'perks' when supplied as part of wage or salary.

Tax return

Income and Capital Gains for year ended 5 April 1984
Allowances for year ending 5 April 1985

P1 tax return 1984-85

Issued by

H.M. Inspector of Taxes

Date of issue

Please use the space below if you need to correct your
name and address or wish to add any details. Is your
postcode correct?

....

....

....

Postcode ....

- Before you start to fill in this form, please read "How to fill in your tax return."
  Look at each section before you write in your entries.
- If you are a woman and the return is addressed to you, make all your entries in the
  "Self" boxes and columns.
- If you are a married man and your wife is living with you, you must show all her income
  and chargeable gains and assets acquired.
- Remember to include all your income, even if you have already paid tax on it.
- Please be brief and give only the details asked for in the notes. If you do need extra
  space for any section, enter the total on the form and attach a separate piece of paper
  with the details.
- Do not forget to sign the declaration at the end of the form.
- Send the form back to me as soon as possible. If you delay you may pay the wrong
  amount of tax.
- If you need help or more information, please ask me.

PI (1984)

The front of Income Tax form P1

Certain allowances can be offset against income tax. These allowances
are given for the following, but must be claimed on Form P1 – the Tax
Inspector will not know the wage-earner is entitled to them unless he is
informed:

- Interest on mortgage repayments to a building society
- Dependants – (man) – earned income allowance, wife, any other
  dependent relatives not earning any money
  (wife) – earned income allowance – if she has a job
  (unmarried woman) – single person's allowance

- Any special protective clothing needed for a job – boots, overalls, spectacles, gloves
- Any special tools required for a job
- Books for teachers
- Subscriptions to trade unions and other official professional organisations connected with a job or profession
- Special income tax allowances for the blind
- Interest on bank loan which qualifies for tax relief (not all do).

Income which is completely tax-free
- Student grant or scholarship
- War widow's pension
- Child benefit allowance
- Maternity pay
- Sick pay
- Industrial injury or disablement pensions
- First £70 interest from National Savings Bank ordinary account

There is no tax relief for National Insurance contributions.

Some tax is paid direct on your behalf, e.g. Building Society interest.

Any of the above information which is relevant should be entered on Form P1 so that the correct code number can be allocated for an employer to know how much tax to deduct from the gross pay.

Employee's Tax Code. A tax code is the amount of annual income an employee may earn before paying tax – e.g. Tax Code 180 means tax-free income of £1800 per annum.

At the end of every tax year Form P60 is sent to every employee, showing the total amount of tax which has been deducted during the previous 12 months. The year for income tax purposes starts on 6 April and finishes on 5 April of the following year.

When changing from one job to another, Form P45 must be obtained from the previous employer and taken to the new one. This shows how much income tax has been deducted up to the date of leaving and also the code number. If Form P45 is not taken, tax will be deducted on an emergency coding, and may be much more than is normally paid.

At the end of the income tax year (5 April) the following should be sent to the Collector of Taxes, by the employer:
- Deduction cards for each employee
- Form P35 (the employer's annual declaration and certificate) which shows both NI contributions and income tax
- Any balance of NI contributions and income tax due.

Form P11. This is the official deduction card for PAYE and NI. If an employee is earning too little to pay tax, a deduction card for NI purposes only should be completed to show the NI contributions payable. The amount of pay need not be entered.

No one pays tax on the whole of their income. Everyone is given a tax-free allowance to set against their income and tax is paid only on what remains after these allowances have been deducted. Income tax is worked out over a whole year and the tax-free allowances are also yearly – the PAYE system spreads the load over a year and prevents tax having to be paid in one big 'lump' at the end of the tax year on 5 April. The idea is that on 5 April each year each wage earner does not owe the taxman any money.

Voluntary Deductions from Pay

In addition to income tax and National Insurance contributions, which are compulsory by law (statutory) an employee may agree to have certain other deductions from his pay.

SAVINGS FUND

Usually this is money put in a fund as a form of saving for a specific purpose, e.g. holidays or purchase of an expensive article such as a car. It may be contributions to SAYE (Save As You Earn), which is a savings fund operated by the Government and from which money cannot be withdrawn for a minimum of five years.

SOCIAL FUND

This goes towards the social activities organised by a firm, e.g. sports, drama, music.

TRADE UNION DUES

This is a regular (usually small, but it varies) contribution made by employees who agree to join a trade union.

CONTRIBUTIONS TO A PENSION SCHEME

The pension may be a private one (in which case the employee is known as 'contracted out') or may be the Government's scheme, in which case the employee is known as 'not contracted out'.

Contributions to a pension scheme provide security in retirement and every worker should make proper provision for old age. Every worker over the age of 18 has to contribute to a pension scheme – either the Government scheme or a firm's own scheme. Upon retirement, a worker will then be entitled to two pensions, one from his firm (or Government) based on his 20 best earning years, and one which will be his basic retirement pension based on his National Insurance contributions.

FOR YOUR FOLDER

53. DEDUCTIONS FROM PAY

Write these notes in your folder, filling in the missing words and phrases.

1) After deductions agreed by the employee together with statutory deductions have been made from pay, the remainder is known as the _____ pay.

2) Statutory deductions are those required by _____ to be deducted from pay.

3) Statutory deductions are National Insurance and _____.

4) National Insurance contributions are calculated on _____ pay.

5) Every person over _____ years of age has to pay National Insurance contributions, whether still at school or not, if they earn over £27 per week.

6) There are three rates for NI contributions – standard, reduced and _____.

7) The amount of income tax deducted from wages depends upon a _____ number.

8) This number is based upon the information contained in a form supplied to everyone earning money – Form _____.

9) There is no tax _____ for National Insurance contributions.

10) The form which is sent to every employee annually showing the total amount of tax deducted during the previous 12 months is Form _____.

11) When changing from one job to another Form _____ must be taken by the employee.

12) The end of the income tax year is _____ April.

13) Voluntary deductions from pay are agreed to by the _____.

14) The official deduction card showing PAYE and NI is _____.

15) PAYE spreads the load of tax due over a year and prevents tax having to be paid in one big 'lump' at the _____.

16) No one pays tax on the _____.

17) The form sent out to all employees annually which must be completed so that the correct coding can be worked out is _____.

18) If this form is not completed, an _____ code number will be

allocated and the amount of tax deducted may be higher than it should actually be.

Exercise 90

WAGES AND SALARIES

1) The words 'wages' and 'salaries' have exactly the same meaning, but over the years, they have come to have a separate meaning. Explain the difference between them.

2) What is payment 'in kind'? What is the importance of the Truck Acts in connection with payment in kind?

3) What is the difference between gross pay and net pay? Why is net pay sometimes quite a shock to a new wage-earner?

4) Explain the importance of Form P1.

5) Explain the importance of Form P45.

6) What has to be sent to the Collector of Taxes at the end of each tax year?

7) What is the importance of Form P11?

8) 'No one pays tax on the whole of their income.' Explain this statement.

9) What is the main object of the PAYE system?

Payment of Wages

Payment of wages can be done by cheque, credit transfer, direct debit (through a current bank account) by National Giro, or by cash (notes and coins). According to the National Westminster Bank in May 1980, over half of the British workforce still preferred to receive their wages in the form of cash. This means that firms must transport from a bank well before the day wages are paid out sufficient money and coins to make up into the exact amount for each pay packet.

In order to calculate exactly how many £50, £20, £10, £5 notes and £1, 50p, 20p, and 10p coins will be needed a cash analysis has to be worked out as below.

When this cash has been received from the bank, it is possible for all the wage packets to be made up exactly to each worker's net amount. Not only does it take a great deal of time to pay wages in cash, but there is also an immense amount of risk involved while the money is in transit. This is the reason for the use of special security vans. It is also a good idea to vary the day, time and person if money is collected weekly from a bank to be paid out in wages.

WAGES CASH ANALYSIS

Clock No.	Name	Wage	£20	£10	£5	£1	50p	10p	5p	2p	1p
351	BROWN J	£31.70	1	1	–	1	1	2	–	–	–
352	WHITE E	39.75	1	1	1	4	1	2	1	–	–
353	GREY S	42.20	2	–	–	2	–	2	–	–	–
354	BLACK P	49.45	2	–	1	4	–	4	1	–	–
TOTAL		163.10	6	2	2	11	2	10	2	–	–

Summary of cash requirements

		£	p
6 @ £20		120.00	
2 @ £10		20.00	
2 @ £5		10.00	
11 @ £1		11.00	
2 @ 50p		1.00	
10 @ 10p		1.00	
2 @ 5p			10
	£	163.10	

A wage cash analysis

In each wage packet is a slip, showing how the money is made up. If a worker does not agree with the contents of his wage packet (i.e. it does not agree with the wage slip) or he does not agree that his wage slip is correct, he must take it to the wages clerk and ask for an explanation. Some firms also use the outside of a wage packet on which to print details of pay instead of a separate pay slip.

PAY SLIP

Name: J Brown   Dept: Packaging   Works No. 351

Basic Pay	Overtime	Gross Pay	Income Tax	National Insurance	Pension	Others	Net Pay
50.00	----	£50.00	£10.00	£6.00	£1.00	£1.30	£31.70

A pay slip

The information for a pay slip is taken from the payroll, which will now be described.

Payroll

A payroll is the document which shows for all the employees:

● Gross pay and amount of income tax deducted
● Statutory deductions (e.g. income tax, pension contributions, National Insurance contributions)
● Voluntary deductions (e.g. SAYE, trade union dues)
● Overtime (if any)
● Net pay

and may also include a cash analysis for the purpose of obtaining the correct numbers of notes and coins from a bank to make up the wage packets.

PAY ROLL																		
WEEK OR MONTH NO	1	DATE	12 April															
EARNINGS	DETAILS																	
	A																	
	B																	
	C																	
	D																	
	E																	
	GROSS PAY	50	00	60	00	65	00	70	00									
PENSION/SUP'N.																		
GROSS PAY FOR TAX PURPOSES		50	00	60	00	65	00	70	00									
GROSS PAY TO DATE FOR TAX PURPOSES		50	00	60	00	65	00	70	00									
TAX FREE PAY		20	00	25	00	26	50	35	00									
TAXABLE PAY TO DATE		30	00	35	00	38	50	35	00									
TAX DUE TO DATE		10	00	12	50	13	25	12	00									
TAX REFUND		−	−	−	−	−	−	−	−									
DEDUCTIONS	TAX	10	00	12	50	13	25	12	00									
	Pension	1	00	1	25	1	50	2	00									
	NAT. INS.	6	00	6	20	6	35	6	45									
	1. SAYE	1	00	−	−	1	50	−	−									
	2. Trade Union		20		20		20		−									
	3. Social Club		10		10		−		10									
	4.																	
	5.																	
	6.																	
	TOTAL DEDUCTIONS	18	30	20	25	22	80	20	55									
NET PAY		31	70	39	75	42	20	49	45									
F																		
G																		
TOTAL AMOUNT PAYABLE		31	70	39	75	42	20	49	45							163	10	
EMPLOYER	NAT. INS.																	
	H																	
	J																	

NAME	BROWN J	WHITE E	GREY S	BLACK P				£20	6
								£10	2
								£5	2
								£1	11
								50p	2
								10p	10
								5p	2
								2p	
								1p	

A payroll

Exercise 91

WORKING OUT WAGES

1) Copy out three pay slips and make out one for E White, S Grey and P Black from the details on the payroll (pp. 386 – 7).

2) Work out wages cash analyses for the following wages:

a   £66.41   A Marshall
   £73.59   D Kenwright
   £84.90   F Rhodes
   £59.37   L Denman
   £79.48   C Price

b £101.22   P Moore
   £144.91   C Parkins
   £56.87   D Dawson
   £73.54   G Martin
   £81.00   F Hines

c   £55.39   C Snow
   £49.80   L Frost
   £59.11   J Iceland
   £61.34   M Fogg
   £77.61   W Rayne

SICKNESS BENEFIT

In June 1982, notes from doctors for illnesses lasting less than a week were abolished. A scheme was introduced whereby employees should complete a form to declare themselves ill and unfit for work. They do not require their employer's signature on this form and are on their honour to tell the truth about their illness.

Forms are available from:

> The Department of Health and Social Security (DHSS)
> Doctor's receptionists
> Hospitals

Forms have to be returned to a Social Security office to entitle the holder to sick pay.

To get sick pay, an employee has to be ill for four consecutive days. For illnesses lasting more than a week, a doctor's sick note is still required. A doctor will still sign a sick note for fewer than four days, but will charge £1.40.

Since April 1983, employers have been required by law to provide sick pay from the fourth day of an illness. Payments for the first three days of an illness by an employer are voluntary. Many firms pay an employee while he is ill and deduct any sick pay he receives in addition on his return.

Anyone injured at work because of an accident gets sick pay under this scheme — not industrial injury benefit, as hitherto.

CHAPTER 17

Money at Banks and Post Offices

How much do you know already? Try the following quiz.

True or false:

1) Banks always charge for looking after people's money?

2) It is difficult to find a convenient time to get to a bank when it is open?

3) It is more sensible to keep savings in a box in a cupboard at home?

4) A great deal of tiresome form filling is necessary to take money out of a bank account?

5) It is not worthwhile having a bank account unless one has a lot of money?

6) To own a cheque book, it is necessary to be over 16 years old?

7) Banks will lend money to anyone who asks them for it?

8) Banks *never* lend money, whoever asks for it?

9) A cheque will be accepted by a bank whatever it is written on – even the side of a large fish?

10) Writing a cheque makes spending money easier – it does not seem like 'real' money?

The answers are on pp. 429 – 30. Don't worry if you got some wrong – just read this chapter.

Why Banks?

There are three major reasons for banks:
- keeping customers' money safe
- transferring money to and from their accounts
- lending money to them.

Banks provide many other useful services, too, which will be explained later in this chapter.

Types of Bank

Several different types of bank have nationwide branches in England and Wales and are the largest clearing house banks (see p. 391).

The Six Main Clearing House Banks

The banks usually referred to as the 'big four' are:

- National Westminster
- Barclays
- Lloyds
- Midland

The clearing house banks are linked with other banks in the clearing house system. This is an arrangement for the quick sorting or 'clearing' of payments, cheques etc. between different banks so that transfers of money can be speeded between accounts held in different banks.

Each bank has its own account at the Bank of England. The Bank of England is the bankers' bank. Each day a daily total is calculated of how much one bank owes to or is owed by another. These totals are advised by the bankers' clearing house to the Bank of England, where a book-keeping adjustment is made to update the account of each bank.

All clearing house banks open at 9.30 am and close at 3.30 pm. The Trustee Savings banks and Co-operative banks are also clearing house banks which open earlier and close later than the big four. Co-operative banks and main branches of the big four open on Saturdays, too, which is a great convenience to customers. The National Girobank (p. 423) is also a clearing house bank. The Bank of England is the nation's banker and is part of the clearing house system — it is a banker to the other banks.

| Coutts | Williams & Glyn's | Midland | Barclays | Lloyds | National Westminster |

Bank Accounts

There are two types of bank account—current and deposit (or savings). In order to encourage customers to leave their money in a deposit account, interest is paid at base rate. For example, if the bank rate is 10 per cent, £100 left in an account for a year will 'grow' to £110.

Most banks allow customers to withdraw money from a deposit account on demand (after completing a withdrawal slip). Giving seven days notice of withdrawal avoids loss of interest.

A current account is quite different. It is the most widely used, although many bank customers have both a current and a deposit account. A current account enables the customer to write cheques to pay bills and to take out any cash needed for day-to-day expenses. Traditionally *no*

A typical enquiry desk at a bank

interest is payable on a current account, but in 1984 the Midland Bank introduced a cheque account *with interest*. A balance left (about £100) in a current account is set by the bank against any charges due, so it is worth keeping about that amount in excess of normal requirements in a current account.

Banks charge customers for a current account only if the balance falls below this amount (and it varies from bank to bank); the charges are based on the number of cheques written and the number of other 'transactions', i.e. standing orders and direct debits (see pp. 406 – 7).

How to Open a Current Account or a Deposit Account

Go into the nearest branch of the big four, or Co-operative Bank, or Trustee Savings Bank and find the enquiry counter.

Tell the clerk you wish to open an account (either current or deposit). You will then be asked for:

- a description of your occupation
- some money (it need only be a few pounds)
- a specimen signature (so that no one else can sign your cheques or withdraw money from your deposit account)
- a reference (your employer would be suitable, or a friend with a bank account).

You will be given (in about a week) a cheque book (for your current account) printed with your name on each cheque (see p. 393).

All you have to do then is to use your account sensibly and, if a current account, avoid writing too many cheques and spending more money than is left in your account (this is known as 'being in the red' – in which case the bank manager will write to you letting you know that he is aware of what you have done and is not pleased with you!).

Cheques

WHAT A CHEQUE IS

A cheque is an order in writing addressed to the bank to pay, when required, a sum of money to the person named on the cheque. It is quite legal for a plain piece of paper to be used, or even a tablecloth or fish (this has actually happened) but it is now the practice for the banks to issue special cheque forms, in books.

A personalised cheque

A cheque made out on a tablecloth

A cheque is not legal tender – as a bank note is – and anyone is entitled to refuse a cheque in payment of a debt, but a cheque is a legal document recognised by Acts of Parliament.

REASONS FOR CHEQUES

One very good reason is that a cheque takes up far less space than a quantity of coins and bank notes. It is also very suitable for posting or carrying and is much safer.

Banknotes and coins . . .

. . . attract thieves

393

WRITING CHEQUES

Cheques must be written in ink or ball-point and *not* in pencil.

Each cheque is attached to the cheque book by a 'counterfoil'. The counterfoil is left in the cheque book after the cheque has been made out and removed, as a record for the customer, so it is sensible to fill it in as a copy of each cheque.

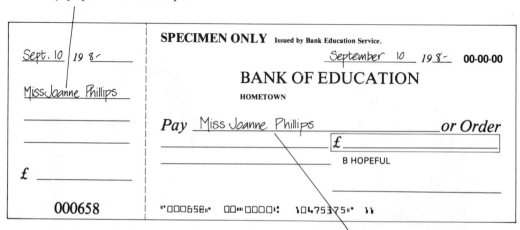

The person receiving the money represented by a cheque is the 'payee'. The name of the 'payee' is written clearly on the cheque against the word 'Pay' and should also be written on the counterfoil, with the date and the amount.

A cheque must be dated with the date on which it is written. Banks will not accept post-dated (dated in advance) cheques, for immediate withdrawal of cash.

On the line beneath the payee's name the amount to be paid is written *in words*. It is written again in figures in the 'box' provided. The two amounts must be the same — if not, the bank will not pay out the money. Any space left should be ruled up so that no one can dishonestly add any figures. 'Noughts' are best avoided as they can look like sixes if written badly. Dots must not be used either — write long dashes instead. The word 'only' may be added after the amount in words as an extra safeguard (see below).

Sept. 10 19 8-

Miss Joanne Phillips

_____

_____

£ 10 —

000658

SPECIMEN ONLY   Issued by Bank Education Service.

10 September   198-   00-00-00

BANK OF EDUCATION

HOMETOWN

Pay   Miss Joanne Phillips   or Order

Ten pounds only ——   £ 10 —

B HOPEFUL

⑆000658⑆ 00⑈0000⑆ 10475375⑈ ⑈

Sept. 10 19 8-

Miss Joanne Phillips

_____

_____

£ 10—

000658

SPECIMEN ONLY   Issued by Bank Education Service.

10 September   19 8-   00-00-00

BANK OF EDUCATION

HOMETOWN

Pay   Miss Joanne Phillips   or Order

Ten pounds only—   £ 10 —

B HOPEFUL

B. Hopeful

⑆000658⑆ 00⑈0000⑆ 10475375⑈ ⑈

The counterfoil does not have to be signed; it remains in payee's cheque book

Signature of 'drawer'

SIGNATURE

The customer signs his (or her) name always in the same way, and it should agree with the specimen signature he gave to the bank when he opened his account. The signature is at the foot of the cheque. This signature is the name of the 'drawer' of the cheque.

CHEQUE-SIGNING MACHINE

This machine saves the time of managers and supervisors who may have many cheques to sign – the signatures are printed on the cheques by a metal plate. Security is provided by a key locking system, and special ink.

A cheque-signing machine

'STALE' CHEQUES

A cheque is 'valid' (that is, it will be cashed by a bank) up to 6 months after it has been made out. After 6 months, it is out of date, and is 'invalid' and will be returned to drawer marked R/D (refer to drawer).

CHEQUES WHICH 'BOUNCE'

Cheques which 'bounce' are dishonoured cheques, for any one of the following reasons:

- if the drawer of the cheque has no money in his current account
- if the amount in words does not agree with the amount in figures
- if drawer's signature looks different from his specimen signature
- if an alteration has not been initialled
- if cheque is postdated (dated in advance)
- if cheque has been 'stopped' by the drawer
- if cheque is 'stale' (see above).

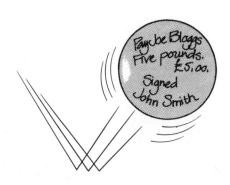

COMPLETING THE COUNTERFOIL

It is useful to the 'drawer' if he has a record of what he wrote a cheque out for as well as to whom and also he may like to deduct the amount of the cheque from his current account balance and make a note on the counterfoil.

CORRECTING MISTAKES ON CHEQUES

Providing it is a simple one, a mistake on a cheque may be crossed through (once only, not scribbled over) and the correction signed by drawer of cheque. If the error is a large one (the wrong payee's name for example), it is better to tear up the cheque, cancel the counterfoil and start again.

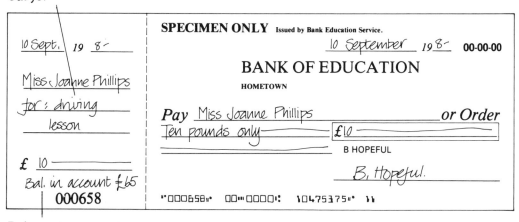

The counterfoil does not require initialling; it stays in the cheque book

A correction crossed through and initialled

What cheque was made out for

Balance in account on 10th September 198-

The completed cheque and counterfoil

397

SPECIMEN ONLY Issued by Bank Education Service.

_____ 19 _____

_____ 19 ___ **00-00-00**

BANK OF EDUCATION
HOMETOWN

Pay _____ _or Order_

£ _____

B HOPEFUL

£ _____

000651

"000651" 00"0000: 10475375" 11

The cheque number is
repeated on the counterfoil

The cheque number

The Bank/Branch number

The customer's account
number

The meanings of the numbers on a cheque

'Stopping' a Cheque

The bank should be informed at once if a customer has lost his cheque book, or a cheque which he has posted has not been received. The bank should be telephoned if possible giving date, number and amount. Then, later, it will be necessary to complete the 'stop instruction' form shown at the top of p. 399.

Stopping Payment

After Mrs Mary Jenkinson had posted her cheque in payment of an account, she was very surprised when, later, the bill was sent to her again. Upon enquiry she found out that her cheque had never been received and must have gone astray.

She immediately went to her bank and found out that the cheque had not been presented for payment. Mrs Jenkinson therefore immediately completed the form overleaf authorising the bank to stop payment of the missing cheque should anyone present it at the bank. She then made out a second cheque in payment of the still unpaid bill. The staff of the bank keep a careful watch for the lost cheque among those which are presented for payment, and a record of the 'stop' is placed on Mrs Jenkinson's computer records. The computer automatically rejects the cheque if it is eventually presented for payment. _But cheques guaranteed by a cheque card cannot be stopped._

THE BANK OF EDUCATION

_____ Hometown _____ Branch

STOP INSTRUCTION

Please stop payment of the undermentioned cheque(s):

Note: Cheques drawn under Cheque Card arrangements cannot normally be stopped

Date _26 September 198-_   Numbered _000779_

Account _Mary Jenkinson_   Account Number _0934150_

Payee _Mark Tyme_   Amount £ _50_

Lost/~~Stolen~~ Cheque(s) ~~or Cheque Book~~-Number(s) of Cheque(s) ___1___

Has a Cheque Card also been lost? Yes/No

Date _30 Sept 198-_ Signature _Mary Jenkinson_

A 'stop payment' instruction form

Withdrawing Cash from a Current Account

This is very simple. A cheque has to be made out by the customer to 'Self' or 'Cash' where the name of the payee is normally written. If it is a crossed cheque, the crossing has to be 'opened' by signing and adding the words 'please pay cash' otherwise the bank will not cash the cheque.

Oct. 4 19 8-	SPECIMEN ONLY Issued by Bank Education Service.
Cash	_4 October_ 198- 00-00-00
	BANK OF EDUCATION
	HOMETOWN
	Pay _Cash_ _____ or Order
	Twenty pounds only £20
	B HOPEFUL
£ 20	Please pay cash B. Hopeful B. Hopeful
000651	"000651" 00"0000: 10475375" 11

A crossed cheque made out to 'Cash'. The crossing has been 'opened' by signing

Most banks have a quick service counter for customers who only want to cash a cheque. This avoids standing in a queue for a long time behind people with other business to transact.

An 'open' cheque has no crossing. It will be cashed by a bank, and is therefore not as safe as a crossed cheque, which has to be paid into a bank account.

If a crossed cheque which has been lost or stolen is later paid into a bank account illegally, it is always possible to trace the person who stole or found the cheque.

	SPECIMEN ONLY Issued by Bank Education Service.
10 July 19 8-	10 July 198- 00-00-00
Cash	**BANK OF EDUCATION**
	HOMETOWN
	Pay Cash _____ or Order
	Fifty pounds only — £ 50
	B HOPEFUL
£ 50	B. Hopeful
000654	⑈000654⑈ 00⑈0000⑈ 10475375⑈ ⑈⑈

An open cheque made out to 'Cash' (for withdrawing money in cash from a current account)

An 'open' cheque can be crossed simply by ruling two parallel lines from top to bottom across the middle, but banks issue cheques already printed with a crossing for people who prefer them. A bank customer may choose which type of cheque book to have. Cheque books are provided free to holders of current accounts.

	SPECIMEN ONLY Issued by Bank Education Service.
10 July 19 8-	10 July 198- 00-00-00
Cash	**BANK OF EDUCATION**
	HOMETOWN
	Pay Cash _____ or Order
	Fifty pounds only — £ 50
	B HOPEFUL
£ 50	B. Hopeful
000654	⑈000654⑈ 00⑈0000⑈ 10475375⑈ ⑈⑈

All cheques sent by post should be crossed, as a safeguard against theft.

It is extremely foolish to sign a cheque and leave the amount blank. The cheque could be filled in for any sum of money and the bank would accept it, even though the writing would be different from the signature. Because the latter is genuine, the cheque would not be queried.

400

1 Nov 19 8⁻

Mr. T Keene

£

000662

1 November 198⁻   00-00-00

BANK OF EDUCATION
HOMETOWN

Pay Mr T Keene _____ *or Order*

£ _____

B HOPEFUL

B. Hopeful

ꞌꞌ000662ꞌꞌ 00ꞌꞌ0000ꞌ: 10475375ꞌꞌ 11

A 'blank' cheque (amount is not specified). Anyone could fill in any amount in words and figures . . .

SPECIAL CHEQUE CROSSINGS

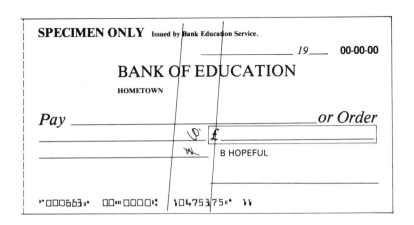

_____ 19___ 00-00-00

BANK OF EDUCATION
HOMETOWN

Pay _____ *or Order*

£ _____

B HOPEFUL

ꞌꞌ000663ꞌꞌ 00ꞌꞌ0000ꞌ: 10475375ꞌꞌ 11

An ordinary cheque crossing (printed on by the banks) consists of two parallel lines which usually has '& Co' printed between the lines, but this is not essential. This is known as 'general crossing'

Issued by Bank Education Service.

_____ 19____ 00-00-00

BANK OF EDUCATION

HOMETOWN

Pay _____ *or Order*

_____

Under £20

£ _____

B HOPEFUL

_____

"000664" 00"0000": 104753 75"))

This cheque must be for an amount under £20 – it is a safeguard against anyone altering the amount by adding an extra nought

Issued by Bank Education Service.

_____ 19____ 00-00-00

BANK OF EDUCATION

HOMETOWN

Pay _____ *or Order*

_____

a/c payee only

£ _____

B HOPEFUL

_____

"000665" 00"0000": 104753 75"))

This is an extra safeguard – the cheque must be paid into payee's account and no other

Issued by Bank Education Service.

_____ 19____ 00-00-00

BANK OF EDUCATION

HOMETOWN

Pay _____ *or Order*

_____

Lloyds Bank Ltd. Carlisle

£ _____

B HOPEFUL

_____

"000666" 00"0000": 104753 75"))

This cheque must be paid into Lloyds Bank, Carlisle

402

FOR YOUR FOLDER

54. BANKS AND BANK ACCOUNTS

Write these notes in your folder, filling in the missing words and phrases.

1) The three major services provided by banks for their customers are:
   - keeping their money safe
   - transferring money to and from their accounts
   - _____.

2) The Big Four banks are:
   - National Westminster
   - Barclays
   - Midland
   - _____.

3) The banks which open during normal shopping hours (which the big four do not) are National Girobank and _____.

4) The two types of bank account are current and _____.

5) The one on which interest is paid is _____.

6) To open a bank account it is necessary to provide:
   - a sum of money
   - a reference
   - _____.

7) Cheques are useful because they take up far less space than a quantity of notes and coins and are suitable for _____ or _____ and are much safer.

8) A cheque must be written in ink or ball-point and not _____.

9) The amount of money to be paid by cheque should be written in _____ and figures.

10) Any correction on a cheque should be _____.

11) Crossing a cheque is a _____.

12) Withdrawing cash from a current account is done by making out a cheque to _____ or _____.

13) A 'personalised' cheque is _____.

14) Another name for a cheque counterfoil is a cheque _____.

15) The payee of a cheque is the _____.

16) The person signing the cheque is the _____.

17) The drawee of a cheque is the _____.

18) A stale cheque is _____.

19) A cheque which bounces is _____.

20) A post-dated cheque is _____.

21) Stopping a cheque means _____.

Cheque Cards

Current account holders may have a cheque card, if they wish (after they have had a current account for about six months and proved that they can handle it responsibly). A cheque card enables them to cash a cheque for up to £50 at any branch of any bank, or write a cheque for goods bought up to the value of £50 in the UK and in the major cities of Europe. A cheque card is an undertaking by the bank issuing it to honour the cheque written in association with it.

There is one disadvantage to a cheque card – a cheque written in conjunction with it cannot be 'stopped' (see p. 398).

Cash Dispensing Machines

Cash dispensing machines have been set up in *some* branches of banks to allow customers to withdraw cash quickly (without waiting in a queue at the counter) or after the bank is closed. The systems used by the banks vary slightly but for most of them the customer is supplied with a special plastic card which is inserted into the cash dispensing machine and the customer taps out his secret number on the keys. The secret number is known only to the computer and the customer. If the card and the number agree, the cash dispenser releases the amount of money that the customer has 'keyed' in.

A cash dispenser

Some machines release only a fixed amount (say £10 or £20). Others release amounts up to a limit agreed with the customer. Others, again, are linked directly to the customer's account through the bank's computer and will therefore release any amount up to the maximum — provided there is money in the account!

These have special buttons to request the print out of a customer's current balance and to request that a full statement or a new cheque book be sent by post. Again, this saves joining a queue at the counter.

Credit Cards

Credit cards are not run by the banks but by separate credit card companies linked to the banks. For example, Barclaycard is linked to Barclays Bank and Access to Lloyds, Midland, Coutts, National Westminster and Williams & Glyn's. There are other credit card schemes such as American Express and Diners Club. The minimum age for anyone to hold a credit card is 18 years.

With a credit card a customer may buy goods, or services (e.g. tickets, meals) at any place linked with his credit card. Such places display the sign. Instead of paying cash at once, the customer signs a special slip which gives the value of the purchase, like a bill. The credit card is made of plastic, embossed with the customer's name and credit number, and carries his specimen signature.

Credit cards

The card and slips (three copies) are placed under a roller so that the customer's name and number are printed out on to the slips through carbon with the shop's name and address. One copy is kept by the customer; the second is kept by the shop; the third is forwarded to the credit card company by the shop paying it into its bank account. The credit card company receives payment in turn from the customer, when he is sent a statement listing all his credit card purchases during the previous month.

If the total is settled before the date shown on the statement, no credit charge is made; but if payment is delayed, interest is charged for the loan by the credit card company.

It is important that cheque cards and credit cards should be signed *in ink* and not in ballpoint, the reason being that ballpoint signatures can easily be removed by criminals, and the signature replaced to match the name on a stolen cheque book; thus making it only too easy to withdraw money from someone else's account.

A credit card imprinter

How to use the Imprinter

1)   Place the customer's card in the imprinter as shown below, embossed side uppermost.

2)   Place the sales voucher over the card with the bottom left-hand corner of the voucher fitting under the section at the bottom left of the voucher guide.

3)   Pull the handle from left to right, then return it to original position.

4)   Remove sales voucher, and check that the details have been imprinted clearly and distinctly.

5)   Remove the card.

Standing Orders

A standing order is an instruction in writing to a bank by a customer (usually on a printed form — see p. 407) to pay on his behalf, from his current account balance, amounts which are paid regularly (insurance premiums, mortgage payments, TV rental, hire purchase payments, savings into a building society or SAYE savings scheme, and subscriptions to clubs). This avoids the possibility of forgetting to pay these amounts at the right time.

```
                                        Standing Order
    TO  COLLEGIATE BANK                  Specimen Only
    Branch   Hometown

                        Date  25th February 198-

    Please make payments and debit my /our  current   account, No. 57367401
    in accordance with the following details, to:
    Bank      Bank of Education
    Branch    Newtown
    Sorting code number  00 - 00 - 04
    For account of  XYZ  Insurance Co.
    Account number, if any  1047575
    Reference, if any          -
    Amount        £ 15 —
    Payments to be made_____weekly / monthly / quarterly / half-yearly / annually*
    Date of first payment  14th March  198-
    Date of final payment  14th March  19--
    This order cancels the existing one * for £ _____
    * Delete as appropriate

                          B. Hopeful.
```

A standing order form

Direct Debit

This is similar to a standing order except that the amount may be varied by the payee without reference to the current account holder. It is a great help to building societies and organisations such as the AA, because a direct debit avoids having to ask for the customer's permission to change (usually increase) the amount payable. Notification that a direct debit is to be changed is sent to a customer by the bank.

Paying Money into a Current Account

Payment is made into a current account at a bank by completing a paying-in slip or a bank giro credit slip (p. 409). These paying-in slips have a counterfoil. The bank clerk date stamps both, one for the bank records and the counterfoil for the depositor to keep.

The paying-in slip (or credit slip) on p. 408 shows:

A   the date
B   the amount
C   the name of the person paying in
D   the name of the person whose account is to be credited
E   the account number.

For the convenience of the bank clerks who have to balance or check their tills at the end of each day, the sum paid in is divided between cash (notes and coins) cheques and postal orders. The 'cash' figure is subdivided into notes and silver and bronze coins.

407

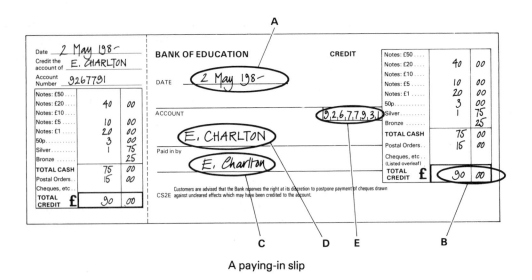

A paying-in slip

In the illustration above, note that two £20 notes have been paid in (i.e. £40), two £5 notes (i.e. £10), twenty £1 notes (i.e. £20) six 50p pieces (i.e. £3) silver coins to the value of £1.75 and bronze to the value of 25p.

Paying-in slip for paying money into your own account (front and reverse)

Details of cheques and postal orders, are written on the back of the paying-in slip (and on the back of the counterfoil). This is useful where there are a number of cheques and/or postal orders. The total is brought forward to the front of the paying-in slip.

The paying-in slip is used when you go to a branch to pay money into your account held at that branch.

Paying-in slips vary slightly from bank to bank.

Paying-in slips are supplied at the backs of cheque books, or a separate book of paying-in slips (personalised — with the account holder's name printed on them) will be supplied to a current account holder, on application to the clerk at the counter. They usually take two or three weeks to be ready for collection.

Bank Giro Credit

Any payment into another account can be made through any bank by Bank Giro Credit, so long as the bank and branch where the account is held are known. Most electricity, gas and water boards encourage customers to pay their bills in this way by printing Bank Giro Credit forms on the bottom of their bills. The bank, branch and account number of the organisation is already printed on the form, so all the customer has to do is to fill in the amount to be paid in, sign the form and hand in the form with the amount.

One cheque may be made out for several bills being paid in this way. Bank Giro Credit slips are available in banks.

Bank giro credit

Bank Giro Credit Schedule

This is a list for paying salaries into employees' bank accounts each month. A cheque for the total sum to be transferred is made out by the firm in favour of the bank itself. This method of payment is safer and more convenient than giving cash, or writing cheques.

BANK GIRO CREDITS		24·2·84 DATE	
To **Lloyds Bank**	HIGH STREET, SUTTON		BRANCH

Please distribute the credit slips attached, as arranged with the recipients
Our cheque £ 750.23 is enclosed.
LIST NO 8

J. Williams SIGNATURE
DIRECTOR

CODE No.	BANK AND BRANCH		ACCOUNT	NET AMOUNT
	BARCLAYS	LINCOLN	A.J.SMITH	58 . 24.
	LLOYDS	BRISTOL	K. BLAKE	53 . 09.
	MIDLAND	SUTTON	P. WEST	58 . 15.
	NATIONAL	CHEAM	T.H. GREEN	61 . 13
	WESTMINSTER			
	LLOYDS	WESTMINSTER	D.M. MORGAN	21 .
	BARCLAYS	CROYDON	F. ROGERS	53 . 00.
	MIDLAND	STRAND	K. JONES	64 . 27.
	COUTTS	BRISTOL	B. WATTS	63 . 55.
			TOTAL (or Forward Total) **£**	750 . 23

Bank giro credit schedule

Bank Statements

These are sent to a holder of a current account at regular intervals, or when he asks for one. It shows all money paid into his current account (money paid in sends the balance up), all cheques written (which send the balance down) and all credit transfers, standing orders and direct debits – as well as any dividends paid into the account. The last figure in the right-hand column is the amount in the account when the statement is made up.

When a customer has overdrawn his account, the letters DR or OD are printed at the right-hand side under 'Balance'. DR and OD mean 'overdrawn balance', i.e. being 'in the red'.

410

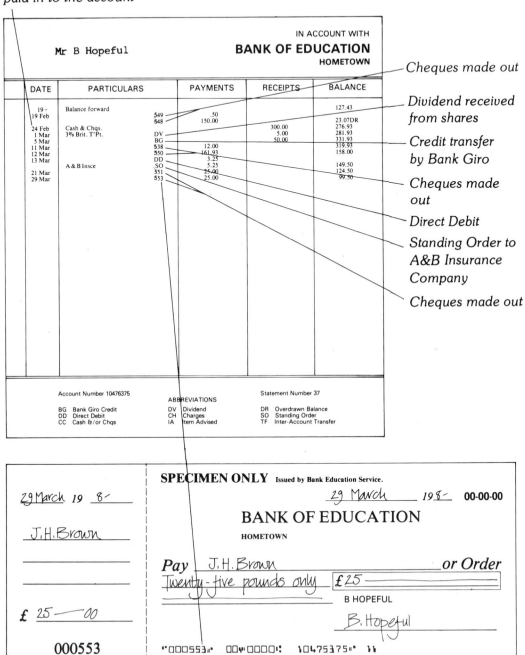

Cash and cheques
paid in to the account

IN ACCOUNT WITH

Mr B Hopeful

BANK OF EDUCATION

HOMETOWN

Cheques made out

*Dividend received
from shares*

*Credit transfer
by Bank Giro*

*Cheques made
out*

Direct Debit

*Standing Order to
A&B Insurance
Company*

Cheques made out

DATE	PARTICULARS		PAYMENTS	RECEIPTS	BALANCE
19 - 19 Feb	Balance forward	549 548	.50 150.00		127.43 23.07DR
24 Feb 1 Mar	Cash & Chqs. 3% Brit. T'Pt.	DV BG		300.00 5.00	276.93 281.93
5 Mar 11 Mar		538	12.00	50.00	331.93 319.93
12 Mar 13 Mar		550 DD SO	161.93 3.25 5.25		158.00 149.50
21 Mar 29 Mar	A & B Insce	551 553	25.00 25.00		124.50 99.50

Account Number 10476375

Statement Number 37

ABBREVIATIONS

BG	Bank Giro Credit	DV	Dividend	DR	Overdrawn Balance
DD	Direct Debit	CH	Charges	SO	Standing Order
CC	Cash &/or Chqs	IA	Item Advised	TF	Inter-Account Transfer

---

29 March 19 8-

J.H.Brown

£ 25 — 00

000553

SPECIMEN ONLY Issued by Bank Education Service.

29 March _____ 198- **00-00-00**

BANK OF EDUCATION

HOMETOWN

Pay J.H.Brown _____ *or Order*

Twenty-five pounds only £25 —

B HOPEFUL

B. Hopeful

⑈000553⑈ 00⑈0000⑆ 10475375⑈ 11

Bank statement of account

Exercise 92

CREDIT AND PAYING-IN SLIPS

Make three copies of (a) the Bank Giro Credit slip on p.409 and (b) the reverse of the paying-in slip on p. 408 and complete each as follows:

1) You pay into B Hopeful's account one cheque for £10.50 and four £1 coins; eight £1 notes; three 50p pieces; £1.40 in bronze; 1 postal order for £3 and one postal order for £1.50.

2) You pay into Messrs Day and Night's account £100 in £20 notes and £150 in £5 notes; £25 in £5 notes; £90 in £1 notes/coins; £256 in bronze; £1.95 postal order; £3.60 postal order; £795 cheque; £4.56 cheque.

3) You pay into I M Broke's account £5 in £1 notes/coins and £4 in 20p; £3 in 50p; £10 postal order.

Other Bank Services

FOR TRAVELLERS

Traveller's cheques are a world-wide form of international currency. Anyone (not just bank customers) can buy traveller's cheques from a bank, in denominations of £2, £5, £10, £20 and £50. The bank makes a small charge.

Drawer has to sign here when presenting his traveller's cheque for cashing; an 'endorsement'

Drawer has to sign here when collecting his traveller's cheques from the bank. He must also take his passport if he is going overseas.

A traveller's cheque

When bought each cheque must be signed at the foot (where it says 'signature of drawer'). A passport has to be taken to the bank and the total sum (currency and traveller's cheques) being taken out of the country overseas is entered on the passport.

When being cashed, each traveller's cheque has to be signed again (endorsed) by the same person who signed when they were collected from the bank. This endorsement has to be made in the presence of the cashier at the bank. Therefore it is necessary to make sure that when traveller's cheques are collected in this country from the bank, that they are signed for by the person most likely to cash them when abroad. It is possibly a good arrangement for a husband and wife to sign half each.

Traveller's cheques are a safe way to carry money abroad (or in this country) as if lost, they will be replaced. Many hotels, shops and restaurants will accept traveller's cheques in payment.

EUROCHEQUES

Eurocheques are offered by the Midland Bank only (up to 1984) and allow holders to pay by cheque in Europe and in Mediterranean countries exactly the same as they would in Britain. Eurocheques can be written in 27 different foreign currencies and cut out the bother of arranging for traveller's cheques before a trip or holiday abroad, and also having to cash them while in a foreign country. The added advantage with eurocheques is that there is no need to pay out a large sum of money beforehand to obtain traveller's cheques.

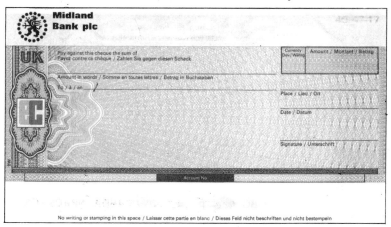

A Eurocheque

Cash may be withdrawn by eurocheque from any European bank displaying the eurocheque sign. Each eurocheque is guaranteed up to the approximate local currency equivalent of £75. There is no limit to the number of eurocheques that can be issued for cash at any one time provided that each cheque does not exceed the guaranteed amount.

413

The usual number of cheques issued to each customer is 15. There is an annual charge of £3.50 for the eurocheque card, plus $1\frac{1}{4}\%$ commission on each cheque cashed abroad, plus 28p per cheque. Eurocheques can also be used in the UK.

The eurocheque service is no cheaper than traveller's cheques, but a great deal more convenient.

FOREIGN CURRENCY

Banks will provide foreign currency in exchange for pound notes (or debit a current account for the value of the foreign currency). It is always useful to carry some foreign money for a journey abroad, so that some money is available for small items on arrival (drinks, bus fares, telephone calls).

SAFE CUSTODY OF VALUABLES

Rather than go on holiday and leave jewellery or other valuables (foreign stamps, silverware) in the house, ready for burglars it is more sensible to take them to a bank for safekeeping. There is a charge for this service, and it is the customer's responsibility to insure the articles deposited at the bank and they must be handed in in wrapped and sealed packages.

NIGHT SAFES

A night safe is built into the outside wall of a bank. The customer has a small box or wallet into which he places his money with a paying-in slip (see p. 408) completed in the usual way. He then locks his bag or

A night safe

seals it with a special punch and takes the box to the bank. He unlocks the hatch in the bank's outer wall and drops the box or wallet down a chute. Its contents are checked the next day by a bank clerk and the amount is credited to the account of the customer. Alternatively, he can collect the box unopened.

Other Services

INSURANCE

Banks will advise on the best type of insurance to take out for children, wives, husbands, and businesses.

WILLS

A will is an instruction to carry out wishes regarding the distribution of someone's property after his death. These instructions are written down in his will. A bank will act as an executor or trustee (a trustee is someone who looks after property or money left in a will to someone who may only be a child, until they are grown up). The bank makes a charge for acting as an executor. An executor carries out the instructions in a will.

INVESTMENTS

Banks employ specialists who will give advice to customers about the best ways of investing their money. The bank cannot force customers to take their advice, and if someone wishes to buy shares in a diamond mine on a remote island that cannot even be found on a map, the bank cannot stop him! Banks charge for advising about investments too, in some cases.

Bank Drafts

A bank draft is a means of transferring money from the account of one bank customer to another, and is preferred by customers to a cheque where a large sum of money is involved. A bank draft is considered to be as good as cash, as the customer pays for it in advance.

BANK OF EDUCATION	
	NEWTOWN Branch
	18 February 198-
On demand pay to the order of	A. Solicitor
Five hundred pounds only	
TO BANK OF EDUCATION Head Office Hometown	£ 500 —— .
	For and on behalf of BANK OF EDUCATION
	J.C.Scott MANAGER

A bank draft

A bank draft is guaranteed by the bank and is useful when two strangers are involved in a business transaction (e.g. selling a car).

The buyer may wish to drive the car away immediately and not wait for the seller to wait for the cheque he has received in payment to be 'cleared' (see p. 391) as it may 'bounce' (see p. 396).

BUDGET ACCOUNT

Some bills such as electricity, gas or telephone cannot be covered by a standing order, as the payment varies each quarter (although the Gas Board and Electricity Board will estimate how much fuel is likely to be used, divide by 12 and arrange a standing order on this basis, with an adjustment for over or under payment at the end of the year). Otherwise, bills for quarterly services such as the telephone may all arrive in one month, meaning a great deal of money has to be found immediately. A budget account with a bank allows these quarterly bills to be spread over 12 months. A customer fills in a form giving his regular expenses such as rent, rates, insurance, hire purchase, electricity etc. the total is added up and divided by 12 to give a monthly average.

The customer agrees to pay this amount regularly each month to the bank and in return the bank clears his cheques for the bills as they occur. At the end of the year, both the bank and the customer will have paid about the same amount of money. The customer has the advantage of knowing exactly how much is going out of his/her account each month. The customer receives from the bank a special cheque book with which to pay bills from his budget account. These cheques are recognised by the bank and are handled separately from other cheques.

The customer is charged a service charge by the bank for a budget account.

BILL OF EXCHANGE

A bill of exchange is the method of payment used by many firms when dealing with overseas customers. It is drawn up by the exporter (the payee) stating the amount owed and the date it is due. The importer signs (thus accepting the bill). The bill of exchange is then a legally binding promise to pay. For a fee, it can be arranged for the bank also to sign the bill of exchange guaranteeing the payment. Bills of exchange usually have a life of three months.

The advantage to the importer of a bill of exchange is that of paying for the goods after they have been received, and, possibly, resold. The exporter has the advantage of not having to give credit to a (possibly) unknown foreigner, and can sell the bill before the date of repayment, if the money is needed.

416

Getting Cash Out of a Branch of Another Bank

A cheque must be written 'Pay cash' or 'Pay self' in the usual way, and when handed in to cashier, a cheque card has to be used for indentification. At present, there is a limit of £50 per day.

By special arrangement in advance, through the customer's own branch, cheques can be cashed up to an agreed amount (i.e. £20 daily) at another specified branch, without producing a cheque card. This is especially useful to bank customers on holiday.

REFERENCES

A bank will provide a reference for a department store, if requested, to the effect that a bank customer is able to manage his financial affairs sensibly and should therefore be allowed to buy goods on credit from the store.

Most firms sell to other companies on credit and may have to wait up to 3 months for their money (though one month is more usual). When a firm receives an order from a new customer, he will ask his bank to make enquiries (from other banks) and let him know if his new customer pays his bills regularly.

Firms engaged in foreign trade find this service especially useful when they are doing business wth a new overseas buyer. Banks have links all over the world with banks abroad.

Confidentiality

All transactions with a bank are confidential. No information will be given to *anyone* about a customer's account without the customer's written permission. The only exceptions to this, of course, are the executors of a will and the Inland Revenue for income tax purposes (see p. 415).

Lending Money

This is one of the three chief reasons for banking, and it is the way banks make their profits – by lending customers' money at interest to other customers in need of it. So that the money is absolutely safe, they will not lend without security (collateral) which means that if a customer wishes to borrow a large sum of money he has to deposit at the bank something of great value, such as the deeds to a house, an insurance policy on which he has paid the premiums for a number of years, or share certificates. If, for any reason the loan cannot be repaid, the bank then has the right to take possession of the collateral. Thus customers' money is safeguarded.

An overdraft is the cheapest way to borrow money – the interest is slightly lower than that for a personal loan, which is the other way to borrow money from a bank. An overdraft means that a current account is overdrawn to a maximum amount and for a maximum period, both agreed with the bank manager.

A personal loan which is borrowed for a certain purpose (buying a car, for instance, or some hi-fi equipment) has to be repaid within a certain period, agreed with the bank manager (the limit is usually 3 years). A personal loan is normally repaid in monthly instalments from a current account. There may be a limit to the amount of cash advanced.

Interest is charged on overdrafts, personal loans and budget accounts – the actual amount of interest varying from bank to bank. Bank interest on loans is always much lower than that of other moneylenders.

Bank Note Counting Machine

This piece of electronic equipment counts both new and used banknotes at the rate of 100 in approximately 7 seconds. It is operated by a photo-electric cell.

FOR YOUR FOLDER

55. BANK SERVICES

Write these notes in your folder, filling in the missing words and phrases.

1) A cheque card enables a current account holder to cash a cheque for up to _____ at any branch of any bank, or to write a cheque at a shop for goods bought up to the value of _____.

2) The machine set in the outside wall of a bank which dispenses packets of banknotes after the customer has tapped out his or her personal number is a _____.

3) Two well-known credit cards are _____ and _____.

4) A credit card can be used for _____.

5) _____ are credit cards and cheque cards combined.

6) A regular payment made by a bank on behalf of a current account holder (e.g. insurance premiums, mortgage payments, TV rental or hire purchase) is a _____.

7) A direct debit is similar to the above except that the amount may be _____ by the payee without reference to the _____.

8) A Bank Giro Credit form is for paying money into _____ bank account.

9) Most electricity, gas and _____ boards encourage customers to pay their bills in this way. One _____ is made out for several bills.

10) A Bank Giro schedule is a list for paying _____ into employees' bank accounts.

11) This method of payment is _____ and more _____ than giving cash or writing cheques.

12) Credit transfer is another name for _____.

13) A safe way to carry money around (either abroad or in this country) is by _____.

14) While you are on holiday, it is sensible to arrange for valuables to be taken care of by a _____.

15) The information sent out to a current account holder about the amount of money he has in his account and the amount he had paid out, is in the form of a _____.

16) Bank services for families and businessmen are advice on insurance, investments and acting as an _____ or trustee.

17) A means of transferring money from one bank customer to another which is useful when two strangers are involved in a business transaction is a _____. A customer pays for a _____ in advance, so it is considered to be the equivalent of cash.

18) No information will be given to anyone about a customer's bank account without the customer's written permission. All transactions with a bank are confidential, except to the executors of a will and the _____ (for income tax purposes).

19) The way banks make their profits is by _____.

20) The cheapest way to borrow money from a bank is by _____.

21) Another way of borrowing money from a bank is by personal loan; this has to be repaid within a certain period, agreed with the bank (limit _____).

22) When a set sum is paid into a separate account each month to cover such bills as telephone, electricity, gas, oil, car insurance and tax, this is known as a _____ account.

23) A bank will provide a reference for a _____ if requested to the effect that a bank customer is able to _____ sensibly and should therefore be allowed to buy goods on _____.

24) A bill of exchange is the method of payment used by many firms when dealing with overseas customers. It is drawn up by the exporter (the payee) stating the amount owed and the date it is due. The importer signs (thus accepting the bill). The bill of exchange is then a _____ promise to pay.

Exercise 93

BANKING

1) What different types of account are offered to bank customers?

2) What information is requested from the customer opening a bank account?

3) Give three advantages of having a bank account.

4) What is a bank statement?

5) Why may a bank ask for 'securities' before lending money?

6) What is the difference between a Direct Debit and a Standing Order?

7) Compare Eurocheques with travellers' cheques. What are the advantages and disadvantages of each?

8) What is a bank draft?

BRIDGING LOAN

Banks have only just started to lend money long term for house purchases with a 20 or 25 year mortgage. Apart from mortgages, special help is often needed for a short period of a few months by someone moving house. The sale of the house lived in may not be completed before the deposit has to be paid on the new house. Here a bank may be prepared to help with a 'bridging loan'. The manager will base his decision on whether to offer a loan on securities which can be offered (see p. 418).

In the last few years, building societies have increasingly offered services which were previously only obtainable through banks. Two examples of these are traveller's cheques (from some building societies) and cheque books. Similarly, banks (in 1982) started to compete with building societies by offering mortgage facilities with longer term repayment arrangements, but these have recently not been so freely available.

Postal Orders

The postal order is the most commonly used Post Office remittance service. It is especially useful for transferring small amounts of money to someone who has no bank account, as it is encashable over the counter of any Post Office. It could, for example, be used to send money as a birthday present.

The maximum amount for which a postal order may be sent is £10. The minimum amount (at the moment) is 25p. As well as the value of the postal order, there is a small additional charge payable to the Post Office, called 'poundage'. There is a scale of poundage which increases with the value of the postal order.

Postal orders may also be sent overseas – the *Post Office Guide* gives full details.

A counterfoil is provided with each postal order for the use of the sender. It should be filled in and kept as a record. It should not be sent with the postal order.

The sender of the postal order should fill in the name of the person (payee) who will cash it and the name of the office where it will be cashed. If the office is not known the name of the town or village should be written here. The postal order will then be cashed at any Post Office in that town or village.

The person cashing the postal order must sign it and the signature must match the name at the top. If it is crossed it must be paid into a bank account (a Post Office Savings account is suitable or another bank account).

Postal orders are valid for six months, after which the Post Office will not cash them without reference to the District Postmaster.

Small amounts may be added to the value of the postal order by sticking on stamps.

CROSSED POSTAL ORDERS

Postal orders may be crossed in the same way as cheques, after which they have to be paid into a bank account – they cannot be cashed over the counter at a Post Office. Postal orders should always be crossed when they are sent away as payment for goods ordered by mail order, or to a football pools firm – uncrossed postal orders are a great temptation to a thief as they are so easily cashed.

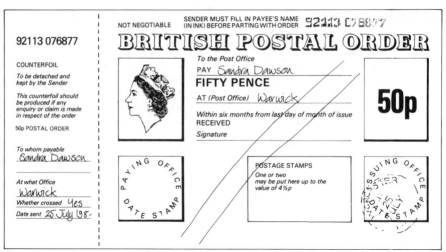

A crossed postal order with counterfoil

FOR YOUR FOLDER

56. POSTAL ORDERS

Write these notes in your folder, filling in the missing words and phrases.

1) The maximum amount for which a postal order may be sent is _____.

2) As well as the value of the postal order, there is a small additional charge called _____.

3) Postal orders may be sent overseas – the _____ gives full details.

4) It is safer to cross a postal order before sending it. If it is crossed, it must be paid into a _____.

5) Postal orders are valid for _____.

6) Small amounts may be added to the value of a postal order by _____.

7) The counterfoil provided with each postal order should be filled in and _____.

8) The counterfoil _____ be sent with the postal order.

9) The postal order is the most commonly used Post Office _____ service.

10) It is especially useful for transferring _____ to someone who has no bank account.

422

National Girobank

The National Girobank is a computerised Post Office bank which offers many similar services as the clearing banks. The Government has the use of all the money held in National Giro accounts.

Post offices are used as branches for National Giro. Directories are kept there of all National Giro account numbers, and an in-payment form may be bought to pay bills over the post office counter to any organisation having a National Giro account.

Extracts from National Girobank application booklet.

APPLICATION FOR A NATIONAL GIROBANK ACCOUNT

NATIONAL
Girobank
BOOTLE, Merseyside GIR 0AA.

Acknowledgement of initial deposit made by

Name of applicant

£

credit account number for use at National Girobank only

amount (minimum £10) (no fee payable at the counter)

.....................19.........

| 12A | 400 | 0528 | £ |

Signature/s (In the case of a joint account both applicants should sign)

Please do not write in the space below

The National Girobank application form (front)

How to apply for your National Girobank Account.

Simply complete the details on both sides of the tear off application form and sign overleaf. Then hand it in at a post office with your initial deposit (at least £10 in cash) which will be credited to your account when it is opened. Or send it with a cheque made payable to National Girobank to: Stephen South, FREEPOST, National Girobank, BOOTLE, Merseyside GIR 0AA.

You will receive an acknowledgement.

Applicants must be 15 or over. Those under 18 will be required to provide a guarantor.

The conditions on which National Girobank accounts are provided can be obtained on request from the address above.

Please do not write in the space below

Surname

1. First names in full Mr/Mrs/Miss

Date of birth

First names in full Mr/Mrs/Miss (for joint accounts only)

2.

Date of birth

Address

Postcode

Home telephone no:

Please give your previous address if you have moved within the last year

Postcode

At which two post offices will you cash cheques?

a

b

In respect of 1 above

Please give your occupation

Please give the name and address of your present employer to whom we may apply for a reference

Postcode

How long have you worked for this employer?

If you already have a bank account please give the name and address of the branch to whom we may apply for a reference. Please also state your account number

Postcode

Account no:

If you have a cheque guarantee/bank credit card please give details

Issuing Bank

Card no:

PTO

The National Girobank application form (back)

All public utilities (water, electricity and gas boards) print at the foot of their bills a National Giro transfer number, with their account numbers already printed on it. Payment can then be made at any post office.

Girocheques are forms for transferring payment out of the National Girobank and may be used exactly as an ordinary bank cheque. Girocheques may also be used to withdraw money from a National Giro account, at any post office.

In addition to the above, the National Girobank offers the following services to account holders:

- personal loans
- standing orders
- budget accounts
- bridging loans
- cheque card (holder must be over 18)
- free bank statements
- traveller's cheques and foreign currency.

There are no bank charges as long as a customer's account remains in credit. When the customer is overdrawn (in the red) 10p is charged for each payment from the cheque account.

The National Girobank is cheaper than the clearing house banks, and also many post offices are open on Saturdays, which is convenient for withdrawing and paying in money. All post offices are open during normal shopping hours, so that National Girobank services are available outside normal banking hours (which are 0930 to 1530, Monday to Friday only). A post office is seldom more than 10 minutes walk away, and National Girobank account holders have the advantage of this network of branches though not of the helpful advice of the bank manager and the full range of bank services.

If you want to open an account, you need to complete an application form like the one on p. 424.

National Girobank and Using a Building Society Account

By an arrangement between a building society and the National Girobank Transcash service a holder of a share account with the building society can pay money in and take money out at any post office. All that is needed is a special card from the building society, the number of which is written on the Transcash form.

This is a useful arrangement for people with a building society account who may find it difficult to get to their nearest branch when they need money (or have money to deposit).
Only one or two building societies operate this scheme so far.

Exercise 94

NATIONAL GIROBANK

1) The National Girobank has several advantages over the clearing house banks. Give two of them.

2) What services are available to clearing house bank customers and *not* to National Girobank customers?

3) At what age is it possible to open a National Girobank account?

4) At what age is it possible to have a cheque guarantee card?

5) How much is it necessary to pay in to open a National Girobank account?

6) Where is this amount paid in?

7) What does the application form mean by 'joint account'?

8) Why does the form ask for details of a previous address if the applicant has moved within the last year?

9) How is bill paying made easy by National Girobank?

10) What is a 'guarantor'?

Exercise 95

ASSIGNMENTS ON CHEQUES AND PAYING-IN SLIPS

1) The balance in your current account stands at £20. Make out a cheque to withdraw cash for your own use (date it for today) for £5. Make a note of the balance remaining in your current account on your counterfoil (cheque 'stub'). (See p. 394.)

```
┌─────────────────────┐
│                     │
│    _____ 19 _____    │
│                     │
│    _____    │
│    _____    │
│    _____    │
│                     │
│  £ _____   │
│                     │
```
A cheque stub   000651

2) You wish to pay some cash and a cheque and a postal order into your current account. Make out a paying-in slip (see p. 408) for the following:

- 2 £1 notes
- 3 50p coins
- 4 10p coins
- 3 5p coins
- 1 cheque for £1.50
- 1 postal order for 50p.

Make a note on the counterfoil in your cheque book of the balance now in your current account.

3) Make out a cheque to Newtown Corporation for £2 with today's date. This will be for an examination entry fee for June 198—. Note balance in your account on the counterfoil.

4) Make out a cheque to R W Phillips Esq for £7.75 with today's date. This will be for a deposit on a record player. Make a note of the balance in your account.

5) Make out a paying-in slip for the following:

- 1 £1 note
- 1 50p coin
- 4 2p coins
- 3 1p coins
- 1 cheque for £1.30
- 1 postal order for 50p.

Make a note on the last counterfoil in your cheque book of balance remaining in your current account.

6) Make out a cheque to withdraw cash from your current account for your own use for £3. Make a note of balance remaining in the account.

Exercise 96

BANKING ASSIGNMENTS

1) You will need:
   - five cheque forms (crossed cheques).
   - paying-in slips (three).
   - a bank statement form.
   - The bank account is in the name of 'F Martin'.
   - The account no is 108976.
   - F Martin runs a small boutique. Its name is 'The Chic Boutique' and the address is: 74 High Street, Hometown.
   - F Martin's account had a balance of £750 on 1 March 198—.

   a *3 March 198—*
   F Martin makes out a cheque for £65.50 to 'The Glen Tweed Co' for 30 yards of cloth.

b *5 March 198—*

The day's cash takings at the boutique are £78.95. Make out a paying-in slip to pay this into the bank. It is made up as follows:

£10 notes 3
£5 notes 8
£1 notes 5
50 pence pieces 4
10 pence pieces 10
5 pence pieces 12
2 pence pieces 15
1 pence pieces 5

On the same paying-in slip, include two cheques: one for £10.50 and the other for £9.64.

c *6 March 198—*

F Martin makes out a cheque to 'Thompson Trimming Co' for £34.81 for buttons, braid and buckles. Takings on 6 March are £108.95, which is paid into the bank on the same day, made up as follows:

£10 notes 9
£5 notes 3
£1 notes 3
50 pence pieces 1
10 pence pieces 4
5 pence pieces 1

d *7 March 198—*

Make out a cheque for 'Cash' for wages amounting to £349.65 and a cheque for £56.11 for NHI and one for £127.31 for PAYE—both made out to the Inspector of Taxes.

e *8 March 198—*

The day's takings are £234.67. Make out a paying-in slip for this amount (divide it up into suitable notes and coins).

Make out a bank statement showing how much money F Martin had in his account on 10 March 198—. This statement should show all the above transactions.

If your calculations are correct, his balance should be £559.33.

2) You have received a private loan of £250 from K G Holding to enable you to buy a car. The cheque is reproduced opposite:

Today's date _____ 19 8- **00-00-00**

BANK OF EDUCATION

HOMETOWN

Pay --- _Your own name_ _____ _or Order_

Two hundred and fifty   £250 —————————

pounds only ————————— K. G. HOLDING.

K. G. Holding

"000851" 00"0000: 10475375" 11

a Prepare a paying-in slip or bank giro credit slip for paying the cheque into your bank current account.

b As you will be repaying the loan by banker's order, fill in a standing order form requesting 24 monthly payments from your account, commencing the first day of next month. (The total amount to be repaid over the two years – with interest – is £300.)

c Complete a bank statement showing the state of your current account, assuming £255.75 was the balance brought forward and including the above transactions, i.e. the cheque paid into your account and the first standing order payment.

d You have also paid:
- a local garage £225 for the car
- an insurance company £60 for insuring the car
- £38.50 for Road Fund Vehicle Licence.

All three cheques have been presented at your bank and your account debited accordingly.

Show one of the cheque counterfoils.

Answers to Quiz on Banking

1) No, they do not always charge – only for current account transactions when the account balance falls below a certain amount (see p. 392).

2) Yes, some Banks do have rather restricted opening hours (see p. 391).

3) No – too easy for burglars to get at!

4) No – all that is needed is a cheque made out to 'Self' or 'Cash' for money from a current account (see p. 399).

5) It is worthwhile to have a Deposit Account – for saving even small amounts.

6) No – there is no minimum age limit.

7) No (see p. 418).

8) Not true (see p. 418).

9) True! (see p. 393).

10) No, not if a record is kept on the counterfoil (see p. 397).

Exercise 97

METHODS OF PAYMENT

1) Describe the services provided through the Post Office for making and receiving payments.

2) State briefly what the following terms used in connection with cheques mean:

   a post-dated **b** stale **c** stopped

3) What action should be taken when:
   a You discover that a cheque sent by you in today's post has been incorrectly made out for £100 more than the amount owed,
   b a cheque which you have paid into the bank is returned 'words and figures differ (R/D)'.

4) What is a 'current account' and how is it used?

5) A cheque which has been sent by you appears to have been lost in the post. What action should be taken?

6) Explain how the credit transfer (Bank Giro) system operates for settling accounts.

7) Complete a blank specimen bank paying-in slip, using the following details:

4 June 1984	1	£20.00 notes
Creditor: A. Brown	3	10.00 notes
Paid in by: A. Brown	4	5.00 notes
A/C no. 10476375	30	1.00 notes
	30	50p coins
	50	10p coins
	15	5p coins
Postal Order (value)		£ 3.60
Cheques		£50.00
Cheques		£15.25
Cheques		£10.40

Insert amount of total credit.

430

General Revision

Exercise 98
MULTIPLE-CHOICE QUESTIONS

Copy out the question, and write the correct letter underneath.

1) A filing clerk in an office would be responsible for:
a opening the mail
b dealing with all the callers to a firm
c filing all papers.

2) An audio-typist would:
a type from written notes
b type from shorthand notes
c type after listening to the dictation through headphones.

3) A copy-typist would:
a have to have accurate typing with a good speed
b have to be able to type in a foreign language
c have to know all about computer programming.

4) One of the following is an essential quality for an office worker:
a high shorthand speed
b conscientiousness
c good looks.

5) One of the following is a *qualification* which a secretary should have:
a excellent English
b initiative
c pleasant manner.

6) The following would be sent by Recorded Delivery:
a gold bracelet
b passport
c £50 in notes.

7) The following would be sent by Registered Post:
a driving licence
b a set of valuable foreign stamps
c worked examination papers.

8) An International Reply Coupon would be used to:
a prepay a letter for a reply from a pen-friend in Germany
b send the postage to a mail order firm for a catalogue
c save buying a postal order for 25p.

9) Post Restante enables:
a people to collect their letters from a post office in a town where they will be staying, when they are not sure of their exact address
b people to have their letters collected by a postman instead of posting them in a letter box
c people to obtain a meal at a post office.

10) Private boxes at a post office sorting office are for:
   a confidential letters
   b firms who wish to collect their mail at their own convenience during the day
   c private detectives.

11) An airmail letter form is:
   a the cheapest seat in an aeroplane
   b a special form sold by the Post Office which is the cheapest way of sending an airmail letter
   c a rubber stamp with the words 'airmail' on it.

12) The airmail service to Europe is called:
   a the 'all-up' service
   b Express post
   c Datapost.

13) The telephone alphabet is:
   a The special language in which telephone directories are written
   b the order in which the *Yellow Pages* is set out
   c for a telephonist to spell out names which the caller cannot hear.

14) A fixed time call is:
   a when the length of the call is set beforehand and the caller is disconnected when the end of the call is reached
   b when a trunk call is booked in advance so that caller is connected at a pre-arranged time
   c a call which wakes you up in the morning.

15) A release symbol is:
   a a message of hope to a man in prison
   b a key
   c a special mark on a document which indicates it can be filed.

16) Spirit duplicating is a method of producing several hundred copies by means of:
   a ghosts who do the typing in the dark
   b hectograph carbon
   c photography.

17) Ink duplicating is:
   a copying by pen and ink
   b many different colours of ink
   c producing copies by stencil on an ink duplicator.

18) An agenda of a meeting is sent:
   a to all those entitled to attend the meeting
   b to all those who don't belong to the Society
   c to old age pensioners.

19) A trade discount is:
   a allowed when goods are returned
   b allowed when goods are exchanged
   c allowed to certain traders because of the quantity they purchase.

20) A cash discount is:
   a allowed for prompt payment
   b allowed only when payment is in cash
   c allowed only when payment is made personally

21) A statement of account is:
   a a story in serial form
   b evidence given in court
   c an account sent to a customer at the end of each month.

22) A cheque card enables the holder to:
   a shop without money
   b write a cheque or obtain cash from a bank up to a maximum of £50
   c obtain money from a service till outside a bank when it is shut.

23) The following account does not pay interest:
   a savings
   b deposit
   c current

24) The payee of a cheque is:
   a the person signing it
   b the bank on whom it is drawn
   c the person to whom the cheque is made out.

25) The drawee of a cheque is:
   a the person signing it
   b the bank on whom it is drawn
   c the person to whom the cheque is made out.

26) The most usual method of organising Petty Cash is:
   a inquest system
   b imprest system
   c outlet system.

27) Gross wages are:
   a wages in a very large pay packet
   b the amount of wages before deductions
   c the weight of a pay packet.

28) Net wages are:
   a wages actually received, after deductions
   b wages in a very small pay packet
   c wages made up in an envelope with a net pattern on it.

29) PAYE means:
  a pay as you enter
  b pay as you earn
  c pass all your earnings.

30) Statutory deduction is:
  a one required to be made by law
  b one which a wage-earner can refuse to have made
  c one made only from people earning over £10 000 a year.

Appendix 1   First Aid

What is First Aid?

First Aid means giving immediate help and comfort to anyone who has been taken ill suddenly, or who has had an accident, until skilled medical attention arrives. *Skilled medical attention* means a doctor, a trained nurse or other trained medical workers such as ambulance men. Instant action by a person who has had some first-aid training may often save a life, and it will always make a casualty feel less anxious and more comfortable.

Minor Injuries and Ailments

A receptionist may have to deal with visitors' minor injuries, such as cuts or scratches, blisters, splinters; and minor ailments — sore throats or headaches. A well-equipped first-aid box will enable her to cope with all of these and should contain the following:

Aspirins
Throat pastilles
Adhesive plasters in assorted
   sizes
Bandages — assorted widths
White lint
Cotton wool
Antiseptic cream

Safety pins
Scissors
Tweezers
Liquid antiseptic such as Dettol
Thermometer
Indigestion tablets
Two or three triangular
   bandages.

More Serious Conditions

NOSEBLEED

This is frightening, both to the patient and to people around. It should be dealt with by putting a bowl under the patient's head, and then by squeezing the nose. The patient should be instructed *not* to swallow, and to breathe through the mouth. This procedure usually stops the bleeding within a few minutes. If it does not, medical help should be summoned. Nosebleeds are not dangerous provided they do not go on for more than 5 minutes.

FAINTING

There are various reasons why people faint — hunger (caused, for example, by starting out without breakfast), standing too long in one position, feeling unwell, shock from bad news, anxiety about something unusual, or exceptionally hot weather. Generally, a faint lasts for only a few seconds and the patient recovers consciousness quite quickly. While still unconscious she should be gently turned on to her side with one leg forward and arms clear. This is known as the *recovery position* (see illustration on p. 437). Any tight clothing — belt, collar, etc. — should be loosened. If patient does not recover consciousness, she should be covered with a blanket and medical help sent for without any further delay.

It may happen that the patient has fallen while fainting, and knocked her head. She may be concussed. She should be placed in the recovery position, and covered with a blanket, but in addition, her pulse should be taken at regular intervals, and reported to the doctor or ambulance men when they arrive. The normal pulse rate is about 80 a minute.

Some people carry treatment cards with them (diabetics and epileptics) showing which drugs they take regularly. These cards are helpful to a doctor to decide what treatment to give to an unconscious patient, and it saves time if they can be produced quickly on arrival.

SHOCK

This is a state where, although the patient is conscious, she feels cold and looks very pale. Shock can be caused by bad news, an accident, or an emotional upset. The important steps are to comfort the patient, perhaps by saying 'I am trained in first aid, and know what I am doing'. Then cover the patient with a blanket, after loosening tight clothing round neck and waist. Patient feels better if she lies on her back with head low and turned to one side and legs raised. Recovery from simple shock is usually quite rapid. A cup of tea or coffee, sweetened (*not alcohol*) can be given if cause of shock is not an injury.

Hot water bottles should never be used, as they can cause serious blisters, especially to an unconscious patient, even through several layers of clothing.

BROKEN ARM (OR SUSPECTED BROKEN ARM)

Support the arm with a sling and keep the patient sitting in a comfortable position. Cover to keep warm. Treat for shock. Send for medical help.

RECOVERY POSITION

The 'recovery' position means simply turning a casualty on her side, with one knee forward, head to one side and arms clear, so that if she is sick, she will not drown in her vomit. Merely doing this may save a life.

Very Serious Conditions

SEVERE BLEEDING FROM CUTS OR OTHER INJURIES

The urgent need is to stop the bleeding as soon as possible. The total amount of blood in the body of an average adult is about 6 litres (about $10\frac{1}{2}$ pints). If an artery or a vein is cut, bleeding may be so rapid that life is endangered very quickly. Blood from an artery is bright red and spurts. Blood from a vein is darker and flows continuously.

Raise the limb which is bleeding, after laying the patient flat. This slows down the heartbeat and reduces the flow of blood around the body.

Control the bleeding by squeezing the sides of the wound together.

Apply a clean dressing — ideally it should be sterile, but a clean handkerchief, a clean tissue or even some folded toilet paper will make a temporary dressing. Bandage very firmly. If bleeding does not stop, add further dressings — do not touch the original ones.

When bleeding seems to have stopped, lower the limb, but tell the patient not to move it.

Cover the patient with blankets and reassure. Bleeding is very frightening and the patient may also be suffering from shock.

An ambulance or doctor should be sent for as quickly as possible, but bleeding must be dealt with first. Someone near at hand can be instructed to telephone for a doctor while the patient is attended to.

BLEEDING FROM AN INTERNAL INJURY

The indications that there may be internal bleeding are:

The patient is very pale, cold and complains of being very thirsty.
There is a very rapid (much more than 80 per minute) and weak pulse.
The insides of lips and lower eyelids are very pale.

The patient should be made comfortable, by loosening tight clothing and covering with a blanket. *Nothing* should be given by mouth. A written note of the pulse rate should be kept.

The ambulance or a doctor should be sent for as quickly as possible.

BROKEN LEG (OR SUSPECTED BROKEN LEG)

Do not move the patient — it may only cause more injuries. Cover the patient or keep her warm, while someone sends for an ambulance or doctor. Treat the patient for shock (but do not administer food or drink).

Appendix 2
Making Tea and Coffee

Tea

In small firms, it is often the job of the junior typist to include making tea amongst her other duties, for other members of staff, for her boss and also, possibly, for visitors to the firm. It sounds a simple, familiar job, but is often done badly, resulting in a poor cup of tea.

The following rules help to make a good cup of tea the norm, rather than the exception:

- Fill the kettle with fresh water – don't boil up the contents left from the last tea-making.
- Make sure the cups and saucers are perfectly clean.
- Wash the milk jug and refill with fresh milk.
- When the water is almost boiling, pour about a cupful into the teapot and leave it until the kettle has boiled.
- Then empty the teapot and place the tea leaves in – one spoonful for each person and 'one for the pot' is a rule which results in a good, strong tea. It can always be made weaker by adding more boiling water, but it cannot be made stronger by any means at all.
- Make sure the water is brought back to the boil and while it is still boiling pour it into the pot. The amount of water depends upon the size of the pot – only trial and error can determine the exact amount, but a mental note should be made of the level the water reaches in the teapot (i.e. below the spout or above the spout) which results in a really good cup of tea, then results will always be the same.
- After pouring on the boiling water, replace the teapot lid and cover the teapot (ideally, with a cosy but anything will do which keeps it warm) and leave for about 3–5 minutes.
- Then stir, allow the tea leaves to settle, and it is ready for pouring into the cups.

Some people prefer to add milk after the tea has been poured; some prefer the milk poured into the cup first, this is not very important. The use of a tea strainer will prevent tea leaves being poured into the cups along with the tea and is quite important. Sugar should be left to the drinkers to add themselves – some people like sweet tea but because of weight control will add their own saccharines.

A little more *boiling* water may be added to the teapot after pouring out the tea, in case anyone would like another cup of tea, but the teacosy must be replaced or it will rapidly go cold. Tepid tea is revolting. Teabags can be used instead of loose tea leaves and they are easier to dispose of but they do not make such a good cup of tea as the leaves are contained inside the bag in a confined area.

Tea should be served attractively on a tray, with sugar basin and milk jug. There should be no tea slopped into the saucers — this spoils the whole effect!

Coffee

The best cup of coffee is made from freshly ground coffee beans, and although modern coffee percolators are excellent, it is very easy to make a perfect cup of coffee with a jug, a saucepan and some freshly ground coffee.

Allow one heaped tablespoonful of coffee to half a pint of water (that is, about two cupfuls). Place coffee in warmed jug and pour over the water when it has boiled. Return the coffee to a saucepan and bring back to the boil. *Do not allow it to go on boiling.* Strain back into the jug.

Ground coffee quickly loses its flavour and should be bought in small quantities, preferably from freshly ground coffee beans. It should be stored in an airtight container — glass if possible, away from daylight.

However coffee is made (and instant coffee *can be* very good) it must be served attractively. Place the cups, saucers and spoons on a tray with a bowl of (preferably) brown sugar and a jug of hot milk. Stir the milk occasionally, or cover it temporarily, to prevent skin forming.

Pour coffee into cups, but do not fill — leave about 1″ at the top so that people who like white coffee can add their own milk. Many people these days drink black coffee.

Serve the coffee as hot as possible.

Try not to slop it into the saucers as you carry the tray into the visitors!

Appendix 3
Looking After Indoor Plants

Plants in offices can be as much a part of the furnishings as the carpets and looking after them is comparatively simple.

Many firms use plants in troughs and tubs as a screen to divide sections of offices (see p. 442) or to make an area visited by the public such as Reception (see p. 451) welcoming and attractive.

It is possible to arrange for a specialist firm to supply the plants, look after them regularly, and replace them when necessary. This relieves the office staff of all responsibility regarding the care of the plants, but is an expensive service which can very well be managed by members of staff. It is a sensible arrangement for one or two people only to be involved in looking after plants in each office, so that their care is not forgotten — few things look worse than drooping, neglected plants.

Guidelines for the Care of Indoor Plants

1) *Position.* All plants need light, but most dislike strong sunshine, so a position near a north or east facing window is ideal. This will get no sunshine (north) or morning sunshine only (east).

2) *Temperature.* No indoor plants will tolerate frost, so do not leave plants touching a window in an unheated room on a frosty night. Move plants away from the windows on to the floor at the end of the day in the winter. Alternatively, plants dislike direct heat from radiators, so do not stand them on top of radiators, or too near them.

3) *Watering.* When the soil surface feels dry to the touch, water from the top until the water seeps out into the container. Drain away any surplus water after a few minutes *so that the plant is not left standing in water.*

4) *Feeding.* Indoor plants require regular feeding which is generally done at the time of watering. Once a fortnight in summer is usually adequate and about once a month in winter. A useful plant food is one which is long-lasting and can be applied once every six months.

5) *Humidity.* Centrally heated offices have a dry atmosphere which most plants dislike. Regular spraying of the foliage with tepid water will be beneficial; also, standing the plant pot on gravel or pebbles which are kept moist keeps the atmosphere moist around the plant.

6) *Pests.* The three most common pests on indoor plants are greenfly, whitefly and red spider. These can be controlled easily by one of the many proprietary chemicals available at plant centres. Spraying will have to be repeated several times to eliminate the pest completely.

7) *Diseases.* The most common diseases on indoor plants are mildew and botrytis and these also can be controlled by using a proprietary brand of chemical. When using indoor sprays, extreme care should be used and the manufacturers' instructions followed closely.

Plants in troughs can be used as screens

Choosing Plants

Buy young plants — they will be cheaper than the larger, more mature plants and will adapt more successfully to the different growing conditions in offices. Choose plants which are short and bushy and have glossy, healthy-looking leaves. Flowering plants should have plenty of buds still to open.

FOLIAGE PLANTS SUITABLE FOR GROWING INDOORS

Shade-loving (can be away from the light)
- Aspidistra eliator (cast-iron plant)
- Asplenium
- Fittonia
- Hedera (ivy)
- Parlour palm
- Pteris
- Senecio mikanioides (parlour ivy)

Light-loving plants (but do not place in direct sunlight)
- Asparagus ferns
- Begonia Rex
- Chlorophytum (spider plant)
- Cissus antarctica (kangaroo vine)
- Dieffenbachia
- Dracaena
- Euonymus fortunei
- Ficus elastica (india-rubber plant)
- Maranta
- Monstera deliciosa (Swiss cheese plant)
- Peporomia caperata
- Philodendron sandens
- Sansevieria (mother-in-law's tongue)
- Tradescantia
- Zebrina pendula (wandering Jew)

Plants which will tolerate some sunlight
- Aloe aristata
- Buxus sempervirens
- Coleus blumei
- Echeveria derenberghii
- Fatshedra lizeii
- Grevillia robusta (silk oak)
- Kalanchoe
- Pittosporum tobira

Flowering plants suitable for growing indoors
The following will be attractive only during their flowering period and will then have to be exchanged for foliage plants:

Spring	Summer/autumn	Winter
Azalea	Begonia semperflorens	Cineraria
Clivia miniata	Begonia tuberhybrida	Hippeastrum
Cyclamen persicum	Chrysanthemum	Saintpaulia
Freesia	Exacum affine	Zygocactus truncatus
Primula	Fuchsia	
Schizanthus	Impatiens	
	Pelargonium	

Post-a-Plant

Plants (chosen from four varieties — parlour palm, grape ivy, sanseveria or devil's ivy) will be delivered by Royal Mail, packed into a box specially designed to protect the plant as it goes through the sorting office, anywhere in the United Kingdom.

A form has to be completed, giving name, address, postcode and telephone number.

State the type of plant ordered and size of pot required. A message card to be sent with the plant has to be completed.

The completed order form and Transcash form should be taken together with cash or cheque to any post office. The counter clerk will date stamp the order and the Transcash form.

Detached order then has to be sent to the address given on the reverse side of the order form.

Appendix 4
Commercial Abbreviations

These are just *some* of the abbreviations you may come across! There are, of course, *many* more in the dictionaries.

&	and
AA	Automobile Association
a/c	account
AD	*anno domini* — in the year of Our Lord
advt	advertisement
am	*ante meridiem* — before noon
asst	assistant
appro	approval
bf	brought forward
BR	British Rail
Bros	Brothers
CA	Chartered Accountant
caps	capital letters
cc	cubic centimetre *or* copies (to)
cf	compare
cm	centimetre
Co	Company, county
c/o	care of
COD	cash on delivery
cif	cost insurance and freight
Cr	creditor
cwo	cash with order
cwt	hundredweight
dept	department
do	ditto
Dr	doctor, debtor
E & O E	errors and omissions excepted
EEC	European Economic Community
Esq	Esquire
ex div	ex dividend
fas	free alongside ship
fig	figure
fob	free on board
for	free on rail
ft	feet, foot

GATT	general agreement on tariffs and trade
GB	Great Britain
GMT	Greenwich mean time
Hon	Honorary, honourable
Hon Sec	Honorary Secretary
HP	Hire Purchase
HRH	His (or Her) Royal Highness
i.e.	*id est* (that is)
Inc	Incorporated
inst	instant (of the current month)
Jr	junior
lc	lower case (small print)
Ltd	Limited
misc	miscellaneous
Mme	Madame
MO	Medical Officer; money order
MP	Member of Parliament
MS	manuscript
NB	note well
np	new paragraph
no	number
nos	numbers
ns	not sufficient (funds to meet a cheque)
OHMS	On Her Majesty's Service
pa	per annum
PAYE	Pay As You Earn
pd	paid
pm	*post meridiem* — afternoon
pp	*per procurationem* — on behalf of
PRO	Public Relations Officer
pro tem	*pro tempore* — for the time
prox	*proxima* — next month
PTO	please turn over
PWD	Public Works Department
RD	refer to drawer (of cheque)
recd	received
RSVP	*répondez s'il vous plaît* — please reply
Ry	railway
SAYE	Save As You Earn
sec	secretary, second
soc	society
supt	Superintendent
TUC	Trades Union Congress
uc	upper case (capital letters)
ult	*ultimo* — last month
VAT	Value Added Tax
yd	yard
Yrs	Yours

Appendix 5
Proof Corrections

The most commonly used signs are given below:

Sign in margin	Meaning	Sign in text
run on /	Do not begin a new paragraph	⌐⟶
stet /	'Let it stand' — ignore the alteration and type the word which has been crossed out	· · · · · Under word to be typed
trs /	Transpose. Change word (or letters) around	⌐_⌐ Round letters or words. Sometimes numbered
⌐	Delete, omit, take out	Word, or words, crossed out
#	Insert space	⋏
⌒/	Close up space	⌒
uc /	Upper case (capital letters)	Two lines under word or words
lc /	Lower case (small letters)	Two lines under word or words
us /	Underscore	One line under word (or words)
NP/	New paragraph	Square bracket
Sp caps /	Spaced capitals	Three lines under word or words
/-/	Insert hyphen	⋏
⊢—⊣	Insert dash	⋏

Appendix 6
Sources of Further Information for Teachers

Telephone

Publicity Division, Education Service, Cheapside House, London EC2.

Schools Officer, British Telecom, (ME/PUB 1.3), 3rd Floor, Seal House, 107/8 Upper Thames Street, London, EC4R 3TH.

The above will supply posters, films and leaflets.

Mail Handling

Films Officer, Room 436, Postal Headquarters, London EC1A 1HQ.

Royal Mail Film Library, Park Hall Trading Estate, London SE21 8EL.

Marketing Department, Postal Headquarters Building, 225 Finsbury Square, London EC2 1PH.

All main Post Offices have up-to-date supplies of (free) leaflets on packing, safeguarding and sending mail. Some Postmasters are co-operative about letting schools and colleges have copies of recent posters for display in classrooms.

Banking

The Bank Education Service, 10 Lombard Street, London EC3V 98T will arrange for a speaker to come and talk to schools or colleges, with a film, if requested.

The Bank Education Service will also send supplies of booklets, and facsimile banking documents.

The Public Relations Division of National Girobank is at 10 Milk Street, London EC2V 8JH.

Safety

ROSPA (The Royal Society for the Prevention of Accidents) publish a useful booklet *Care in the Office* as well as a picture competition, both of which are reasonably priced. Address: Cannon House, The Priory, Queensway, Birmingham B4 6BS.

Miscellaneous Publications

Two monthly publications which give up-to-date information about all types of office machinery and furniture are *Business Systems and Equipment* (Circulation Department, Maclean-Hunter Limited, 30 Old Burlington Street, London W1X 2AE) and *Office Equipment News* (109—119 Waterloo Road, London SE1 8UL). These are issued free to lecturers and teachers.

The Inland Revenue office in most large towns and cities will supply out-of-date tax forms upon request, for practice purposes.

The AA or RAC have, on occasions, out-of-date copies of their handbooks which they pass on to schools and colleges, upon application, free of charge.

It is also worthwhile getting into touch with local librarians, with a request for out-of-date copies of any reference books they may be replacing.

An example of a well planned reception area

Index